# THE FALL OF EMPIRES

Dedication:
*For Lauren and Berit*

First published in 2009 by Pier 9, an imprint of Murdoch Books Pty Limited

Murdoch Books Australia
Pier 8/9
23 Hickson Road
Millers Point NSW 2000
Phone: +61 (0)2 8220 2000
Fax: +61 (0)2 8220 2558
www.murdochbooks.com.au

Murdoch Books UK Limited
Erico House, 6th Floor
93–99 Upper Richmond Road
Putney, London SW15 2TG
Phone: +44 (0) 20 8785 5995
Fax: +44 (0) 20 8785 5985
www.murdochbooks.co.uk

Publisher: Diana Hill
Project manager: Emma Hutchinson
Editor: Christine Eslick
Designer: Annette Fitzgerald
Illustrator: Iain McKellar



ISBN: 978 1 741 96313 7

Printed 1010 Printing International Limited in 2009. PRINTED IN CHINA.

# THE FALL OF EMPIRES

## FROM GLORY TO RUIN, AN EPIC ACCOUNT OF HISTORY'S ANCIENT CIVILIZATIONS

Cormac O'Brien

PIER 9

# CONTENTS

# INTRODUCTION

*"All that is human must retrograde if it does not advance."*

*Edward Gibbon, The History of the Decline and Fall of the Roman Empire*

Reaching out across the span of centuries, ancient empires continue to capture our imagination. It is easy to see why: their ingenious accomplishments, their martial strength, and, of course, their chilling brutality. The gulf of time that separates them from us only brightens the light of their achievements. How could they have done so much in a world that, at least to us, seems to have been so unstable and benighted?

As fascinating as these questions are, it is another to which we invariably turn: How and why did these empires come to an end? From the Parthenon of Athens to the pyramids of Egypt, the epic monuments of the ancient world not only remind us of their builders' greatness—they also make us wonder at the forces required to topple such vigor and genius, and suggest a reality much more dangerous than our own.

In such a world, might was a virtue. If, as Voltaire said, "history is nothing more than a tableau of crimes and misfortunes," we need only look at the empires of the past to understand why. Ruthless, acquisitive, and domineering, those who would rule on an imperial scale have littered the story of humanity with misery and subjugation.

But like any grand human endeavor, the complete truth is hardly that simple. Representing the control and mobilization of immense resources and manpower, empires have been able to leave legacies in art, engineering, science, and law that stand as testaments to power and centralization. Rome drove throngs of unfortunates into slavery during its military campaigns and reveled openly in blood sport; but it also built wonders of architecture and laid the foundations of governmental and legal concepts still in use today. Puissance made manifest can look like many things, from the wonder of a pyramid to a corral of shackled women and children. Both had their roles to play in the rise and fall of empires.

In the twenty-fourth century BC, Sargon the Great of Akkad conquered a swathe of territory stretching from the Persian Gulf to the Mediterranean Sea, establishing what some scholars consider history's first empire. Though little is known of the Akkadian realm (even the location of Akkad, its capital city, remains a matter of debate), the expansion of Sargon established a familiar pattern: military campaigning in neighboring lands to secure tribute and enhance prestige, followed by the establishment of control, however imperfect, over large subjugated populations to ensure the future availability of resources and manpower. Glorification of the throne throughout this process was as palpable a benefit as booty itself; a dynasty's notoriety served to overawe quarrelsome neighbors and quell recalcitrant subjects, making a necessity of regular military campaigning, which in turn brought in more tribute for the purchasing of more troops, and so on.

The use of force to acquire wealth and territory, cultivate reputation, and subdue regional threats would be common to all ancient empires. But when it came to the means of governing their own expanding populations, a wide variety of strategies arose across the planet and over the centuries. The Assyrians employed terror and propaganda, while the Achaemenid Persians relied on local autonomy to win loyalty. For Alexander the Great and his Hellenistic heirs, a merging of Eastern and Western customs and institutions, it was hoped, would supplement revolutionary methods of military power to forge a new and stable society. Other states, like the Egyptians, deified royalty as the basis of centralization. Little more than feudal relationships between great families formed the basis of Parthian rule, while the Romans wove a complex suite of carrots and sticks into their legalistic approach to empire, backing it up with a military machine the like of which the world had never seen.

Despite their widely varying approaches, all of these ruling powers struggled with a fundamental paradox: the securing of peace within an empire won by war. "One who conquers the lands of others places priority on deceit and force, but one who brings peace and stability honors obedience to authority," observed Jia Yi, a Han scholar writing during the second century BC. "This means that seizing, and guarding what you have seized, do not use the same techniques." Jia Yi was writing about the Qin, the first (and very short-lived) dynasty to unite China's Warring States, but his observation holds for all ancient empires—supra-states whose relative success often depended on the skill with which they negotiated the awkward balance between violent acquisition and harmonious stability.

In the chapters that follow, we will see this issue arise again and again, exacerbated by a broad range of factors: religious strife, class conflict, environmental mishap, commercial competition, and, perhaps most often, aggressive neighbors who ultimately prove too tough to resist. The perils and pitfalls of power take many forms, from scheming priests and jealous aristocrats to military disasters on which the fate of millions could hang. It all makes for a varied and colorful look at mighty states of the deep past that have one thing in common: the fact that they all failed to stave off their own demise.

Finally, an explanation is in order. Because a truly comprehensive and authoritative narrative of imperial decline is beyond the modest scope of such a book as this, choices had to be made that balanced the most powerful and legendary empires of the ancient world along with those that, though lesser known, take readers off the beaten path. As a result, while some empires that may appear in a greater work did not "make the cut" here, a few that did might not even be considered empires by some authorities—a consequence in part of the ongoing debate among scholars over what constitutes an "empire" in the first place. That said, I can only ask the indulgence of the reader and hope that the range of states and peoples covered is as fascinating and instructive as I believe it to be.

CHAPTER ONE

# PHARAONIC EGYPT

## THE LONG DESCENT FROM THE APEX

As a group these structures, lustrous in their limestone finish, would have shone like beacons in the desert that surrounded them. This mountainous necropolis in the sands, which included the two neighboring pyramids built by Khafre and Menkaure as well as the sensationally enigmatic Sphinx, must have been an otherworldly sight to behold.

Incredibly, the Giza structures were built toward the beginning of Egypt's greatness; for all their skyscraping grandiosity, they were the creations of a culture that had yet to truly find its stride. That is one of the most arresting of Giza's messages. But a deeper, more ominous issue exercises everyone whose eyes behold the wonder that is Giza: What could possibly have brought down such a civilization?

The answer is hardly as simple as the question, not least because Egypt represented a collection of beliefs and traditions that were nearly as immutable as the stone that built the pyramids. One of the ancient world's richest cultures, Egypt endured long after it had stopped being a great power, converting its own conquerors with its dazzling sophistication. But there was a time, however long and open to definition by scholars,

## A SHIP TO SAIL THE SKY

Ironically, the only likeness known to exist of the pharaoh who built the greatest monument of the ancient world is a single figurine, just three inches in height. Khufu's legacy stands in inverse proportion to his only statue—and he left much more to posterity than the Great Pyramid.

Everyone knows about the ancient Egyptians' skill with stone. The pyramids, after all, are some of the most recognizable and widely praised icons of ancient genius in the world today. But the Old Kingdom culture that produced the marvels of the Giza plateau also excelled at shipbuilding—evidence of which was found in the unlikeliest of places.

Discovered by accident during clean-up operations in 1952, Khufu's royal barque had been left, disassembled, in its own immense pit near the foot of the Great Pyramid. (Nearby, another pit, also containing a disassembled boat, was confirmed in 1985.) Over the ensuing years, archaeologists undertook the painstaking task of putting the vessel back together, gradually giving shape to one of the most remarkable artifacts of ancient history.

The boat, built of meticulously shaped cedar wood planks and held together exclusively with wooden pegs and rope made of grass fibers, measures 142 feet from stem to stern.

It seems probable that it was intended to carry Khufu on his final voyage to the sun god, Re, with whom he would sail across the sky every day from dawn till dusk. What is certain is that ancient Egyptians knew how to build sturdy, sophisticated sailing vessels—skills that allowed them to exploit the Nile to become a great power.

that witnessed the gradual weakening of ancient Egypt's ability to chart its own course by the wisdom that had originally defined it. And that, it seems fair to argue, was the fall of pharaonic Egypt.

## FOUNDATIONS OF GREATNESS

*The pyramid of Khafre, seen from one of the many funerary structures on the plateau at Giza.*

For most of its enormous length, the Nile River shoots like a shimmering green stem through the Egyptian desert, emerging at the shores of the Mediterranean in a great delta that ancients compared to a lotus blossom. It is, and has been since prehistoric times, a thoroughfare for life and trade through an otherwise desiccated wilderness. The "black land," a rich agricultural belt that hugs the river, contrasts dramatically with the "red land" of the desert, creating a demarcation that is distinct and abrupt—verdant abundance stands weirdly close to lifeless, dun-colored outback.

The river's two primary tributaries, the Blue Nile and the White Nile, carry water north from the Ethiopian highlands, merging near modern-day Khartoum for the long, lonely journey toward the Mediterranean. With so little rainfall along the vast majority of its length, the Nile is subjected to a degree of evaporation as it runs through the desert, but its rich, undiluted silt has been the great treasure of Egyptian farmers for millennia.

The Nile *was* ancient Egypt, the river's various peculiarities coming together to form the ideal incubator for civilization. To begin with, its cycle of flooding and receding produced an unbeatable combination for productive agriculture. From mid-summer to October the river, fed by the summer downpours in Ethiopia, rose enough to inundate the surrounding plains. This period of inundation, called *akhet*, sowed the alluvial fields with the sludge that made them Egypt's beloved "black land." When the waters receded in November, the time of *peret* began, during which the land could be sown. From March through June was harvest time, or *shemu*, after which the whole process began anew. Without rain, the river offered just the right amount of ready water to span the rich soil that stretched along its banks in vast, easily flooded basins. The result was a staggering yield of emmer wheat and barley—as much as four times that of rain-fed regions. Egypt became a land of granaries.

Such abundance could be put to long-term use thanks to another of the Nile's unusual traits: its isolation. Scholars continue to debate the relationship between Mesopotamia and Egypt, and whether the first cities in the former gave rise to civilization in the latter. Whatever the truth, Egypt had an advantage that the cultures of Sumer, Akkad, and Babylonia did not. While the peoples of Mesopotamia dwelt in a region crisscrossed with trade routes and avenues of invasion, the early Egyptians enjoyed the convenient proximity of desert—lots of it, both east and west. Surrounded by arid buffer zones, they could exploit the wealth of their precious Nile unperturbed by the kind of strife that characterized the Tigris–Euphrates cockpit.

To the north was the Mediterranean, as much a venue for trade as anything else, and to the south lay Nubia, with which the Egyptians would share a long and contentious history. But in that direction the pharaohs could rely on the Nile's cataracts—six of them, each a chokepoint that hindered commerce and invasion equally. In time, threats would emerge, particularly from the direction of Palestine in the northeast, but Egypt's remote location served it well—and paved the way for the gigantic building projects that turned it into a great power.

## THE PYRAMID BUILDERS

The first pyramid for a pharaoh was built during the reign of Djoser, a king of the Third Dynasty who reigned sometime in the middle of the twenty-seventh century BC. Called the "Step Pyramid," it resembles a series of flat mastabas of decreasing size placed one on top of the other. Though not a true pyramid, it marked a dramatic departure from previous tombs and symbolized the growing significance and authority of the pharaoh.

By the Fourth Dynasty (2613–2498 BC), pyramid construction reached its zenith, literally and figuratively. This was the dynasty of the Giza builders: Khufu, Khafre, and Menkaure. And the scale of their tombs was entirely on par with the dizzying heights of power they had achieved.

The pyramids of Giza, built with relatively crude technology, required organizational efforts of incredible duration, complexity, and forethought. Nothing but a centralized state with absolute control over the whole of Egypt's population could have pulled off such feats. Though we stand agape today at the technical expertise of the Great Pyramid, its grandeur conceals a much larger accomplishment: the recruitment of legions of laborers (slaves were not used), the organization and building of communities to house them, the gathering of grain and other stores to feed them, and the managerial genius to bring it all together in a project whose sheer mass and exacting specifications demanded a consuming obsession with perfection over decades of work.

Scholars often maintain that the pyramids in effect built Egypt, their enormous requirements allowing the pharaoh to unify the people in a long-term, giant project and to perfect the bureaucratic skills of his court. If the irrigation efforts of the Euphrates River gave birth to the organized cities of Mesopotamia, the pyramids gave structure to Egyptian civilization.

## THE EDIFICE CRUMBLES

This was the state of affairs in the Old Kingdom: a prosperous people directed by an all-powerful monarch who was nearly as much god as man. The origins of his deification stretched back to the mythic unifier of Egypt, a king called Narmer. Until that time there had been two separate Egypts: Upper Egypt, a sinewy ribbon of green along the Nile River valley, and Lower Egypt, whose wild marshes stretched across the broad, wet delta in the north. Some time around 3100 BC, the legendary Narmer unified these two kingdoms, ruling all Egypt from a single throne in the royal city of Memphis and wearing a crown that combined the white crown of Upper Egypt with the red crown of Lower Egypt. In the pharaoh was merged the papyrus of the Valley and the water lily of the Delta—he was, among other things, the "Lord of the Two Lands," this being the most important of the many titles he bore.

With unification came connection to the gods. Since predynastic times Egyptians had believed that their king was the direct descendant of Re, the sun god. Aided and protected by Horus, the son of Isis, pharaoh battled to maintain order against the chaotic forces of Seth—a struggle in which the union of the two kingdoms featured prominently. With such important credentials, and with the organizational ability to make the most of the Nile's bounty, it is little wonder that the early kings were able to construct their lofty stone tombs, solidifying an already considerable power base.

The pattern was set for stability in Egypt. At its apex stood the pharaoh, whose godly pedigree ensured success in the battle against Egypt's enemies, foreign and domestic. As long as the kingdom remained unified and the Nile flooded as scheduled, all would be well—the king, godhead of the nation, would retain his unassailable position and fulfill his people's need for direction and security.

By the Sixth Dynasty (2345–2181 BC), however, the nobles and local officials who had benefited most from the prosperity of the state had consolidated their own degree of authority, dispersing the power of the king. The pace of this rarefaction of power at the top was perhaps imperceptible, until catastrophe exposed it. During the reign of Pepi II, the Old Kingdom's last great pharaoh (with a reign of perhaps ninety years), the Nile suffered a series of low flood levels, sparking a famine that not even the massive granaries of Egypt could alleviate. Starvation stalked the land for decades, and strife came right along with it as local lords struggled to feed their own people and maintain order in a desperate countryside. The world of the pyramid builders came crashing down.

## A CULTURE REDEFINED

What followed was what scholars refer to as the First Intermediate Period; there would be three in all, each characterized by political division. During such times, the unity of the two Egypts that was so fundamental to a pharaoh's prestige and validity was either a sham or altogether nonexistent.

In 2055 BC a king named Mentuhotep II brought the discord of the First Intermediate Period to an end. Based at Thebes, he defeated his principal foes and sacked their

*Above: Tombs of the pharaohs were decorated with richly colored wall paintings. This one shows the pharaoh between the gods Horus and Anubis.*

capital, the northern Egyptian city of Herakleopolis. An ambitious warrior prince, Mentuhotep II eventually assumed the title "He who unifies the two lands," an epithet pregnant with significance. Indeed, he would be hailed by later generations as the founder of a new Egypt.

But there was no going back. Gone were the tyrants of old whose egos and outsized ambitions could harness an entire people for the creation of a single mountainous tomb. In the chaos that followed the collapse of the Old Kingdom, pharaonic power had taken a beating. As the Nile harvests failed and the kingdom foundered for want of a single ruler to quell the chaos, the people came to a new understanding of leadership: the pharaoh came down to earth.

He was still, however, the lord who protected his people and provided for their culture's flowering—and in this the new pharaohs would excel. What emerged in the Middle Kingdom following Mentuhotep II's crushing of the Herakleopolitans was a wiser, more sophisticated civilization that many scholars dub Egypt's "Classical Age." Rather than rely only on family members to fill important posts, the kings of the Eleventh and Twelfth Dynasties cultivated a burgeoning bureaucracy. Writing became the most sought-after skill in the land, and scribes proliferated in a large and meticulous administration.

An intellectual shift seems to have occurred. In an atmosphere in which the pharaohs stood almost chastened by the excesses and failures of the past, a cult of righteousness and humility became the vogue. Literature, some of the greatest in Egypt's history, appeared during the Middle Kingdom, much of it offering lessons in charity and conscientious living. The favor of the gods, it was widely believed, was bestowed on the forgiving and the just.

Stability reigned. Nubia, rich in gold, amethyst, diorite, and other resources, was now brought more closely into the Egyptian orbit, with forts built beyond the First Cataract. Trading missions were sent as far as Lebanon, which soon came under heavy Egyptian influence. Goods from all over Asia and Africa flowed into Egyptian markets, and the pharaoh's image seemed secure both at home and across the sands and sea.

From the perspective of these halcyon days, it seemed as if Egypt had become eternal. But by the Thirteenth Dynasty (1773–c. 1650 BC), the kingdom's foundations were gradually eroding, beginning a cycle of disruption and recovery that would ultimately compromise Egypt's ability to steer its own course. And a new element was added to the mix of Egypt's vulnerabilities during this period: foreign intervention. It would prove an enduring and tenacious problem for those who would strive to rule the Nile.

Egypt was becoming an international power. Though the sands had long acted as a barrier, the kingdom's dazzling prosperity now acted as a magnet.

## THE PENDULUM SWINGS BACK

Who were these foreigners? They were called the "Hyksos," literally "rulers of foreign lands." Originally hailing from Palestine, they had been settling in the eastern Delta for generations, forming an immigrant community within the borders of Egypt, but one that the pharaohs, at least initially, found little cause to fear.

That would change. By the middle of the seventeenth century they were established enough within the local elite to take control in the Delta. That this was even possible, however, was mostly to do with the old problem of erosion of pharaonic power: for years the kings of the Thirteenth Dynasty, most of them with short, troubled reigns, had been losing control. As the prestige of the throne declined yet again, the borders became more porous. This time, the collapse of the kingdom would happen from within *and* without.

Known as the Second Intermediate Period, the confusing age that followed the rise of the Hyksos was hardly a cultural decline. Indeed, the "invaders" brought with them many intriguing things, including the harnessed horse and a few new musical instruments, not least the lyre. But despite an infusion of foreign impulses and the creative flowering that resulted, alien suzerainty within the sacred realm of Egypt was no small psychological blow. The Egyptians, accustomed to centuries of homogeneity within the cushioned realm they had long taken for granted, could not abide the loss of territory to outsiders with foreign names, foreign ideas, and foreign gods. Millennia of continuity had bred a conservative people who craved, above all things, stability and order. Now, with the two lands driven asunder, they had neither.

## THE ANCIENT ART OF CHRONOLOGIES

In the third century BC an Egyptian priest named Manetho wrote a chronology of the nation's kings called *Aegyptiaca*. A cleric commissioned by Ptolemy II, second of the Ptolemaic rulers (r. 285–246 BC), Manetho grouped the pharaohs into thirty dynasties, creating a rough framework for pharaonic history that has endured to this day. Unfortunately, it survives only in excerpts compiled by later writers such as Josephus and Eusebius. Enhanced and contextualized by other written sources as well as extensive archaeological work, Manetho's work is vital to modern historians' division of ancient Egypt into "kingdoms" and "intermediate periods."

And that was not all. To the south, in Nubia—Egypt's precious goldmine—the kingdom of Kush was making rumblings of independence. It was not long before the Hyksos and the Kushites were talking to each other, threatening to encircle Egypt in a hostile pincer. Seth, the god of chaos, seemed to have triumphed at last.

A response eventually came around 1550 BC from Thebes, ancient city of the god Amon and seat of the last house to reunite Egypt, during the Eleventh Dynasty. Beginning with Seqenenre, the Theban kings of the Seventeenth Dynasty—who had maintained control of Upper Egypt since the coming of the Hyksos—dedicated themselves to reuniting the kingdom once more. The Hyksos, initially accepted as de facto rulers of the north, were now the enemies of sacred Egypt. "I will close with him that I may slit open his belly," proclaimed Kamose, son of Seqenenre, "for my desire is to rescue Egypt and to drive out the Asiatics."

## THE STORM BREAKS

The mummy of Seqenenre is a testament to the brutal days that capped the Second Intermediate Period. In addition to a shattered cheekbone, the pharaoh's skull has a gash in the forehead in a shape that bears a conspicuous resemblance to the damage profile of a Hyksos axe. As if that were not enough, the back of the corpse's neck gapes with an ugly dagger thrust that was likely delivered when the victim was prone. Here was a king who led his army personally, and who paid dearly for it.

His son Kamose probably ruled only three years or so but proudly bore the name "Kamose the Brave." Moving north by land and river, his army dealt the Hyksos a series of blows but failed to conquer them. Ahmose, Kamose's successor, finished the job, successfully besieging the Hyksos power bases in the north, cutting off their retreat to Palestine, and hitting their demoralized forces at the city of Avaris. There the Hyksos surrendered and, depending on which source you believe, either succumbed to slaughter or signed a treaty and departed from Egypt en masse. Ahmose drove into Palestine itself, returned to Egypt, and then wheeled south to deal with Kush, securing the vassal status of Nubia once again.

With the campaigns of Ahmose, the Eighteenth Dynasty reunited the two lands. Like his hallowed predecessor Mentuhotep II, founder of the Middle Kingdom, Ahmose ushered in a new era—the New Kingdom—by sheer force of will. And the Egyptian elite had learned its lesson: the outside world, strange and intractable, presented challenges too threatening to leave to fate. The discord sowed by the Hyksos must never happen again, and the only way to ensure that was to go beyond the borders of Egypt and see to it personally.

## EMPIRE

By driving out the Hyksos, the Thebans of the Eighteenth Dynasty had set the martial pattern of future pharaohs. From this point on, kings were compelled by sacred honor to be as much soldier as ruler—to secure the devotion of the two lands by campaigning abroad. Once upon a time, it had been enough to build up the bureaucracy, secure the frontiers, ensure the harvest, and build monuments to ensure one's place in the afterlife. No more.

All pharaohs since the Old Kingdom had portrayed themselves in monumental architecture as smiters of foreign enemies, but not until Ahmose had this become so central to the pharaoh's image. Now, in the New Kingdom, it would become increasingly important for aspiring kings to emulate Ahmose's bloody deeds. The bureaucracy and its institutionalized learning had been the hallmark of the Middle Kingdom. In the New Kingdom, military readiness and domination of foreigners mattered most. Egypt's imperial age had begun.

This was the age that saw some of Egypt's most famous rulers, including—perhaps most sensationally—Queen Hatshepsut (r. 1473–1458 BC). Though originally governing as the co-regent of her young stepson, Thutmose III, Hatshepsut soon declared herself sole ruler, presiding over a period of peace and prosperity that included a much vaunted mission to Punt, a rich land beyond Nubia. After her disappearance in 1458 BC, Thutmose III assumed sole kingship—and not long afterward virtually every representation of Hatshepsut in the monuments and temples was systematically desecrated. Whether it was because of Thutmose's resentment at his stepmother's regency, or because of some other unforgivable slight on the part of the queen, Hatshepsut was nearly wiped from the record—an act of deliberate cruelty, as one's representation in this world was believed to guarantee eternity in the next.

Thutmose III did a lot more than wage war on his stepmother's memory. When Egypt's hold over the Levantine cities was threatened by the kingdom of Mitanni, the pharaoh began a military intervention in Asia that would last most of his reign

*Head of a pharaoh of the Eighteenth Dynasty, possibly the great Hatshepsut herself.*

and include no less than seventeen expeditions. Egypt's access to the region's resources, especially copper and Lebanese cedar, was the *casus belli*, but Thutmose ended up bagging much more than that during his conquests. The spoils taken after the siege of Megiddo alone included 894 chariots, over 2,000 horses, and some 200 suits of armor. Clearly military might had its rewards.

Other pharaohs did their best to follow suit. During the Eighteenth Dynasty much of Nubia, perennial stomping ground of campaigning pharaohs, now became an outright possession of Egypt, its valuable mines worked directly by Egyptian authorities who could rely on forts that were being built farther and farther south along the Nile. Precious metals and luxury goods were brought from as far away as Cyprus and Syria, and hostages from neighboring lands filled the court as guarantors of good behavior. Truly the Lord of the Two Lands had become an emperor.

All of this grandeur found expression in new waves of monument building, fueled by an artistic revival and made possible by the dizzying influx of raw materials that came with conquest. Most spectacular of all was the temple complex at Karnak near Thebes, the city whose families had twice reunited the two lands. Already the site of sacred construction since the Middle Kingdom, it was the Eighteenth Dynasty pharaohs who began turning Karnak into a vast construction project—the glorious religious court of a proud, wealthy state. And, ironically, therein lay an insidious vulnerability for the kingdom's future.

The accretion of wealth and religious influence at Thebes would have dire consequences in years to come. Though no one could know it at the time, of course, the growing power of the Theban priests was the final element required for Egypt's eventual decline, adding itself to the kingdom's other weaknesses: the fragility of north–south cooperation, growing agitation from foreign powers, increasing reliance on war, and the inexorable hemorrhaging of pharaonic power. Centuries in the future, these circumstances would conspire to bring about the civilization's fall. All that was needed was a jolt to get the long process started.

It came in 1352 BC and it had a name: Akhenaton.

## THE SUN RISES OVER EGYPT

By the middle of the Eighteenth Dynasty the priests who maintained the temples at Thebes had become more than clerics. Much more. In fact, during this period as much as a quarter of all the land under cultivation in Egypt was owned by the priests of Amon at Karnak. With so much wealth, the priests began to expand their traditional roles as keepers of the faith to include regional administrators and even military commanders.

It was not long before the real power in Upper Egypt lay in the vast religious compound at Thebes.

The pharaohs were all too aware of this development; after all, their conquests and patronage had helped it to happen. Suspicion of the Theban priests soon became standard in the ruling house—a schism that spread into spiritual realms.

Amon, the god whose worshippers had long been based at Thebes, was a deity as mysterious as he was powerful. In the primordial days he had been associated with air and wind—his name, in fact, means "unseen one." By the era of the New Kingdom, however, his stock had risen considerably, and he was widely worshipped as the king of the gods.

Long associated with Upper Egypt, Amon was deep and elusive. His opposite was the Aton—the physical disk of the sun god Re—a luminous, life-affirming deity popular in Lower Egypt. Amenhotep III (1390–1352 BC), wary of the growing power of Thebes, ensconced his court in the north at Memphis, where he favored the heliocentric world of Re. A division was clearly emerging along the traditional lines of north and south, but it was Amenhotep III's successor who would dramatically raise the stakes in this conflict.

Amenhotep IV is known to history by the name he adopted for himself: Akhenaton, meaning "he who acts on behalf of the Aton." Just five years into his reign as pharaoh (1352–1336 BC), Akhenaton broke completely with the Theban establishment and did what can justifiably be called a very rash thing: he proclaimed the Aton sole god, dismissing the rest of Egypt's hallowed pantheon as false. As far as Akhenaton was concerned, Egypt was now a monotheistic state and he would tolerate no ideas to the contrary.

The renegade pharaoh even built his own capital, called Akhetaton, or "Horizon of Aton." From there he directed a revolution in Egyptian life, overturning ancient institutions and ushering in a new regime that would change the course of history.

## THE TREMORS OF HERESY

Akhenaton's new order marked a reversal of much of Egyptian orthodoxy. New temples to the Aton, for example, celebrated open space, rejecting the traditional columned halls and confined, lightless inner sanctum. In art, an unmistakable realism crept into paintings, emphasizing true forms and perspectives over the ossified formality that had dominated Egyptian art since the Old Kingdom. Figures appear free, loose, and spirited, evoking a break with convention that was clearly deliberate. All of society, it seemed, was reborn, just as the sun was reborn every morning in the east. Akhenaton saw himself as nothing less than a savior.

*Relief from the royal palace at Tell el-Amarna, showing Akhenaton, Nefertiti and their daughter Meritaton making an offering to the Aton.*

The priests at Thebes were not impressed. Moreover, they were out of a job. Amon, who had even been reimagined in earlier dynasties as a politically correct Amon-Re, hybrid of the Theban god and his sunny Delta colleague, had been dismissed out of hand. As far as the disenfranchised priesthood was concerned, the new order was an abomination. And they had allies—after all, Egypt was a land of pious people, each of whom had a precious deity whose favor meant more than anything in the course of everyday life. Whether north or south, in the Delta or in the Valley, people since time out of memory had depended on a vast pantheon of gods as eternal as the pyramids. Now the pharaoh, at a whim, had made them all extinct.

And that was not all. Akhenaton had not only promoted the Aton; he had promoted himself. If the Aton was the only god, his agent on earth, Akhenaton, was the only connection to him. All worship, therefore, must now be directed to the pharaoh and the pharaoh alone. By royal decree, deification had been restored to the king. The megalomaniacs of the Old Kingdom would have been jealous.

From his new capital at Akhetaton, a site known today as Tell el-Amarna, Akhenaton pushed the rays of his new solar faith outward to every corner of Egypt. The people, however, merely averted their eyes and kept to the old ways. The pharaoh, it seemed, was an apostate.

Akhenaton died in 1336 BC and was probably succeeded by Neferneferuaton, who died only two years later. The next pharaoh presided over the rejection of Akhenaton's fragile order, his very name representing a civilization's return to the past. Though coming to the throne as Tutankhaton, he soon changed his name to Tutankhamen, attaching himself to the traditional god of kings whose temple formed the heart of Karnak. (Some thirty centuries later, he would become famous as "King Tut" after the discovery of his undisturbed tomb by Howard Carter.)

## FINAL GREATNESS

The Eighteenth Dynasty ended not long after Tutankhamen's death at an early age. Horemheb, a general, succeeded to the throne and devoted much effort to erasing Akhenaton's legacy. Then came Ramses I, founder of the Nineteenth Dynasty—the last dynasty that can be called truly great.

The experiment in monotheism had shaken Egyptian civilization to its core. That it managed to recover, albeit temporarily, had much to do with the quality of leadership showed by those who held the throne from 1295 BC. Most famous of the Nineteenth Dynasty pharaohs was Ramses II (r. 1279–1213 BC), who grappled with the Hittites at the battle of Kadesh, maintaining control over Syria-Palestine and ensuring peace

*Laborers cart new sculptures into an Egyptian temple, some time during the Nineteenth Dynasty. This reconstruction gives an idea of the elaborate decoration used on such buildings.*

by marrying a Hittite princess. In the west he fought off the Libyan tribes, which had been aggressively encroaching on the Delta from their desert homelands. His military achievements were more than matched by his building program: he further enhanced the majesty of the Temple of Amon at Karnak, covered the countryside with monumental statues of himself, and oversaw the creation of his impressive mortuary temple at Thebes, the Ramesseum. At Abu Simbel, in northern Nubia, he left a magnificent temple hewed from the mountain face, perhaps his most impressive legacy.

Ramses II also usurped a host of temples and statues left by previous pharaohs, a coopting of the past that mirrored his belief in a resurgent Egypt harkening back to the days before Akhenaton. Things were indeed good: trade flourished with Asia and the south. Ramses II reigned for over sixty-six glorious years, lived to be over ninety years old, produced a veritable horde of offspring, and enjoyed an unprecedented fourteen *sed* festivals (the jubilees, beginning in a pharaoh's thirtieth year of rule and then occurring every three or four years, that celebrated his vitality). Little wonder that he dominates the history books as Ramses the Great. He remains the capstone to his empire's golden age.

By the end of the Nineteenth Dynasty, however, great pharaohs were as rare and precious as the lapis lazuli used to grace their death masks. The next dynasty confirmed this—and though the pharaohs of the Twentieth kept adopting Ramses's name (there were eleven of them in all), they could not hide the hard facts.

## A TUMULTUOUS TIME

As the first millennium BC approached, all of Egypt's chickens—to borrow an apt anachronism—started coming home to roost.

To begin with, the schism between Thebes in the south and Lower Egypt was widening. Akhenaton's attempt at overturning the kingdom's religion had left two indelible wounds. By his reckless ideological excess, he had undermined faith in the pharaoh, furthering a process that had been underway for centuries. And by attacking the Theban priests of Amon, he had inspired their resolve to expand the power base that had been so rashly stolen from them. Pharaohs like Ramses II had been strong enough to keep Thebes in its place but the weaker kings of the Twentieth and Twenty-First Dynasties were not up to the task.

The Theban priests gathered their strength and began to assert greater influence over Upper and Middle Egypt. And why not? The pharaohs, for the most part, were busy validating their status with campaigns in foreign lands. Empire had become convenient: if it brought in the goods and resources necessary for a thriving commercial economy, it also provided kings with a *raison d'être*. War, or at least raiding, was a necessity on the frontiers in Asia and Nubia. And in the wake of Akhenaton, a pharaoh was more likely to impress cynics with corpses and captives than with bureaucratic reform.

Nevertheless, in reaction to the Akhenaton period, the cult of Amon waxed considerably. In fact, his aura came to encompass the kingship itself, and he became the primary deity to whom the most important Egyptians directed their devotions. Amon was the manifestation of royal power—a development that elevated the status of the Theban priests even as it compromised the pharaoh.

These trends were exacerbated by the issue that in time became Egypt's bane: the interests of foreign peoples. During the thirteenth and twelfth centuries, a wave of migration was set in motion throughout the eastern Mediterranean, probably by widespread crop failures in the lands around the Aegean. Collectively known to the Egyptians as the "Sea Peoples," these invaders moved into the Levant and northern Egypt with fire and sword, throwing the whole power balance of the ancient world into disarray. Though the impact on Egypt was smaller than it was on other civilizations, Palestine and Syria were lost and trade throughout the empire suffered a severe setback.

The greatest foreign threat, however, came not from the north or east, but from the west, once Egypt's quietest border. Driven into the Delta by a Sahara that was becoming more and more barren, the Libyans came as immigrants whose numbers eventually afforded them influence in Egyptian affairs—not unlike the Hyksos of old. That their presence in the north was growing at precisely the time when pharaonic power was waning during the Twenty-First Dynasty (1069–945 BC) would prove fateful.

## WHO RULES?

Civil war sparked the Third Intermediate Period. During the reign of the last Ramessid, Ramses XI (r. 1099–1069 BC), a noble named Panehsy, viceroy of Nubia, charged with governing that region on behalf of the pharaoh, marched on Thebes to quell the chaos that reigned there in the wake of economic woes. The viceroy's rash move, apparently done on his own authority, started a civil war that Egypt could ill afford. When it was over, Nubia lay beyond the reach of Egypt's authority, depriving the kingdom of invaluable resources, and a military junta that formed around the high priest of Amon ruled Thebes and all Upper Egypt.

The kings of the Twenty-First Dynasty were happy to admit the limits of their authority, ruling Lower Egypt from the Delta city of Tanis, while the Theban priest-commanders in the south built a string of forts near the entrance to the valley known as the Faiyum in Middle Egypt, formally marking the division of the two lands.

The Libyans, now a pervasive force in the military of Lower Egypt, gradually assumed greater control there. Eventually they achieved a first, becoming the first non-Egyptians to sit on the pharaoh's throne: the Twenty-Second Dynasty (945–715 BC), founded by Sheshonk I, would be known as the Libyan period.

Foreign control of the kingship was a watershed. Egypt's awesome civilization overwhelmed the Libyans, inspiring them to adopt Egyptian culture, but the exchange went both ways. Hailing from a semi-nomadic society far to the west, Libyan notions of kingship were less elaborate and less focused than Egypt's. Localized power along the lines of chiefdoms was not as unpalatable to them. Consequently, as Thebes consolidated its hold on Upper Egypt during the Third Intermediate Period, Lower Egypt divided into smaller power bases with semi-autonomous governorships—most of them held by Libyans—jockeying for resources in a land that had lost its immense stature on the world stage.

It had not, however, lost its immense allure—and this would work to Egypt's detriment. The greatness of the pharaohs had become a farce, with competing dynasties claiming simultaneous rule in a fugue of authority that makes a jumble of the ninth and eighth centuries. To outsiders, Egypt's lost glory had become alarming. And no outsiders were more thunderstruck than the Nubian kingdom of Kush, whose power and independence had increased since the end of the New Kingdom. Concerned by the chaos on his northern border and sensing an opportunity, Piy, king of Kush, marched down the Nile with an army in 730 BC. The Twenty-Fifth Dynasty he established harkened back to the old pharaonic traditions—the Kushites, in perpetual reverence of the land of the pyramids, became almost more Egyptian than the Egyptians.

## CONQUERED

It fell to the Kushite pharaohs to defend Egypt from the powerful Assyrian Empire, but to no avail. The war, sparked by conflict over influence in the Levant in the mid-seventh century, proved devastating and mercifully short. It also shook things up considerably: after sweeping the Kushites back into Nubia, the Assyrians found themselves overstretched. The result was a power vacuum that—thankfully for Egypt—was filled by an extraordinary leader.

Libyans, Nubians, Assyrians—everybody, it seemed, was capable of controlling Egypt except the Egyptians. But the Twenty-Sixth Dynasty, founded by the energetic Psamtik I (r. 664–610 BC), was an exception, marking the last long period of successful, unified, native rule. After wresting independence from Assyria and capturing the Delta by force, he marched south, quelling or conquering opposing princes and even wooing the Theban priests to his side. It is significant, however, to recall just how he did it: by relying on a large army of foreign mercenaries, including Greeks, Phoenicians, and Bedouins. Remote and traditional, Egypt had always had to deal with the risk of falling behind in the arms race of the Near East. And now military juggernauts like the Assyrians and Persians were pulling ahead once again.

Psamtik ushered in a period of prosperity, complete with unprecedented trade throughout the Mediterranean and successful military campaigns in Asia, but with Egypt's fate now inextricably attached to the rise and fall of military powers vying for supremacy in the Near East its days were numbered. The Twenty-Sixth Dynasty had inherited a deflated throne, its once-hallowed authority eroded by centuries of sectionalism. Such a government could not expect to last in a world full of predators whose greater martial abilities were matched by an appetite for Egypt's prizes.

In 525 BC Achaemenid Persia, unchallenged bully-boy of the Near East, descended on Egypt with unprecedented strength and determination. Not even the might of old Assyria could compare with that of the Achaemenids, whose armies would ultimately carve out an empire spanning three million square miles. Pelusium, a fortified town on the far eastern edge of the Delta, had guarded Egypt's northeastern frontier for centuries. It was near its walls that Cambyses II, king of the Persians, clashed with Egypt's armies.

The Persians had prepared their march across Sinai by organizing way stations through the desert, complete with water provided by friendly Arab tribes. Emerging from the desert, the Persians routed their outnumbered Egyptian foes and quickly captured Pelusium itself, clearing the way for an invasion of the Delta. Memphis fell soon afterward, and the Persians gradually assumed control of the whole country. Two millennia after Khufu built the Great Pyramid, Egypt of the pharaohs effectively passed into memory.

From 525 BC—with a brief respite between 404 and 343—Egypt would be an occupied country, first under the Persians and then, after 332, under the Macedonians. The Romans would come as well, assuming direct control over Egypt from 30 BC. All of these peoples became as thoroughly conquered by Egyptian customs as Egypt itself was by military superiority. The Persian and Ptolemaic rulers adopted the trappings of pharaonic majesty, being cognizant of its ability to channel timeless tradition into civil obedience and entranced by its wonder and ritual.

This is the legacy of Egypt's "decline"—one of cultural endurance in the face of political and military failure. Few cultures thrived for as long as ancient Egypt's. Not until the sixth century AD were the last pagan temples destroyed there, falling prey to a new order—Christianity—that in turn would fall to Islam. An incredible feat, indeed, for a nation whose political fortunes had collapsed almost a millennium earlier.

CHAPTER TWO

# THE MINOANS

## A TALE OF TWO PEOPLES

IN 1876 Heinrich Schliemann, a German entrepreneur and adventurer with a passion for Homeric Greece, plumbed the stony depths of a great Bronze Age ruin in the Peloponnese and struck gold. It was not the first time. Before coming to the Mediterranean to make history, he had made a fortune in California selling supplies to the dreamers of America's Gold Rush. He then became a dreamer himself, setting his mind on proving the veracity of Homer's tales through archaeology.

In the early 1870s he achieved the incredible by locating Troy itself, the ancient Anatolian city whose fall at the hands of the Achaeans in Homer's epics had long been written off as myth. In what became the infamous climax of the excavation, Schliemann and his Greek wife, Sophia, entered a recently breached chamber and emerged with "Priam's treasure"—a hoard of gold jewelry that in the coming days would adorn Sophia's head for the photo op of the century. Whether it was appropriate for her to fancy herself a nineteenth-century Helen was the least of the Schliemanns' worries, as rumors began to surface of something even more tasteless—specifically, the planting of the treasure itself, a possibility that exercises scholars to this day.

Scandal would forever shadow Schliemann, not least because his excavations were usually carried through with all the subtlety of siege warfare. But Troy's glories had made him into an international celebrity, and in 1876 he went to the Peloponnese with the intention of exposing Mycenae, the fabled heart of Homeric Greece. There, opening the dark tombs beneath one of the Bronze Age's most formidable citadels, he found perhaps his greatest legacy: a royal burial, as "rich in gold" as any king's cache out of legend. As Schliemann himself explained, he reached for the gold death mask and, for a brief instant, "beheld the face of Agamemnon."

A quarter century later, the Englishman Arthur Evans went digging in the shadow of a figure

*Previous pages: Contractura column from the Palace at Knossos.*
*Above: Gold funerary mask from Mycenae, mistakenly thought by Schliemann to be that of Agamemnon.*

nearly as legendary as Agamemnon: King Minos. What he unearthed at Knossos in central Crete was an impressive palace complex with storage chambers, or magazines, full of enormous storage vessels called *pithoi*. Dazzling frescoes on the crumbling walls took his breath away, while the ruin's labyrinthine nature reminded him of the mythic Minotaur to whom Minos sacrificed youths brought from Greece. Inspired by this, Evans dubbed the palace's builders "Minoans."

Evans also had his fair share of scandal. With little to go on, he proceeded to reconstruct some of the Knossos rooms, bringing something of their long-lost glory back to life. Though guided by a rational interpretation of the evidence, Evans's "restoration" of Knossos has made more than a few archaeologists cringe.

These two intrepid men, for all their faults, helped to force open the long-shut window on the Bronze Age Aegean. Schliemann had not, in fact, seen the face of Agamemnon (the mask he discovered was too old to be that of Troy's conqueror), and the Knossos that greets visitors to this day owes as much to Evans's imagination as it does to painstaking fieldwork. Nevertheless, they risked everything for dreams of discovery—and they turned myth into history.

Moreover, they had begun to assemble the story of an amazing time and place—a tale of two peoples whose fates seemed bound together. As scholars soon discovered, understanding the fall of the Minoans meant getting to know their Aegean neighbors, the Mycenaeans.

## BUILDERS AND ADMINISTRATORS

Crete is a long, narrow island measuring over 150 miles from east to west. From the eight-thousand-foot mountains that form its spine to the harbors that dot its long coastline, it presents a breathtaking variety of physical environments. And there is plenty of good arable land, where farmers have been growing vines, olives, and grain in profusion since time out of memory.

Emerging out of the mists of the Late Stone Age, the "Minoans" (we do not know what they called themselves) thrived in their island paradise, eventually organizing themselves into a highly structured society. The physical expressions of this civilizing impulse—Crete's impressive "palaces"—began to emerge some time in the mid-twentieth century BC. Knossos, though certainly important, was hardly the only one of these capital centers. There were also palaces at Phaistos in the south, at Mallia on the northern coast east of Knossos, and probably at Khania and Zakros in the far west and east, respectively.

These were remarkable buildings, each characterized by a central court around which rooms and halls were clustered. A second court was typically situated to the west.

Though each palace featured distinctive elements, they all had a common purpose: to serve as the organizational heart of the surrounding countryside.

Proof of this was found in the magazines, or storage chambers, which usually lay on the palace's ground floor. Here excavators have found the amazing *pithoi*, enormous ceramic vessels, resting in long rows as if they had been abandoned just months ago. Standing up to six feet in height, they were used to store the bounty of Crete, from wheat and barley to olives, pomegranates, wine, and oil. They offer silent testament to the administrative role of the palaces, which gathered local produce for measured redistribution to surrounding towns and villages.

Or so it seems. The fact is, scholars can only speculate, however insightfully, on what Minoan society was truly like. This is because the Minoans left no literature and very few records, leaving to archaeology the burden of answering our questions.

## TANTALIZING PEEKS AT A DAZZLING CULTURE

And we have so many questions!

For instance, who led? The Minoans may well have been ruled by queens. Much of their art portrays women as equals of men—a rare cultural practice indeed in the Bronze Age Mediterranean and Near East. Even feats of daring and athleticism included females: frescoes portraying bull-jumping, in which participants appear to vault over an oncoming bull, feature female performers as well as male.

How united were the Minoans? Knossos clearly dominated through most of Minoan history, but it is anyone's guess as to how completely. This is an issue particularly in the earliest years, though it persists throughout the history of ancient Crete. Conflict between the major palace centers clearly occurred at some points during the Bronze Age, not unlike the wars between Greek city-states in later centuries, but did any one dynasty ever control the whole island? We do not know.

What deities did they worship? Minoan goddesses, either separate deities or different manifestations of the same Great Mother, abound. Representing these female spirits was a host of sacred symbols, which included serpents, stylized bull's horns, and the ubiquitous double-headed axe. Much about Minoan religious life remains mysterious, however.

Without more certain answers to questions such as these, efforts to see the Minoans as they really were are bound to be inconclusive. But on certain matters there is agreement. Around 1700 BC, the palaces of Crete suffered a widespread calamity. All of them burned to the ground, whether because of outside invasion, earthquake, internecine warfare, or

something else. This destruction of Minoan architecture marks the end of what scholars call the Protopalatial Period of Minoan history.

## MARINERS AND TRADERS

Just as interesting as the end of Crete's first palatial period is the swiftness with which the Minoans recovered. In fact, they simply rebuilt their palaces. Neopalatial, as the next period has been called, covers the zenith of classic Minoan culture.

Though no larger (and in some cases even smaller) than their predecessors, the second palaces were brilliant displays of Minoan building and artistic prowess. The central and western courts remained, with a maze of connected rooms extending outward from each. Blending cloistered and open spaces, light wells, and multi-storyed structures in asymmetric layouts, the palaces were built with ashlar masonry faced with plaster and strengthened against seismic activity with wood beams. Porticos, broad staircases, distinctive pillars (usually painted red and, in the characteristic Minoan style, tapering from top to bottom), and elegant facades would have overwhelmed the visitor from all sides—a calculated miscellany of color and structure, awe-inspiring in its mathematical

*Above: Fresco from the palace at Knossos showing the three stages of bull jumping. Both men (red skin) and women (white skin) took part in the ceremony.*

articulation. Little wonder that Knossos, the "Palace of Minos," endured in Greek memory as a labyrinth.

Bringing together a wide variety of societal functions, the palaces fulfilled religious, social, and governmental requirements, all of which may have blended seamlessly in the Minoan world. The grounds included workshops, living quarters, administrative chambers, temples, and public spaces, and were connected with local residential districts. The great magazines were still there as well, jammed with *pithoi*. Water and drainage systems, such as the one that has survived at Knossos, were meticulously conceived and built, displaying an outstanding level of civil engineering. Indeed, the Minoans even built the first paved roads in European history, linking far-flung regions with a network of thoroughfares constructed of stone.

The Neopalatial Period also witnessed the appearance of country villas. These smaller complexes, built in remote areas well beyond the palaces and their accompanying towns, were clearly linked to the power structure centered at the palaces, though it remains unclear precisely how. Perhaps they were subsidiary power centers, or country homes for the aristocracy.

All of these structures—the roads, the villas, the palaces and their towns—formed the infrastructure of a great civilization whose influence spread throughout the Aegean. Crete stood at the heart of a vast trading venture built on maritime strength. Throughout the eastern Mediterranean, Minoan satellites—whether colonies, outposts, independent settlements, or some combination of these—sprang up during the Bronze Age, propagating Minoan tastes in pottery, architecture, and ritual as far away as the Peloponnese and Asia Minor.

Evidence points to close links with Syria and Palestine, Egypt, and the northern Aegean, and many of the islands of the eastern Mediterranean reveal a Minoan presence during this time. Such an expansion of culture would not have been possible without extensive trade; these were people of the sea with an impulse to take their thriving way of life to distant shores and to barter its products for luxuries, precious metals, and exotic produce.

Self-sufficient in timber and agriculture, the people of Crete built a water-borne domain whose many varied contacts spurred creativity and gave birth to a unique people—they were as much the western outpost of the Near East as they were Europeans. But despite their location at the crossroads of Bronze Age civilizations, the Minoans left precious little evidence of war. Fortifications, in fact, are almost entirely absent. Whatever the truth behind this enduring puzzle, it seems fair to view the Minoans as dedicated seafarers whose ships not only plied the trade routes but also secured the coastlines.

## OF GRAVES AND GOLD

A different reality was taking shape to the north. There an Indo-European people, having migrated from Eurasia, had moved into the Greek mainland and established themselves in settlements dominated by hilltop strongholds. This was the culture that scholars have named for the greatest of its citadels, Mycenae. And the Mycenaeans hardly lacked for signs of warrior culture.

Evidence for this has emerged from the tombs in which they buried their rulers and warrior princes. Of two types—*tholoi*, featuring a dramatic beehive-shaped dome at the end of a processional path or *dromos*, and shaft graves, in which the deceased were lowered to rest at the bottom of a deep rectangular shaft—the tombs of Mycenaean Greece open a window, however skewed, on the formidable civilization that produced them.

The interred themselves must have seemed like giants in their time. Standing nearly six feet tall, they were well fed and heavily muscled, clearly the elite of a martial aristocracy. The goods that accompanied them into the afterlife bear this out: brilliantly crafted swords, spear points, daggers, and other weapons, along with helmets covered with boar's tusks and pieces of bronze armor. Gold artifacts abound—evidence of extensive trade abroad, given Greece's lack of gold deposits. And the presence of Minoan jewelry and seal rings points to close links with Crete.

If the Mycenaeans were clearly influenced by the Minoans, however, the differences between them were acute. The frescoes of Crete, rich in scenes of playful youths, frolicking animals, and worshipping priestesses, stand in stark contrast to the art of Bronze Age Greece with its chariots, clashing warriors, and hunting parties. And the differences went deeper than depictions of war and peace. Though the rulers of Mycenae and the other citadels of the mainland were able to tap into the wider Aegean world that Crete dominated, they were as landward-oriented in their hillside strongholds as the Minoans were tied to the sea-lanes.

These distinctions would become more blurred with time. Mycenaean Greece was just coming into its own as the Minoans were at their zenith, dominating the eastern Mediterranean with their commercial prowess and deep cultural sophistication. But shortly after 1400 BC, the Mycenaeans started building the colossal citadels for which they would become famous—hilltop fortifications with massive bastions built of stones so huge that later Greeks believed them to be the work of the Cyclopes, huge craftsmen with superhuman strength. To this day the style is known as "cyclopean."

These marvelous halls of stone, the ultimate expressions of a warrior aristocracy, bore grim testament to the Mycenaeans' arrival as a Mediterranean power capable of expanding outward. And they came right on the heels of Minoan Crete's sudden downfall.

## A GREAT POWER LAID LOW

Between roughly 1450 and 1380 BC, the Minoan world suffered a catastrophic collapse. While Knossos endured as a shadow of its former self, every other major palace on the island of Crete was destroyed by fire. The Minoan culture's widespread influence, once unassailable, ended seemingly overnight. What could possibly account for this?

Anyone who has visited Santorini, closest of the Cyclades Islands to Crete, has seen firsthand what was believed for years to be the smoking gun of the Minoan collapse.

*Above: The most famous of the* tholos *tombs at Mycenae is the so-called Treasury of Atreus, or Tomb of Agamemnon.*

Standing in the streets of Phira, largest of the island's towns, one can teeter on the very precipice of what appears to be an enormous, crescent-shaped cliff, its great arc bowing forward to hug Santorini's harbor with two massive arms. A similar geography can be seen opposite the town on Therasia, Santorini's smaller neighbor and, upon closer inspection, a mirror image of the larger island.

Stunning in the Mediterranean sun, the tranquil idyll of Santorini (also known as Thera) belies an incomprehensibly violent past. The cliffs, in fact, are merely the top of a gigantic caldera that has filled with water to become one of Europe's most beloved tourist destinations. Where a harbor full of cruise ships now laps against the rocks, a huge volcano hissed and rumbled in antiquity. And then, around 1600 BC, it blew sky-high in the noisiest, most destructive seismic blast in history.

The apocalyptic plume of ash would have blotted the sky for miles, dumping deadly debris as far away as the Nile Delta. Crete certainly was affected, and probably dramatically. Tsunamis must have devastated the Aegean, smashing coastal settlements to pieces. All of which seems to say that Cretan civilization must have been destroyed by Thera's eruption, but this is almost certainly incorrect.

Why? Because while experts continue to disagree over the exact date of Thera's eruption, almost all of them acknowledge that there was as much as two hundred years of thriving Minoan settlement throughout the Aegean *after* the event. Thera's destruction

## BRONZE AGE TIME CAPSULE

When Thera exploded some 3,600 years ago, it did more than just terrify the Aegean world—it also, ironically, saved for posterity a jewel of modern archaeology. Buried beneath the scalding ash on the very island of Thera itself, a Minoan town—now known as Akrotiri—was preserved for eternity much as it had been on that fateful, violent day about 1600 BC.

The site was first excavated by the late Spyridon Marinatos, one of the most esteemed archaeologists of the twentieth century. Like Herculaneum and Pompeii, Akrotiri held a moment in deep time waiting to be discovered. Marinatos and his successors have found *pithoi*, multi-storyed houses full of frescoes, milling installations, and other features. Though not a palace complex like those on Crete, the town features elements typical of Minoan genius—pipe systems for hot and cold running water, for instance, as well as water closets and a complex drainage system.

Akrotiri was clearly a community of wealthy merchants, craftsmen, and fishermen. Not even Knossos has given us a clearer look at this extraordinary civilization.

may well have wreaked havoc on Crete and elsewhere, but it did not bring about the demise of the Minoan "empire" all by itself. The fiery end of the palaces happened generations later.

## THE THIRD MAN

So what *did* bring down the great Minoan centers?

To shed more light on this engrossing and tenacious issue, we need to jump forward once again, to the twentieth century. It was then, during the 1950s, that Michael Ventris brought together the two worlds that Schliemann and Evans first began to resurrect. In one of the most important archaeological breakthroughs of the century, Ventris—with the help of John Chadwick—deciphered the script called Linear B.

Linear A, which remains undeciphered to this day, was an older script employed throughout the Minoan world. Linear B, by contrast, appeared on tablets at Knossos and elsewhere only after the collapse of the palaces. Ventris's triumph was to prove that, contrary to scholarly belief at the time, Linear B was an early form of Greek. In other words, it was a Mycenaean script and the Mycenaeans had brought their own indigenous script from the mainland to Crete in the wake of the catastrophes of about 1400 BC—proof that Mycenaean culture replaced that of the Minoans, both on Crete and elsewhere in the Minoan diaspora.

The manner of that replacement, however, is open to question. It is not unreasonable to imagine a Mycenaean conquest of Crete and its extensive trade networks—to see the events of 1400 BC as the culmination of a generations-long struggle between the two cultures over control of the Aegean, with the Mycenaeans triumphant. On the other hand, archaeologists are keen to point out that Mycenaean control of Knossos did not commence until well after the palace's near-destruction. This, it would seem, leads to a scenario in which Minoan strength is long spent by the time that Mycenaean Greeks, scavenger-like, move in to assume control.

So what are we left with? Around 1600 BC, Thera erupted with otherworldly force, spreading mayhem and who-knows-what throughout the eastern Mediterranean. Such a singularly calamitous event could well have brought Cretan agriculture to its knees, even if it did not wipe out the Minoans.

Around two centuries later, two things occurred within close temporal proximity to each other: the vast domain of the Minoans centered on the palaces of Crete collapsed dramatically, while Mycenaean Greece rose to new heights as evidenced by the tremendous stone works at Mycenae and other citadels. Then, within a generation or so, the extensive maritime civilization that was once distinctly Minoan succumbed to a Mycenaean takeover. If Thera erupted too early, and the Mycenaeans came too late, what happened to the Minoan palaces? As of now, no one knows for sure. The Mycenaeans were clearly competitors, and warlike ones at that, but why would they have destroyed the palace settlements they wanted to possess themselves?

Perhaps they were invited in by one particular faction in a war between Minoans for control of the island, participating in a long, destructive war that ultimately helped them to enforce their own agenda. Who knows? All that can be said with confidence is that a shift in power had occurred in the region—the Mycenaeans gradually stopped living in the shadow of their illustrious Minoan fellows and replaced them as dominators of the Aegean.

As archaeologists continue to unearth treasures from the ancient Mediterranean, the shadows concealing Crete's deep past may well be dissipated completely. But for the moment, the fate of Minoan greatness remains a mystery—and one of the many reasons this glorious culture continues to fascinate us.

## AFTER THE FALL

The great conflagrations of the mid-to-late fifteenth century BC throughout the Minoan world may have destroyed the status quo, but they hardly did away with the Minoans themselves. What emerged in Crete has been called "Mycenaeanization," referring to the gradual assumption there of Greek cultural elements and institutions—Linear B being the most famous. But these merged with, rather than replaced, the indigenous customs, creating a new Bronze Age culture that managed to flourish for another two centuries. The Mycenaeans may have taken control, but like so many occupiers throughout history, they also took on much of the local flavor. Crete had lost its native control and preeminence in the Aegean but it endured as part of the burgeoning Mycenaean world.

That world, on Crete and elsewhere, came to an abrupt end at the dramatic conclusion of the Bronze Age, after 1200 BC. The twelfth and eleventh centuries, a period of tumult and violence marked by the widespread movements of peoples throughout the eastern Mediterranean and Near East, spelled the end of many civilizations, including the Mycenaean.

On Crete, archaeologists have discovered numerous mountaintop sanctuaries from this period—makeshift homes of people fleeing inland from invaders. By the end of these still mysterious convulsions, the lights of Aegean high culture had all but gone out: Linear B, for instance, was lost, and writing would not reappear in the Greek world for another three centuries.

CHAPTER THREE

# THE HITTITES

## VICTIMS OF THE SEA PEOPLES

IN May 1286 BC, one of the most spectacular events in all antiquity occurred along the banks of the Orontes River in modern-day Syria. The fortress-city of Kadesh, of major importance to those who wanted to control the northern Levant, became the focus of a struggle between two of history's first empires.

One of them was Egypt, then in the midst of a martial revival under the New Kingdom's Nineteenth Dynasty. Five years into his reign, Ramses II led his army out of Egypt, across the Sinai, and up the ancient invasion route of Palestine to resolve, once and for all, an issue that had been festering for many years: the extent of Egyptian influence in Syria and Lebanon. His claim was being challenged by a powerful Anatolian empire based on the kingdom of Hatti, whose people have become known to us as "Hittites." Their King Muwatallis reigned at the zenith of his nation's history, ruling a swathe of Anatolian territory that stretched from the Aegean coast to the Levant and east to the Euphrates. His people, strong in war, had humbled the toughest kingdoms of the Near East, and now they meant to trounce the cultural heavyweights of distant Africa, the Egyptians.

What happened at Kadesh was not unlike a fight between modern street gangs: as the Sharks and the Jets did in *West Side Story*, so the Egyptians and the Hittites, antagonists

*Previous pages: Stone carving from the Lion Gate at Hattusa.*
*Above: In an early example of propaganda, this Egyptian wall painting shows a large Ramses II in his chariot, attacking the city of Kadesh.*

in a match for control of the Levant, seem to have agreed on a location to iron out their respective grievances by force. Kadesh, an ancient settlement under Hittite control that stood guard on the frontier with Egyptian Syria, was an obvious choice for this prearranged showdown. The two-day clash that followed was the first well-documented large battle in history, and probably the greatest collision of chariot forces in the ancient world.

## A PHARAOH HUMBLED

Four divisions constituted the pharaoh's army, each named for a patron god: Amon (which was led personally by Ramses), Re, Ptah, and Seth. As Ramses approached Kadesh, his forces drawn out in a long line of march, his officers questioned a pair of local Bedouins, who insisted that Muwatallis's camp was still far to the north, well beyond Kadesh. Comforted by this bit of intelligence, Ramses marched northwest of the city with the division of Amon and began to set up his camp.

The rest of the army was still some distance away when the Egyptians captured two Hittite scouts. Beaten into talking, the captives told the pharaoh what he definitely did not want to hear: his earlier intelligence had been faulty—not only was the Hittite army not far to the north, it was just across the Orontes to the east, perhaps a few miles away at most.

Ramses browbeat his officers for their faulty intelligence work and sent orders for the rest of the army to come up at the double-quick. The division of Re, whose columns were just southwest of Kadesh, arrived first on the scene, as a dreadful sight came into view: hundreds of chariots bearing down on them from the east. Muwatallis had struck.

Drawn by a pair of horses, each Hittite chariot carried three men into battle, as opposed to the two in Egyptian chariots. The significance of this remains a topic of debate, but some scholars suggest that Hittite chariots could have been used not only as platforms for loosing arrows and javelins, as was common with all chariot forces of the Bronze Age, but also as a means of delivering more direct punishment. Support for this idea comes from the difference in designs: while the Egyptians constructed light chariots with the axle to the rear, affording maximum speed, the Hittites built theirs heavier, with the axle in the center to support another armored combatant. If the Egyptians intended their chariots purely as swift missile platforms, the Hittites, it seems, were not as bothered by the idea of taking theirs directly into harm's way, where the extra fighter—a dedicated shield-bearer—could help ensure the team's survival and perhaps even cause damage to enemy troops with spear and sword. The precise truth, of course, will never be known unless more ancient evidence surfaces.

In any event, the hapless soldiers of Re now reeled from the punishment of the Hittite chariots. Strung out in column for the march, they were wholly unprepared for a lightning strike in the flank by speeding charioteers who, it appears from the sources, had been hiding just out of sight behind the walls of Kadesh. The Egyptians broke and scattered.

Back in his camp, a pensive Ramses tried to make sense of the dust clouds to the south while prodding his officers to ready the corps for battle. But before the men could be drawn up, Hittite chariots emerged from the roiling dirt, the thunder of hooves announcing their imminent arrival as they came on in galloping fury. Having made a mess of the division of Re, they had wheeled north in a great sweeping arc, and now meant to savage the division of Amon—and Ramses himself.

## ORDER FROM CHAOS

The pharaoh was in trouble. With arrows falling out of the sky and his soldiers attempting to sort themselves out in the bedlam, all seemed lost. A running melee now raged from the approaches to the camp to within the camp itself, as the retreating soldiers of Re struggled to make a stand while their fellows in the corps of Amon fought to maintain order in the face of mounting disaster. Indeed, most of the Egyptian horses in camp had been unhitched from their chariots, a process that was difficult to remedy in the middle of battle.

A relatively small cadre of chariots was up and running, however, and Ramses himself now led them out in a desperate gambit to throw the Hittites off balance. (The pharaoh's official account of the battle insists that he rode out literally alone to do battle at this point, a notion that can be safely dismissed as preposterous.) We cannot know how many there were, but Ramses and the charioteers of Amon swung around behind the camp to strike at the rear of the Hittite forces from the west. With desperate fighting, they managed to cause enough havoc to allow the rest of the army room to regroup.

Muwatallis, directing affairs from the walls of Kadesh, now sent another large force of chariots splashing across the river to finish off the Egyptians. Perhaps a thousand strong, this reserve force was led by the king's brothers and included numerous units from Hittite subject states, led by their chieftains and rulers, their myriad helmets and regalia making a dazzling panoply in the bright Syrian sun.

In the shadow of Kadesh, along the west bank of the Orontes, the fight now surged back and forth, with thousands of chariots maneuvering for advantage in a battle of speeding combatants. Discipline must have been difficult at best in the swirling dust clouds, and the exact role played by infantry—let alone chariots—in such a maelstrom remains a mystery. We know that tens of thousands of infantrymen were present on both sides, but the chariots dominated the action.

There are other mysteries regarding the battle of Kadesh, including the denouement of the first day's fighting. Despite their initiative and superiority in numbers, the Hittites were unable to deal the pharaoh's army a decisive defeat, perhaps because of the timely arrival of the corps of Ptah from the south. There is also the suggestion in Egyptian sources that auxiliary forces from Syria came to the pharaoh's aid, setting upon those Hittites who were busy plundering the Egyptian camp and slaughtering them.

Another day of fighting followed, the details of which are unknown. Despite this anticlimax, the two-day battle was an event of immense significance, ultimately leading to an international treaty—the first ever to be well documented—that helped to establish peace between the two empires.

For the most part, Egypt would remain supreme throughout most of the Levant. But it was the Hittites who could boast of a strategic victory at Kadesh, for Ramses had been prevented from laying siege to the city and was compelled to return to Egypt with little to boast about save his bold intervention on the first day. And boast he did, portraying himself as a superhero surrounded by incompetents—a king who "entered in among the [Hittite] enemies, being like a storm which goes forth from heaven."

We can forgive Ramses his hubris. After all, he was a pharaoh (and one who would go down in history as "Great"). In fact, it is not hard to imagine him infusing the narrative with glorious deeds out of spite for his formidable opponents.

So who were these people who had foiled one of the most famous warlords of the ancient world?

## MASTERS OF ANATOLIA

The Hittites were relative outsiders to the Near Eastern world in which they would play a leading role. Based in central Anatolia, in what is today Turkey, their mountain fastnesses could not have been more different from the river basins of Egypt and Mesopotamia. They also spoke a different language from their Semitic neighbors to the east and south: though the Hittites adopted cuneiform writing, their tongue was Indo-European, placing their still-obscure origins somewhere to the north in Eurasia.

At some time in the third millennium BC, they and a host of other Indo-European peoples moved into Anatolia, eventually becoming established throughout most of the peninsula. Those speaking the Hittite language ultimately settled in the region around the bend of the Halys River, in central Anatolia. Evidence suggests that they formed a feudal aristocracy that dominated the indigenous population, a people known as

Hattians from whom the Hittites would adopt many cultural institutions, including gods. Only after they settled in this land of Hatti would the invaders, despite speaking an unrelated language, assume the identity that has gone down in history as "Hittite."

The central Anatolian plateau, a high tableland bound by mountains and hammered by extremes of temperature, is nevertheless sliced by river valleys. Orchards and wheat fields produced food that was more than adequate for the local population. Deposits of iron, silver, and copper brought Mesopotamian merchants bearing woolen cloth and tin, and the area's close proximity to the intersection of ancient trade routes going east and south from the Aegean and the Black Sea helped establish Hittite wealth and power.

The Hittites, a society led by warrior elites, and their fellow Eurasian newcomers excelled at fighting—for several centuries, in fact, they excelled at fighting each other. Evidence from the early second millennium points to multiple Indo-European principalities, of which Hatti was merely one, vying for control of the area. Dates are fuzzy, to say the least, but by around 1650 BC a single Hittite kingdom had emerged with its capital based firmly at Hattusa, near modern-day Bogazkoy.

## THE OLD KINGDOM

The founding figure who established his court at Hattusa renamed himself Hattusilis, "Man of Hattusa." To this dynamic leader and campaigner the Hittites traced the origins of their greatness as a Near Eastern power.

Like all rulers of the age, Hattusilis engaged in the sport of kings—war—to secure his stature among his people, particularly his fellow aristocrats, but he also had a much more pressing reason for expanding the power of Hatti. Since the early second millennium the region's settlers had relied on Assyrian traders from Mesopotamia to connect them with the wider world and its treasured goods. Long before they became an empire, the people of Assyria had been merchants of the first order, busy bargainers who went out to foreign lands to establish a network of colonies connected to their capital, Ashur. Most valued of the products they brought to the early Hittites and their neighbors was tin, which could be paired with local supplies of copper to forge bronze.

Not long after 1800 BC the northern Assyrian trade networks disappeared, probably because of the predations of Hurrian invaders, a people who would go on to create the kingdom of Mitanni. Anatolia's bronze industry all but came to a halt. Only with a united kingdom under his yoke could a Hittite ruler hope to strike south, beyond the Taurus Mountains, and seize control of the other route between Mesopotamia and the Mediterranean coast, that running along the Euphrates River. Such a scheme would secure access to the tin that came from the distant east. Hattusilis was now that ruler.

Any army hoping to pass between the Anatolian plateau and the plains of Syria must go through the Cilician Gates, the most important pass through the Taurus Mountains. King Hattusilis first conquered the cities that stood between him and the Gates, expanding Hatti's borders farther south and east. Once in control of the Gates, he moved on Cilicia itself, at the northeast corner of the Mediterranean, and used it as a base for operations against the kingdom of Aleppo, whose capital was the northern terminus of the trade route Hattusilis meant to control.

The prize would remain out of reach. Although, in addition to his achievements in the south, Hattusilis succeeded in expanding Hatti's control into western Anatolia at the expense of Arzawa—a kingdom near the Aegean coast that would remain a thorn in Hatti's side for centuries—he failed in the effort to break Aleppo, and died on campaign. His grandson and heir, Mursilis, continued the effort and smashed Aleppo in the first decade of the sixteenth century BC. Hittite power now dictated events in northern Syria and, therefore, along much of the Euphrates as well. Tin and all the other goods coming from the east would again be Hatti's for the bartering.

Still greater triumphs beckoned. In less than two generations, the Hittites had built a dynamic kingdom, swiping themselves a ticket into antiquity's busiest arena. Now, riding his momentum and spurred by the prospect of military glory, Mursilis undertook one of the most legendary acts of aggression of the Bronze Age. In 1595 BC, he took his army down the Euphrates and destroyed Babylon. The dynasty begun by the great Hammurabi was finished, the city plundered of its treasures and the conqueror, never intending to occupy his prize, returned home with captives and booty. Hatti had arrived.

## KNIVES IN THE DARK

It is suggestive of reality at the Hittite court that Mursilis, conqueror of Babylon, was assassinated in a palace coup after returning to Hattusa. Hatti may have shaken the pillars of heaven with its warrior audacity, but it was still a kingdom trying to take on more than its institutions could handle. Its noble families still plotted against authority like they had nothing to fear.

Mursilis's assassin was Hantilis, his brother-in-law, whose son-in-law Zadantas had helped make the murder a family affair. Hantilis assumed the throne and had a long reign, but he suffered the horrible fate of outliving his son and grandsons—who were murdered by none other than Zadantas in *his* bid to seize the throne.

And so it went. Zadantas was eventually killed by his own son, Ammunas, who in turn became king—and lived a relatively long life. Upon his death, his sons were slain by agents working for Huzziyas, a relative of Ammunas's through marriage. Huzziyas's attempt to take out the next in line for succession, Telipinus, was discovered in time for the latter to strike first and seize the reigns of power.

Rather than bathe his first days on the throne in blood, Telipinus drove Huzziyas and his family into exile. With this act of restraint, the new king brought an end to generations of court intrigue. Nevertheless, the damage had been done—by the time Telipinus could devote his attentions to matters of state, Hatti's borders had shrunk, pushed back by neighbors who had taken advantage of the years of chaos in Hattusa.

To the west, Arzawa had won its independence, while Syria slipped beyond Hittite control, once again putting the southern trade routes beyond reach. Telipinus had to content himself with keeping the northern barbarians at bay and maintaining defensible borders around the Hittite heartland. His heirs, who ruled during a period of stagnation for which we have no detailed sources, seem to have fought over the succession nearly as often as his predecessors. Supremacy became a memory.

## A FIGHT IN EVERY DIRECTION

Called the "Old Kingdom," the age that fizzled with Telipinus and his successors had put the potential of the Hittites in bold relief. The New Kingdom, also referred to as the Empire, began around 1450 BC with a resurgence in Hittite fortunes and saw Hatti exploit that potential to build a realm of historic proportions—to pour out of its borders and secure a powerful state that would last two and a half centuries.

Hittite military and political leadership must have been extraordinarily dynamic, as little else can account for the empire's success. Their weapons were typical of the age. Though masters of the building and use of chariots, the Hittites hardly had a monopoly on this technology; indeed, no state of the later Bronze Age would have dared to show up on the battlefield without chariots. For fighting in the mountains that ringed their homeland, the Hittites relied on infantry but, again, nothing about their armaments—axes, swords, bows, spears, scale armor—stands out as particularly unusual. Though evidence of Hittite iron working has surfaced, it was used at this early date mostly for statuary and ceremonial weapons.

Constant, vigorous campaigning and imaginative leadership were employed by the Hittites to carve out and maintain their polyglot domain. Indeed, enemies were everywhere, a burden that would play a role in Hatti's eventual destruction. Taken together, the exploits of Hittite rulers during the New Kingdom read like a map of Anatolia rendered in blood and flame. Tudhaliyas I smashed a confederation of enemy states to the northwest and led his army east to deal with Isuwa, a hostile kingdom on the northern Euphrates. Suppiluliumas I, one of Hatti's most effective kings, crushed

*The Sphinx Gate at Alaca Höyük bears two human-headed sphinxes, evidence of Egyptian cultural influence even at the height of the Hittite Empire.*

the vaunted Mitanni in northern Mesopotamia, pounced decisively on Aleppo and Syria, captured Carchemish on the Euphrates, and strengthened his hand on the lower Euphrates with a marriage to the daughter of the king of Babylon. Mursilis II cut loose into hated Arzawa to the west, placed a puppet on its throne, and emasculated its irksome neighbors with treaties ensuring vassal status. And then there was Muwatallis, who refused to let the burning of Hattusa by rampaging northern barbarians put a kink in his successful bid to check Ramses II at Kadesh with a multinational force that put the long arm of Hatti influence on impressive display.

To put it simply, central Anatolia was a rough place to rule an empire. Though Hattusa looked out over a fertile plain and could rely on a wealth of nearby minerals, Hittite greatness was directly dependent on the kingdom's ability to both secure its borders and ensure access to the trade routes that brought it needed materials. Add to this short but daunting list of challenges a host of aggressive neighbors in every direction and you have a scenario in which survival itself was a tall order, let alone the building of an empire.

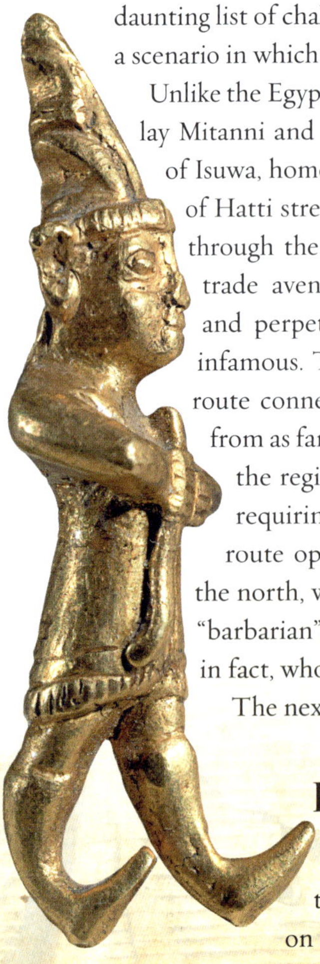

Unlike the Egyptians, the Hittites could only dream of splendid isolation. To the east lay Mitanni and Assyria, both of which ended up clashing with Hatti over the land of Isuwa, home to some of the richest copper deposits in the Near East. Southeast of Hatti stretched Kizzuwadna, another kingdom capable of blocking the passes through the Taurus Mountains in times of conflict and putting the Euphrates trade avenue beyond reach. Hatti's neighbors to the west were numerous and perpetually troublesome, the kingdom of Arzawa being only the most infamous. This area was greatly complicated by the presence of another trade route connecting central Anatolia with the Sea of Marmara and bringing tin from as far away as Britain. Funneling wealth and commercial opportunity into the region, this link to Europe brought competitors like moths to a flame, requiring an unusual degree of vigilance on the part of Hatti to keep the route open. The west would ever be a bane to Hittite security—as would the north, where a string of fortifications was required to keep out the Kaska, a "barbarian" hill people who regularly raided Hittite territory. It was the Kaska, in fact, who burned the Hittite capital in the reign of Muwatallis.

The next time such a thing happened, Hattusa would not rise again.

## INTERNATIONAL PROMINENCE

A continental, land-locked power, the Hittites succeeded in using their central position and interior lines to reinforce areas of conflict on the expanding frontiers. Theirs was a feudal society, becoming more

*Gold pendant in the shape of a Hittite god. He wears boots, a kilt and a conical hat decorated with horns, and holds a curved staff in his right hand.*

so with every generation as greater numbers of minor nobility were required to operate and maintain a growing chariot army. Transmitting this hierarchical system outward, Hatti bound conquered subjects to it by treaties that made vassals of them; though not ruled directly, they were required to pay tribute and fight for their Hittite superiors, and they were forbidden from acting independently on the international stage. Every treaty was slightly different, reflecting the range of peoples and predicaments that bordered the Hatti homeland and producing a patchwork empire built in the face of changing circumstances. But for over two centuries, this system kept the trade routes open and the kings of Hattusa in regal splendor.

By the fourteenth century BC the Hittites had joined the select group of Near Eastern superpowers—a handful of states whose kings communicated copiously, addressing each other as "brother" and engaging in elaborate rituals of flattery that often included the exchange of lavish gifts. Though war never disappeared, this mutual admiration society—including Egypt, Mitanni, Assyria, and Babylonia—presided over a period of relative peace and prosperity, even as border areas were chafed in the ongoing jockeying of imperial opportunism. The trade routes provided plenty for everybody, and the courts supplied each other with rare and precious items, including gold, lapis lazuli, and iron.

It all came crashing down in the twelfth century, during one of the most convulsive and mysterious moments in ancient history. And when the dust had settled, the Hittite Empire was in dire shape.

## CONFLAGRATION

Following Muwatallis's clash with Ramses at Kadesh, the Hittite kings found themselves dealing with a series of mounting crises. Hatti may have turned back the Egyptian foe, but that was no guarantee against strife on other fronts.

That included the home front. On his death around 1285 BC, Muwatallis left a kingdom in chaos. Mursilis III, the late king's son and heir, quickly came up against a plot by his uncle, Hattusilis, to seize the throne. Worse, the empire itself became sundered, with opposing factions backing one or other of the respective claimants. By the time Hattusilis had ousted his nephew and kicked him out of the country, many of the vassal states in the west had gone their own way, having probably taken advantage of the dynastic struggle to assert their independence.

Even more ominous was Assyria's rise to the southeast. After defeating Mitanni and appropriating much of its territory, the increasingly alarming Assyrian war machine was poised to steal the copper mines along the northern Euphrates, an eventuality that not even a Hittite–Egyptian alliance could stop.

Though things had clearly heated up, Tudhaliyas IV, Hattusilis's heir, proved that the Hittite Empire was still a force to be reckoned with. Amassing a fleet from his Levantine vassals, he invaded the island of Cyprus, whose ample copper deposits more than made up for the loss of Isuwa to the Assyrians. And treaties with client states in Syria ensured commercial access to the old southern trade routes. One of Tudhaliyas's successors, Suppiluliumas II, succeeded in winning battles off Cyprus and in Mesopotamia, but he would be the last ruler of the Hittite Empire. Sometime around 1186 BC his capital lay in ruins.

Why? Ask ten different scholars, and you will get twelve different answers. One thing they will all agree on: beginning around the year 1200 BC, massive movements of peoples swept the eastern Mediterranean, overturning the status quo throughout Greece, the Aegean, the Anatolian coast, and the Levant. Records from the time, which are scant and somewhat obtuse, recount violence and political turmoil throughout the broad expanse of these migrations, suggesting waves of raiders running wild from the city-states of Syria along the Mediterranean coast (which they plundered and destroyed) to the Nile Delta (where they were driven back by Ramses III). The Bronze Age came dramatically to an end, writing disappeared for three centuries in the Greek world, and all of the Near East's great palace cultures were shaken to their foundations.

Who were these people—or, as some prefer to call them, "invaders"? Owing to an Egyptian inscription from the reign of the Nineteenth Dynasty pharaoh Merneptah, which explicitly refers to "foreign peoples of the sea," it has become fashionable to call them the "Sea Peoples." Debate over their nationalities, based on transliteration of the names assigned to them in inscriptions such as that of Merneptah's, has only sparked more debate and added considerably to the mystery. Some experts see them as originating in Europe, others in the islands along the western Anatolian coast, while others see the whole scenario as the historical backdrop of Homer's Trojan War, in which an alliance of powers aligned behind Troy waged a destructive regional war against a coalition of Mycenaean warlords. According to a common line of argument, it is impossible to sort the instigators from their victims—by the time Egypt was fending them off in the 1180s, the Sea Peoples had become a veritable tsunami of displaced migrants seeking new homes in the wake of massive demographic chaos. Many of the peoples involved in the depredations in Egypt, for instance, were once employed by the Egyptians as mercenaries.

Further complicating the ongoing debate are theories about drought and famine sweeping the eastern Mediterranean, evidence for which is compelling. But if the causes of this widespread shakeup of the ancient world remain a mystery, there is little doubt about its most conspicuous casualty.

The Hittites, already engulfed in struggles to maintain access to the raw materials that underpinned their empire, were in no position to sustain a seismic shift in the Anatolian balance of power—but that is just what they got. States such as Egypt and Assyria suffered declines during the twelfth and eleventh centuries, but they managed to survive, due in no small measure to their relative geographical remoteness. Hatti, however, dwelt in constant contact, for good or ill, with the peoples along the Anatolian coast—nearly all of whom were profoundly affected by the crisis of the Sea Peoples. More importantly, Hatti's vital foothold in Syria disappeared with the utter despoliation of the Levant.

In the early twelfth century BC someone burned Hattusa to the ground, destroying it for all time. The Sea Peoples, whoever they may have been, were unlikely to have made it all the way to the Anatolian plateau to take place in the razing of one of antiquity's most powerful capitals, but they did not have to. With the trade routes severed in what must have seemed like a world gone mad, the embattled Hittite aristocracy probably had to fight for their lives—their opponents any one of a host of inveterate enemies. Perhaps it was the Kaska, the implacable hill people to the north. In any event, the destruction was as complete as it was sudden, and the first Indo-European-speaking empire of the Near East passed into history.

## THE "OTHER" HITTITES

Hittite history did not end with the collapse of the empire. In the tumultuous migrations that defined the twelfth and eleventh centuries BC, much of the old Hittite culture remained where it had taken root, even as the Anatolians were swept up in the displacement of peoples that followed the razing of Hattusa. In the ensuing centuries, "Neo-Hittite" kingdoms emerged in Syria and Anatolia, many of which—such as Carchemish and Aleppo—continued from earlier days, their years of vassalage having inculcated in them an enduring Hittite culture.

But what of the "Hittites" mentioned in the Old Testament? Were they also heirs to the Indo-European empire that fell centuries before? In fact, this is a question as likely to spark debate as the end of Hatti itself. Referred to in the Bible as Canaanite descendants of Heth, the "Hittites" are portrayed variously as a rustic hill people or, more impressively, as military equals of the Egyptians: in 2 Kings 7:6 their arrival is heralded by the "sound of chariots, and of horses, the sound of a great army." This just muddies the water, giving us a dual portrait of people who *might* be the intimidating inheritors of Hittite war craft, or not. The name "Hittite" itself could be a mere coincidence. The academic world remains divided on this subject, as it does with so many aspects of Hittite history.

CHAPTER FOUR

# ASSYRIA

## DYING BY THE SWORD

"3,000 of their soldiers I felled with weapons ... Many of the captives taken from them, I burned in a fire. Many I took alive; from some of these I cut off their hands to the wrist, from others I cut off their noses, ears and fingers; I put out the eyes of many of the soldiers ... I burnt their young men and women to death ... "

Such was the fate of those who defied the king of Assyria. This passage, written by the ninth-century BC King Ashurnasirpal II about one of his many military campaigns, is typical of much of the language that survives from the Assyrian royal annals. Ashurnasirpal, like all Assyrian rulers, was eager to record his martial excesses so that Ashur, his god, would look favorably upon him.

The language of brutality abounds. Ashurnasirpal went on to record other conquests, complete with the skinning of rebel leaders: "I flayed many within my land and spread their skins out on the walls." A later monarch, Sargon II (r. 721–705 BC), recorded his victory against Urartian forces with equal enthusiasm: "I killed large numbers of his troops, the bodies of his warriors I cut down like millet, filling the mountain valleys with them. I made their blood run down the ravines and precipices like a river."

Assyrian kings leveled cities, smashed open granaries, scorched the earth, and carried off cartloads of booty. It was not uncommon for their vanquished foes to have their tongues ripped out or to be impaled en masse, and the atrocities meted out could get even more imaginative: the royal annals tell of those who had been bound and buried alive in enormous heaps of severed heads, or walled up inside pillars erected to commemorate their defeat at Assyrian hands. Those who survived an Assyrian onslaught might be forcefully deported, or simply left to deal with a wasted landscape: Shalmaneser III, Ashurnasirpal's successor, was known to leave capital cities alone, only to annihilate all their outlying settlements. Still others might face a stranger fate—such as being forced to grind into dust the bones of their recently exhumed ancestors.

In a world in which a select few were literate, however, written records were hardly enough to convey a dynasty's sanguinary accomplishments. Those visiting the Assyrian kings in their throne rooms would have been assailed from every wall with images guaranteed to impress: mutilations, mass burnings, decapitations, the crumbling of enemy towers and the routing of troops, the trampling of wounded and the subjugation of families. One seventh century BC king, Ashurbanipal, had himself portrayed at a sort of garden party in which he and his queen recline in serene luxury while gazing at the head of the defeated king of Elam, which hangs from a nearby tree, its hair dangling above the shoulder of a palace servant bearing food for the royal couple.

*Previous pages: Head of a winged bull from the palace gate at Dur-Sharrukin.*

Even Assyrian hunting scenes smack of sadism, vividly capturing lions and other prey animals in the moment of defeat, their bodies bleeding and hobbled, their faces grimacing with pain.

The Assyrians, in other words, were not to be trifled with.

## HISTORY'S FIRST TRUE EMPIRE

Were the Assyrians as brutal as they seemed? The answer, like all questions about the deep past, depends on your point of view and how much evidence you have. Assyrian ferocity remains a controversy in its own right, pitting those scholars who cannot stop focusing on it against those scholars who dispassionately assert that Assyrian records and art were little more than a colossal propaganda campaign intended to cow friends and enemies alike. Though there can be little doubt that all the tales and images of gore must have given potential enemies pause, it is also safe to say that such propagandistic efforts would have been pointless or even silly had there not been plenty of hard facts to back them up. Whether the Assyrian rulers razed all the cities to which they laid claim is impossible to say, but deeds of stunning carnage must certainly have been a standard *modus operandi*.

Though emerging in a world full of sparring power centers, each with its own history of war and oppression, the Assyrian kingdom was uniquely immersed in the cult of cruelty. No great civilization's art had ever shown such a meticulous, consuming preoccupation with martial prowess and the grinding humiliation of foes. Though they

*Above: Stone relief from Nineveh, showing King Ashurbanipal and his wife taking refreshment in a garden, while the head of the defeated king of Elam hangs in a tree.*

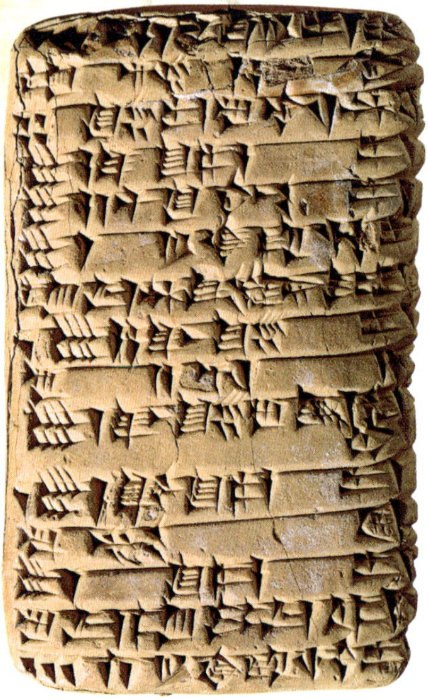

built prodigiously, their legacy, unlike those of the Egyptians or the Hittites, was overwhelmingly concerned with the concentration of a king's assets in the cause of war.

Perhaps it is no coincidence, then, that the Assyrians also built the first true empire in history—an international, fully centralized polity dependent on complex tools of organization and governance, rather than merely a powerful kingdom built on the tribute of clients and vassals. Every empire that came after, from the Persians to the Romans, emulated the institutions of conquest and domination codified by the Assyrians. This is the beginning of imperial history.

The ability to wield weapons and terror on an unprecedented scale characterized Assyria's historic accomplishments, but it also accounted for the empire's fall, sowing the seeds of resentment that would grow to ominous proportions. It was a formula that ultimately proved too much even for the power of Assyria.

## URBAN GENESIS

Assyria's roots ran deep into the past of Mesopotamia, "the land between the rivers." Bordered on three sides by mountains and desert, the region fed by the Tigris and Euphrates rivers was always two lands: one in the north, later known as Assyria, where proximity to the Taurus Mountains offered rain-fed agriculture, and one further south, comprising Akkad and Sumer, where lack of precipitation required farming of a different sort. It was in Sumer, nearest the coast, where the world's first cities appeared some 5,500 years ago. Deprived of the rain that watered Assyria, Sumerians built vast irrigation ditches along the Euphrates, their engineering projects spawning urban development.

Each city had a patron god, whose temple stood prominently above all other structures. There was an *ensi*, or ruler, also known as a *lugal*, who usually dwelt in a modest palace with a courtyard and whose responsibilities could be numerous, from running the temple and gathering tribute for the god to settling disputes and maintaining irrigation ditches. Major cities had impressive defensive walls built of mud brick, within which the community's specialists—weavers, bakers, builders, priests, etc.—lived on the bounty of harvests brought in from the surrounding countryside.

It was not long before Sumer was crowded with cities—indeed, some sprang up within sight of one another, causing friction over precious agricultural land. Unlike Egypt,

*Above: Cuneiform tablet with wedge-shaped symbols impressed into the clay. For almost two thousand years this was the writing system of the Near Eastern empires.*

which did not see an early eruption of powerful city centers, Sumer—and eventually all of Mesopotamia as the urban phenomenon crept up the rivers—became a civilization of independent, walled communities. Each had its own beloved deity, and each had its own laws, customs, dynasties, and armies.

They did share a culture, of course. Mesopotamians spoke a common language (actually, two—Akkadian in the north and, at first, Sumerian in the south), and their scribes all employed cuneiform, the script used to record deeds, transactions, and inventories on clay tablets. Though every city jealously favored a particular god, the regional pantheon was familiar to everyone, from Anu, god of the sky, to Ninkasi, the

## THE FIRST SCRIPT

Most Assyrian kings were illiterate. A notable exception was the last great king, Ashurbanipal, who boasted of his reading skills and collected an impressive library of texts from around the known world.

Nevertheless, every king had a coterie of scribes at his beck and call. For most of Assyrian history, these men of learning employed the oldest form of written expression on earth: cuneiform. With its roots going back as far as the fourth millennium BC, this ancient script was typically pressed into clay tablets with a stylus, creating distinctive triangular characters that inspired the name "cuneiform" (which means "wedge-shaped"). Interestingly, it existed wholly apart from the spoken languages it represented, meaning that any given cuneiform impression could represent a concept in Sumerian or Akkadian with equal felicity. It was, however, complicated, requiring the memorization of huge numbers of characters—one reason why so many Assyrians, even in the aristocracy, never bothered to learn it.

Later on, however, many of the court's scribes started learning a new language. The Aramaean invaders of the eleventh century BC brought with them a tongue whose script was phonetic, like modern English, making it a far more practical medium for record-keeping. In time Aramaic became popular with scribes who saw it as a practical alternative to cuneiform, not only because it was simpler to learn, but also because it could be written on papyrus or parchment, eliminating the need for cumbersome clay tablets.

Assyrian kings, however, were slow to embrace the new language, insisting that most of their scribes remain schooled in the traditional script of Mesopotamia. Despite this, Aramaic continued to grow in popularity and usage. By the seventh century BC, both written forms were thriving, existing side by side and requiring two types of scribes at official residences.

Cuneiform's days were numbered, however. In time Aramaic would become the lingua franca of the Near East.

patron goddess of brewers. Moreover, some institutions for concerted action seem to have been put in place: the "King of Kish," for instance, was a vaguely defined post whose purpose was to settle disputes between cities (or at least to attempt to settle them) and to lead pan-Mesopotamian armies in emergency situations, though the selection process remains a mystery.

Such realities, however, only served to put the region's fractiousness in bold relief. Power and loyalty in Mesopotamia were local affairs; war became all too common.

## THE IMPERIAL IMPULSE

It was against such trends that the Assyrians, a people on the northern fringe of Mesopotamia who reached their zenith in the first millennium BC, had to struggle in the creation of an empire. But they were hardly the first to try.

Throughout the third and second millennia BC, many rulers attempted to extend their authority over more than one city, and some of them succeeded. But true regional hegemony remained elusive in Mesopotamia until the arrival of Sargon of Akkad.

Little is known of Sargon (r. 2334–2279 BC), who became the first ruler to conquer virtually all of the Fertile Crescent. Indeed, archaeologists have yet to discover his capital of Agade. One legend holds that Sargon, like Moses, was found in a reed basket on the river when he was still an infant. Another tale insists that he was the son of a royal gardener.

The one certainty through all of the stories that surround Sargon is that his father is never named—meaning, essentially, that Sargon was illegitimate and, therefore, a usurper, probably of King Ur-Zababa of Kish, a city near the border between Sumer and Akkad.

By around 2300 BC Sargon had united both regions under his warrior crown and expanded his territory all the way to Syria and Lebanon on the Mediterranean coast. His even more ambitious grandson, Naram-Sin, would proudly wear the title "King of the Four Quarters of the World," but this "empire" did not last; within a few decades of Naram-Sin's death, Akkadian rule disintegrated amid a flurry of revolts.

Though an impressive achievement of military conquest, the brief Akkadian period showcased the challenges of unifying Mesopotamia. The next imperial enterprise, referred to rather prosaically as the Third Dynasty of Ur (2112–2004 BC), took Sargon's efforts a few steps further by ushering in a period of multifaceted diplomatic and bureaucratic governance. During their century of dominance, the Ur III kings (Ur was a Sumerian city) perfected new standards of record-keeping and diplomacy, holding sway over a united Mesopotamia with methods of unprecedented sophistication.

It all sounds impressive, and it was. The Ur III period left piles and piles of records to posterity, testifying to the kingdom's humming success. But it, like the Akkadian effort before it, collapsed under foreign pressure and internal decay.

Then there was Hammurabi of Babylon (r. 1792–1750 BC), the mercurial, hot-tempered warrior-king and lawgiver who turned his city-state into the center of a regional power that encompassed all of southern Mesopotamia. Pious, assertive, popular, and famous for all time for his law code, Hammurabi created a stable kingdom that lasted a century and a half until it was sacked by the Hittites. His accomplishment confirmed the arrival of territories, rather than cities, as the principal players in the Tigris–Euphrates arena, and made Babylon the region's unofficial capital. Marduk, patron deity of Babylon, became the most important figure in the Mesopotamian pantheon.

Each of these three bids for imperial supremacy left an imprint on Mesopotamia, contributing its lesson to a class in leadership that would teach the Assyrians well. Indeed, Assyria was already a regional power to be reckoned with by the time Hammurabi was forging his Babylonian enterprise.

## A BUMPY ROAD TO SUPREMACY

Ashur, capital of Assyria, was originally little more than a stronghold on the Tigris River in northern Mesopotamia. Named after its patron god, the city went on to become the heart of a realm that ultimately stretched from the shores of the Persian Gulf to the whole of Egypt.

Scholars traditionally divide the kingdom's history between "old" and "new." The Old Assyrian period stretched roughly from 2000 to 1750 BC, and witnessed the creation of a successful web of trade routes that stretched out of Ashur to merchant colonies as far away as Anatolia and Palestine. However, decline and obscurity overtook the kingdom after the reign of Shamshi-Adad, a contemporary of Hammurabi's. Assyria even became a vassal of the Mitannians, whose dominance stretched across northern Mesopotamia and the southeast corner of Anatolia.

Sometime in the fourteenth century BC, the kings at Ashur acquired enough prestige and power to throw off Mitannian control, with Ashur becoming once again a fully independent member of the group of great states—Egypt, the Hittite realm, and Babylonia among them—that dominated Near Eastern affairs. The so-called Middle Assyrian Empire that followed began spreading militarily at the expense of the crumbling Mitannian kingdom, adopting the tools of government that would become famous (and infamous) in the centuries to come. By the thirteenth century BC Ashur was collecting tribute from all over northern Mesopotamia.

Then came the convulsions associated with the so-called Sea Peoples. Power centers from Greece to Palestine succumbed to crisis and the destructive migrations of raiders and fugitives, and Assyria was no different. By the eleventh century BC, no region of the Near East could boast of its own prosperity or stability.

As its borders collapsed, the Assyrian kingdom fell back onto its heartland once again, in what was becoming a regular cycle of expansion and withdrawal, boom and bust. Assyria's next comeback, however, would be spectacular, as if the centuries of tumult that brought down states like that of the Hittites had merely hardened the rulers of Ashur and galvanized their imperial mission. The roots of empire had already been laid during the Middle Assyrian Period; in the centuries to come, they would blossom formidably.

## ASHUR FLOODS ITS BANKS

Of all the threats posed by the dark, confused century after 1100 BC, none so bedeviled Assyrian kings as the Aramaeans, a powerful nomadic people who—like so many during the era of the "Sea Peoples"—were on the move at someone else's expense. They seem to have originated in or around Syria, spreading out in nearly all directions to put pressure on the Mediterranean coast, Assyria, and Babylonia. Tiglath-pileser I (r. 1115–1077 BC), famous for his battles against the Aramaeans, struggled manfully against them during his reign, only to watch Assyria's borders shrink.

By the time the Aramaeans had exchanged their violent peregrinations for settled kingdoms in the tenth century, regular record-keeping had made a comeback in northern Mesopotamia, and Assyria's war machine, though battered and humbled, had acquired plenty of practice. Peopled by prominent kings eager to go campaigning, the Assyrian story from hereon becomes much fuller and more dynamic, in a chapter known as the Neo-Assyrian Period.

Assyria's armies campaigned in the mountains to the north and east, extended their borders at the expense of Babylonia, and crushed the last pockets of Aramaean resistance, enforcing upon the tribes a lucrative and regular system of tribute.

Then, in 883 BC, one of the empire's greatest rulers came to the throne. Ashurnasirpal II, who ruled until 859, left a treasure trove of records detailing his considerable achievements, making him a point of reference for this period of Near Eastern history, as well as a sort of poster child for Neo-Assyrian greatness.

By the time of Ashurnasirpal's reign, the militarization of Assyria's national demeanor was complete. Generations of warfare, not least against the Aramaeans, had bred a lean, spirited, dedicated, professional military. Provided with up-to-date weaponry and seasoned by yearly campaigning, the army had achieved unrivaled status as an expression of the state's prominence—and Ashurnasirpal did not squander it.

So much of the state's efforts under previous dynasties had been spent in reconquering and securing what were believed to be Assyria's traditional boundaries that few Assyrians understood anymore what it was like to subdue new territories. A natural strategist, Ashurnasirpal initiated a new era in which Assyria's borders were ever-expanding. He added new territory in the Zagros Mountains to the east and marched his armies all the way to the Mediterranean, receiving tribute from new subjects as he expanded the borders of his growing kingdom. "I destroyed them, tore down the walls and burned the towns with fire," reads one typical account of his accomplishments. "I caught the survivors and impaled them on stakes in front of their towns." To his son and heir, Shalmaneser III (r. 858–824 BC), Ashurnasirpal left an education in extremism and a greatly expanded inheritance.

He also left a new capital at Nimrud (known as Kalhu in ancient times), whose royal palace was adorned with a new form of art: stone relief. On long panels, the king carved depictions of his wealth and power, complete with scenes of murderous conquest and subject peoples offering tribute of everything from monkeys to textiles. Times were good.

They would get better during the reign of Shalmaneser, who continued his father's expansionist policy. After fighting an alliance of Levantine states to a draw, he managed to secure their submission and tribute, further establishing Assyria's influence on the crucial Mediterranean coast. He also pushed Assyrian control further into Anatolia, acquiring valuable iron deposits. By this time, Assyria was probably the mightiest power on earth.

## THE ASSYRIAN JUGGERNAUT

How had kings like Ashurnasirpal and Shalmaneser been able to do it? In a word, *force*. The kings of Assyria could count on what can justifiably be called the first large standing army in history. Previous exercises in national aggression, whether by Egyptians or Hittites or Babylonians, had been with armies raised principally from peasant populations when they were not busy with the harvest. There had, of course, always been a cadre of retainers attached to the king—men of training whose only craft was fighting—and all the great states of the ancient Near East had depended at some time or other on significant numbers of professional fighters, whether indigenous or mercenary. But these were nothing compared to the armies of fulltime professionals utilized by the Assyrians. By the late eighth century BC, through a series of reforms, the Assyrian army became as effective as it was massive.

## A MATTER OF PERSPECTIVE

The inner courtyards of Assyrian royal palaces were typically guarded by two imposing relief statues of winged beasts with human heads. Representatives of the gods, these mystical beings projected power to all who approached, reminding visitors that the king had the favor of Ashur. But their most distinctive feature was not their braided beards, or their massive wings: it was their legs—they each had five of them.

This was a "cheat" by Assyrian sculptors to allow passersby to see a natural form from both the front and side perspectives. From directly ahead, each colossus presented two front legs standing straight and parallel, but from the side, one of those legs would be hidden behind the leg closest to the viewer. The solution was to add a fifth leg, extending backwards as if the statue were in the middle of a stride, that would not be visible when the relief was viewed from the front but was clearly visible when it was viewed from the side. Unfortunately, viewing the colossus from the front corner exposes the ruse, presenting the image of a freakish beast with an extra appendage sticking out of its underside.

The Persians, who inherited so much of Assyrian culture and administration, found a solution to this awkward problem by more realistically rendering their four-legged statues.

The tactical quality that made Assyrian armies so formidable remains a matter of some debate. What seems certain is that they relied on a diverse range of forces, all of which were coordinated to an unprecedented degree—combined arms tactics, Iron Age style. Most numerous were the archers, many of whom were foreign auxiliaries from subject peoples. There were other types of auxiliaries, such as Syrian spearmen, equipped with their own distinctive arms and armor. Assyrian infantry, the most formidable in the world at the time, wore scale armor almost to the feet, a conical helmet, and carried a giant round shield. They fought either with heavy spears or swords. Slingers were also employed in great numbers, their stones adding considerable weight to the archers' fire.

Chariots, without which no early Iron Age army would be recognizable, provided overall maneuverability and striking power. They also became increasingly heavier with time, acquiring larger wheels, more armor, and greater numbers of passengers wielding bows, spears, and other weapons. In addition, the Assyrians created the first dedicated cavalry units in history, employing masses of mounted archers and lancers who were better able to fight in mountainous or broken terrain than chariots.

Coordination and direction of the Royal Army (*sab sharri*) depended on a command system of unprecedented detail. At the military pinnacle was the king, who relied on a pair of *turtanu*, or field marshals. A long line of officers answered to them in descending order, the lowest of which commanded just ten men. The Royal Cohort, or *kisir sharruti*, shielded the monarch and formed an elite cadre. All told, the Royal Army and its foreign contingents numbered around half a million by the final decades of the eighth century.

## MOVERS AND BREAKERS

The army rarely went anywhere without a corps of engineers. These specialists were required to build roads and bridges along the campaign trail, just like pioneers of later armies. "I equipped my sappers with strong copper picks," boasted Sargon II (r. 721–705 BC), "and they shivered the crags of steep mountains to fragments as though limestone, and made a good way." Their most conspicuous achievements involved that exclusive purview of great military powers: siege craft.

With a few minor exceptions, the art of ancient Near Eastern civilizations to this time is devoid of any detailed depictions of sieges. Then, in the Assyrian period, there is an embarrassment of riches. The Assyrians not only spent considerable time and effort denying enemies any safe haven, they also reveled in portraying that fact in impressive detail. The ability to penetrate a city's defenses was the ultimate proof of a kingdom's efficacy and authority, and the Assyrians elevated siege warfare to a science.

Often merely isolating the city had to suffice, whether because its defenses were too formidable or because the Assyrian king wanted to avoid incurring huge casualties. On such occasions, he would rely on the range and speed of his units of chariotry and cavalry to police the surrounding countryside, denying the city all contact with the outside world and gradually starving the urban population into submission. The Assyrians might also decide on circumvallation, constructing a great wall around the besieged city. Archers and slingers could then fire on the defenders from a height. Passive tactics could take an incredibly long time, however—it took three years for Tiglath-pileser III to take the city of Arpad. For this reason, more direct methods were quite popular with the Assyrians.

When the direct means were used, security for the attackers was paramount. Whether going over, under, or through a city's defenses, the besiegers needed to get right up against the wall, exposing themselves to intense and accurate enemy fire. This was where the Assyrian archers came in: they maintained a steady volley of arrows to force as many of the city's defenders as possible from the walls. To protect themselves, Assyrian archers employed large shields—almost like portable walls—that could be moved and positioned where needed. Some battle scenes also show them relying on spearmen with great tower shields to deflect incoming missiles.

*The Assyrian city of Nimrud towers over the Tigris River: a romantic reconstruction of the city by Austen Henry Layard, the first excavator of the site.*

The sappers themselves were heavily armored, with conical helmets and padded scale mail that extended past the knees. While hacking away at the wall with picks or tunneling underneath it, they could depend on a portable shield—perhaps a different variety of the sort employed by the missile troops. The sappers' primary purpose was to undermine the city defenses, excavating a space beneath the wall and filling it with wooden support beams. The timbers would then be fired, bringing that section of the wall down.

Though not necessarily elite troops, the sappers were well trained. Those who went over the walls, however, must have been quite extraordinary. Assyrian siege ladders were designed to double as fighting platforms, allowing archers to pause and fire at defenders while swordsmen and spearmen—all heavily armored—savagely fought their way onto the ramparts. This was dangerous work, with clouds of arrows no doubt flying from defending archers desperate to thwart any such escalade. Any successful assault would have required huge numbers and probably incurred a ghastly price in lives.

In light of such unpleasant realities, the Assyrians developed their most spectacular weapons: the siege engines. They were particularly fond of the battering ram, which was housed in a massive structure on four or six wheels, its roof and sides covered with wicker shields and leather skins. Arrow slits afforded opportunity for defensive fire. The ram itself was often tipped with a great iron wedge for prying bricks apart in the walls and could be used either for smashing gates or, time permitting, making a breach. Defenders typically attempted to destroy such behemoths with flaming arrows, but the Assyrians even had a way of dealing with this, equipping every ram with water that could be used to douse flames from within the protection of the armored housing by way of a purpose-built pole with a bucket at its end.

The engineers often enhanced the hitting power of these monstrosities by building huge earthen ramps. Once the ramps were completed, the engines were rolled up to strike at the upper wall, which was invariably weaker than the base with its sloped glacis.

With as many as seven siege engines employed against one stretch of wall, the Assyrians could deliver tremendous destructive power to force a capitulation. Indeed, the sight alone of the Royal Army preparing for a siege was usually enough to persuade cities to surrender.

## MAINTAINING CONTROL

Assyria's army was the fiercest, best organized in history up to that time, but that did not mean that a good king was not needed at the helm to secure the empire's success. The solid father-and-son team of Ashurnasirpal and Shalmaneser ensured sixty years of victory and stability for Assyria. However, the empire entered a fifty-year period of chaos after Shalmaneser's death, perhaps because of powerful local governors who had become disloyal.

In any event, the empire found its stride again in the eighth century BC. Beginning with Tiglath-pileser III (r. 744–727 BC), Assyrian rulers perfected the old institutions of imperial control and even added a few, completing the realm's transformation from feudal super-state into empire. Before long Assyria would achieve a degree of centralization worthy of the army that had established its dominion.

Not surprisingly, simple ruthlessness was a frequent tool in Assyrian government. King Ashurbanipal once promised the weight in gold of a rebel leader to anyone who would turn him in, dead or alive, but there were plenty of more advanced methods of control. While the Assyrians, like other Near Eastern empire builders, had long relied on cowing subject peoples into remaining loyal and offering up tribute, they depended increasingly on more direct administration of the empire, by elevating a puppet ruler from the local population or installing an Assyrian governor answerable directly to the Assyrian king himself. Tiglath-pileser established the custom of appointing eunuchs to such posts in the hope of preventing the creation of local dynasties. Such methods had the effect of carpeting the empire—even areas at great distances from the capital—with Assyrian royal customs and bureaucracy, and creating a more uniform establishment. Provinces themselves were made smaller, giving each local governor a narrower power base from which to launch potential rebellions. To facilitate communication throughout the empire, the Assyrians built an unprecedented road network, complete with way-stations built every twenty miles and stocked with supplies for the exclusive use of the king and his messengers.

Perhaps the most infamous tactic for maintaining mastery of Assyria's vast realm was deportation. After one successful military operation in the Levant, Sargon II removed some 27,000 people from Israel to other parts of the empire, particularly Syria. Such enormous forced migrations were common. The purpose was twofold: first, to break up subject communities that might otherwise revolt; and, second, to transfer artisans or agricultural labor to newly settled areas.

The Assyrians had achieved a watershed in Mesopotamian history, having blended the military dynamism of old Akkad with the administrative complexity of the Third Dynasty of Ur. Around 710 BC, they also coopted the cultural gravitas of Babylonia when Sargon II defeated a rebellious leader there and assumed the crown of Babylonia himself, ending that region's semi-autonomy within the greater empire. From the Persian Gulf to southern Anatolia to Phoenicia, the massive Assyrian domain now stretched like a great crescent around the Arabian Desert in the south. Nothing like it had ever been seen before.

## STORM CLOUDS ON THE SOUTHERN HORIZON

Like his famous Akkadian namesake fifteen centuries earlier, Sargon II was a usurper who achieved great things. After naming himself king of Babylonia he stayed for several years, investing considerable time and treasure in rebuilding Babylon's temples and other public buildings. Such personal devotion was emblematic of the Assyrian reverence for the great city of Hammurabi. Because of this fondness, Assyrian control in the region was always exceptional—while other provinces were subject to harsh tributes and oppressive eunuch governors, Babylonia, sacred city of Marduk, was handled with kid gloves: no deportations, no mass burnings, no destruction of farmland, and often no taxes.

The irony could not have been more acute, for Babylonia, proud in its heritage and wealth, was never a willing subject of its brutal neighbor to the north. If anyone in the empire needed strict minding, it was the Babylonians.

Worse, Babylonia itself was flanked by Assyrian enemies who were more than happy to encourage Babylonian disloyalty. Chief among these was Elam, an Iranian kingdom that bordered Babylonia to the east. Old allies of Babylon, the Elamites were alarmed by Assyria's might and aggression. Then there was "Sealand," the vast marsh that stretched along the shore of the Persian Gulf in the south, home to a race of fishermen and sailors whose way of life had changed little since Sumerian days. To the Assyrians, these reed-dwellers were little better than bandits for hire to their Babylonian neighbors.

Assyria's final days would play out against this background of tension and hostility in the south—the region, significantly, that gave birth to civilization in Mesopotamia. With an empire built on tribute, fear, and military authority, the Assyrians had sown the seeds of their own downfall by breeding animosity virtually everywhere. Aided by this, Babylonian intransigence would become the bane of Assyrian fortunes and lead to its downfall—a process set in motion by the usual catalyst of dynastic tribulation.

## THE SINS OF SENNACHERIB

Sargon II, one of the empire's greatest rulers, presided over Assyria at its prime until he died campaigning against a nomadic people known as Cimmerians in the north. Some historians have suggested that the nature of his death—falling to enemies on the battlefield—was a bad omen to the Assyrians, perhaps because it compromised the notion that he was the center of the moral order, divinely ordained to fight against the kingdom's enemies.

It may have been for this reason that his son and heir, Sennacherib (r. 704–681 BC), abandoned Sargon's brand-new capital at Dur-Sharrukin and relocated the court to Nineveh. Sargon's successor was an able general and administrator—and he needed to be, because the series of crises he had to face virtually from the moment he sat on the throne seemed to verify the bad omen of his father's death.

Trouble came in the Levant when recently conquered regions in Syria-Palestine revolted, probably with the encouragement of Egypt. Sennacherib responded with characteristic Assyrian alacrity, personally leading a massive army west to sort out his subjects, including laying siege to the Judean cities of Jerusalem and Lachish in 701 BC. Though Lachish fell, the Judean capital held out—a drama famously captured in the Old Testament. Nevertheless, Judea had been humbled, and just in time—for Sennacherib's real troubles were just beginning back east in Babylonia.

With encouragement from Elam, a rebel named Marduk-apla-iddina II had pronounced himself king of an independent Babylonia. Returning from the western campaign, Sennacherib moved south, chased the pretender into the watery wastes of Sealand, and put his own son on the throne of Babylonia. More importantly, Sennacherib stopped treating the Babylonians with the politeness that had characterized their previous relations. In fact, he deported over 200,000 of them to Assyria, determined once and for all to put an end to the region's infuriating disobedience.

He then launched a seaborne invasion of Elam itself. An impressive expression of Assyrian might and resourcefulness, the invasion fleet was led by naval experts brought from Phoenicia, who sailed Sennacherib's army down the Persian Gulf and landed them in the south of Elam. The stunned Elamites responded boldly, sending an army into Babylonia. After capturing Sennacherib's son Ashur-nadin-shumi there, they dragged him back to Elam and executed him.

With all-out war now raging between Assyria and the Babylonian–Elamite alliance, things had gotten quite out of hand in the south. But they were about to get much worse. Having lost his son, King Sennacherib abandoned all restraint and laid siege to Babylon in 689 BC. When the city fell, he vented his rage on the fabled jewel of the Euphrates with frightful thoroughness.

Capital of an ancient civilization that had risen because of its management of water, Babylon now fell victim to the river itself: "Through the middle of that city I dug canals," proclaimed Sennacherib. "I flooded its ground with water ... and made it like a meadow."

He also claimed to have thrown down the temples and set whole neighborhoods to the torch. Leaving a wasted, smoldering metropolis in his wake, the king headed back to Assyria with the cult statue of Marduk as a prize.

## FALLOUT

The rape of Babylon sent shockwaves throughout Mesopotamia, convincing many that this was too much even by Assyrian standards. Sennacherib, in fact, became a kind of heretic—a kidnapper of Marduk and defiler of his mighty city. Eight years later, Sennacherib met his death at the hands of assassins—who happened to be his sons. More than anything, this profound act offers a window on the polarization that Babylon's ruin had wrought within the Assyrian elite.

Before his disturbing demise, the king had named Esarhaddon, one of his younger sons (who, interestingly, was not involved in Sennacherib's murder), as his heir. The new monarch had inherited a situation that, to say the least, was full of pitfalls—his late father was a blasphemous scourge, his older brothers were parricides, and the empire seemed on the brink of complete disorder and invasion.

Esarhaddon moved deftly between and over these obstacles, beginning with the rebuilding of Babylon. Like his grandfather, Sargon II, he committed himself to the complete restoration of the city, personally seeing to much of the project's detail. Esarhaddon meant to distance himself from his father's shattering sacrilege, and to win over what remained of Babylonian loyalty.

But if severing himself from the past was of vital importance, so was avenging it. This paradoxical relationship with his father served to put the significance of Assyrian kingship in bold relief: though Sennacherib had done an unforgivable thing, his patricidal sons had also, and Esarhaddon must make them pay for it. In 672 BC he led an army into the Taurus Mountains, where his brothers had found sanctuary in the kingdom of Shubria. Awed by the Royal Army's approach, the Shubrian king begged desperately for forgiveness, but to no avail; he was killed along with the outlaw princes he so stupidly sheltered.

With his house in order, Esarhaddon moved west against Egypt and conquered it, achieving immortality even as he extended the boundaries of his empire beyond the court's ability to police them. Perhaps the greatest prize in all the Near East, Egypt nevertheless was too distant for even the formidable Assyrians to control. It would soon slip from Assyria's grasp, making its conquest more of an excuse to boast than a triumph of imperial ambitions.

Esarhaddon's true legacy lay much closer to home—in fact, it involved his own family. Before his death, he had arranged for a succession that he believed would ensure peace for years to come. Shamash-shuma-ukin, his oldest son, was to become king of Babylonia, while Ashurbanipal the younger was made heir to the Assyrian throne. Such an arrangement, Esarhaddon believed, would put Babylonian fears to rest by binding both crowns with blood. Whether he anticipated Shamash-shuma-ukin's all-too-predictable jealousy of his younger brother we shall probably never know, but perhaps he should have—for it sparked the destruction of the Assyrian Empire.

## A DYNASTY IN CHAOS

Ashurbanipal (r. 668–c. 627 BC) was the last king of Assyria about whom we know a great deal—only two more would follow him on the throne, and their reigns would be swallowed in war and darkness. It is a notion that no one at the time would have predicted, given the empire's unassailable strength and vitality, but in a variation of the old saying about pride before a fall, an empire's hubris often looks to enemies like an opportunity to strike.

By around 652 BC, Ashurbanipal was facing threats from both Babylonia and Elam. In the east, the Elamites under their king, Teumman, took advantage of Assyria's burden in Egypt and launched an attack. It ended badly: Ashurbanipal drove them back into their own kingdom and returned with Teumann's head (which, you will recall from earlier in this chapter, ended up hanging from a tree). Meanwhile, Shamash-shuma-ukin had had enough of reporting to his younger brother and conspired with Elam and the Chaldaean peoples in southern Babylonia to oust him. Ashurbanipal's intelligence network was better, however, and he got word of the plot in time to act first. What followed reads like

## ROYAL IMPOSTER

Esarhaddon, conqueror of Egypt, was a surprisingly sickly man. Because the king was viewed as the very manifestation of Assyria's might and prosperity, this was hardly a satisfactory situation, and Esarhaddon—like any hypochondriac—resorted to all manner of methods in an attempt to cure himself.

The most interesting of these involved an exchange of identity with a commoner. An ordinary Assyrian, perhaps a farmer or laborer, was chosen by the court to literally take the king's place on the throne for a select period of time. While the king retired to the countryside to get a taste of the simple life, his substitute would, as it were, "soak up" the illness-causing spirits that surrounded the person of the king. When the real king and his officials were satisfied that all the spirits had been properly fooled, the imposter was killed, thereby banishing the spirits to oblivion.

It is not clear whether the tactic worked to Esarhaddon's complete satisfaction.

a Greek tragedy: with his brother laying siege to Babylon, Shamash-shuma-ukin set his own palace ablaze and immolated himself in the flames. Babylon's seemingly insatiable hunger for lost causes had struck again.

Shamash-shuma-ukin's grandiloquent sacrifice, however, had set in motion events that his younger brother, for all his piety and ability, was powerless to stop. Indeed, Ashurbanipal—his hand having been forced—rode his wrath like a wave into Elam, as if circumstances were controlling him rather than the reverse. The Elamites, long the thorn in the Assyrian side, now reaped the whirlwind: their country was ravaged utterly, their cities razed, their temples destroyed, and their cult statues hauled back to Assyria like souvenirs. Ashurbanipal recorded his triumph with sneering pride: "I counted their gods and goddesses as powerless ghosts ... I pulled down and destroyed the tombs of their earlier and later kings ... I exposed them to the sun. I took away their bones to Assyria, I put restlessness on their spirits." So much for Elam.

*Ashurbanipal kills a lion. The lion had been released into a cordoned area so that the king could take part in this royal "hunt."*

## THE LAST DAYS OF THE FIRST EMPIRE

In crushing Elam, Ashurbanipal paved the way for his empire's destroyers. Western Iran surged with conflicting peoples, and Elam's weakness was the strength of its more dangerous foes. Chief among these were the Medes, about whom archaeologists know little—and only from the records of other cultures—but the Medes shared one very significant characteristic with the Elamites they displaced: they were more than willing to join the great crusade to rid Mesopotamia of the Assyrian monster.

The scarcity and confusion of surviving records from this time exacerbate the efforts by scholars to reconstruct precisely how Assyria came to its end. What seems clear is that Ashurbanipal, extremely vindictive and always more of a scholar than an emperor, did not provide a secure enough succession—upon his death in 627 BC, Babylonia had little trouble exerting its complete independence. Almost immediately, an enterprising Chaldaean leader in Babylon's elite, named Nabopolassar, assumed full control of the city's throne, ruthlessly quashing all local resistance. By 616 BC he had managed to build an alliance with the Medes against Assyria, their combined hatred of the old empire providing the fuel to see this fight to its end. Before long the Scythian horsemen of the north were enlisted as well, sealing the empire's doom. After a joint invasion, they quickly conquered the cities of the Assyrian heartland, including Ashur itself, and, in 612 BC, Nineveh. By 610 BC—only two years later—the Assyrian Empire had completely collapsed.

Though there is evidence in the records from this time of a conflict within the Assyrian dynasty itself over succession, it is easy to dismiss this as a symptom of the larger maelstrom rather than a cause. By the end of the seventh century, too many crimes had been committed on behalf of the empire for it to be forgiven by its victims, who had at last found the opportunity to overturn the balance of power. At no time in history had any government so completely mastered the use of widespread violence to secure so vast a stretch of territory.

That Assyria also mustered the administrative institutions to govern its enormous realm was impressive, but it was unequal to the task of overcoming the seething rage of a Near East that had been so badly mishandled in the quest for empire. "All who hear the news of you clap their hands at your downfall," proclaimed the Old Testament prophet Nahum upon hearing of Nineveh's destruction. "For who has not felt your unrelenting cruelty?"

Nevertheless, Assyria had set the pattern for all who came after. Though later empires never embraced the propaganda of brutality as warmly as Assyria, they all adopted Assyria's methods to construct their own grand empires. A new age had dawned.

CHAPTER FIVE

# NEO-BABYLONIA

## SWAN SONG FOR MESOPOTAMIA

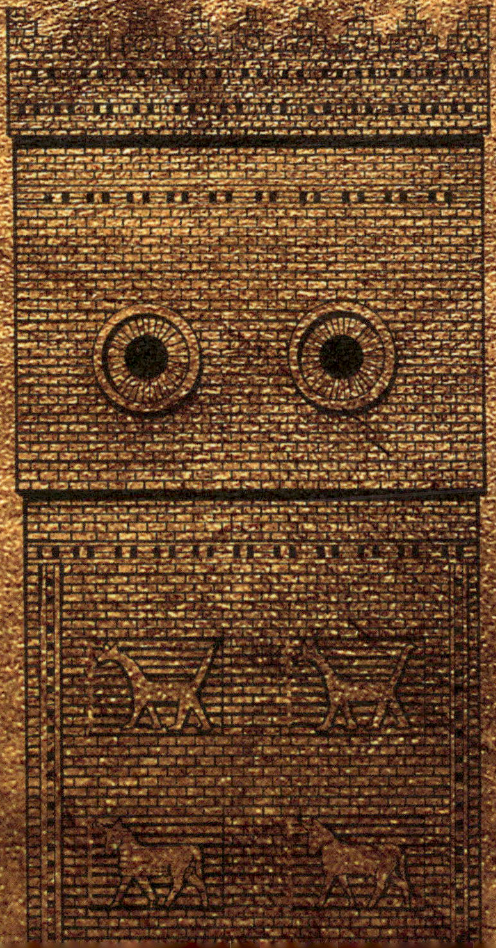

IN 1982 Iraqi workers began a very ambitious project in the ruins of Babylon. For Saddam Hussein, the Iraqi president, remembering the glories of ancient Mesopotamia was not good enough. He needed to bring them back to life, and he began by ordering the reconstruction of Nebuchadnezzar's palace. The pleas of archaeologists, aghast at the damage being done to the 2,500-year-old ruins, were simply ignored. Just as the legendary Babylonian king had done, Saddam ordered his name pressed into the bricks, connecting his reign directly to the restoration of a long-lost "golden age."

Clearly Saddam was mesmerized by Nebuchadnezzar, and for obvious reasons. Most famous of the kings who ruled over what is now known as the "Neo-Babylonian" Empire, Nebuchadnezzar was a relentless builder, turning his already revered city into the marvel of the ancient world. He oversaw the construction of titanic defenses, magnificent palace grounds, and the "Tower of Babel" itself. This was a man who left his imprint on history as few have ever been able to. But there was another reason why a man like Saddam Hussein would try to emulate Nebuchadnezzar. For Nebuchadnezzar was the conqueror of the kingdom of Judah who sent thousands of Jews into exile, an event remembered in the Old Testament as the "Babylonian Captivity."

Acts of subjugation had become ubiquitous in the Near East by the heyday of the Neo-Babylonians. With its great population centers, its rich agricultural land, its strategic location astride the richest trade routes, and its complex mixture of peoples and cultures, the cradle of civilizations had become a viaduct of imperial ambitions. Any dynasty seeking to control events in the region had to play tough, as the Assyrians and the Akkadians before them had proven. After orchestrating the downfall of the hated Assyrian Empire, the Neo-Babylonians took their place in the long list of supreme rulers. Their reign, however, would be as short as it was glorious, ending as it had begun—by the sword. The last empire of indigenous Mesopotamians, the Neo-Babylonians would fall to an even greater power from the east against whom they had no hope of victory. Military power now trumped everything else in the Fertile Crescent.

## THE FABLED CITY

The Assyrians, sanguinary braggarts *par excellence*, reveled in portraying all other rulers as cowering, diminutive lightweights. There is a remarkable exception: in the ninth century BC Shalmaneser III commissioned a throne base at Nimrud showing him

*Previous pages: Parapet from the Ishtar Gate at Babylon.*

and the king of Babylon, Marduk-zakir-shumi, shaking hands. The two figures are of equivalent height, standing erect and gazing stoically into each other's eyes. In every way, the relief depicts them as equals.

This is a startling break with Assyrian convention, and a clear indication of the esteem with which all Mesopotamians held the ruler of Babylon. Even Shalmaneser, self-important sower of terror and lamentation, considered it prudent to boast of his friendship with Marduk-zakir-shumi on the very platform above which he rested his regal behind. Babylon and its rulers were clearly in a league of their own.

That had not always been the case.

Once upon a time, Babylon was just another city on the Euphrates. Other cities in the region had achieved celebrity status. Uruk, legendary home of Gilgamesh, had been a great regional power around 3000 BC—a populous commercial center that set the standard for Mesopotamia's bustling city-states. Then there was Nippur, Mesopotamia's first religious capital. Rulers seeking regional influence in deepest antiquity had to make a pilgrimage to Nippur, where they would seek the favor of Enlil, the city's patron deity. And Ur became the base of one of history's earliest imperial efforts in the twenty-first century BC.

*Relief from a throne base showing Shalmaneser III of Assyria (centre right) shaking hands with Marduk-zakir-shumi of Babylon.*

It was not until the time of Hammurabi, in the eighteenth century BC, that Babylon became the mistress of Mesopotamia. An energetic diplomat and general, Hammurabi conquered much of Mesopotamia to create the first regional empire based on Babylon. He was a creature of his time and place, selling himself to the masses (and more importantly to the gods) as the natural successor to the rulers of Sumer and Akkad (the oldest kingdoms of the Tigris–Euphrates region), manifesting a pan-Mesopotamianism that would find its fullest expression in his city.

Of all his accomplishments, Hammurabi's "law code" endures as his greatest. It is far from being the comprehensive assault on lawlessness of popular imagination, but nevertheless it offers one of the first serious efforts to put the "law of the land" in stone—and to put it beyond the reach of a capricious king. Preserved in the Louvre, the seven-foot-tall stele engraved with Hammurabi's laws in forty-nine columns represents a milestone of civilization. From divorce to theft to careless construction, the terse decrees cover a broad range of transgressions with an earnestness that impresses the reader even today.

Despite this, Hammurabi's stellar standing with the people of his age had more to do with his military ability. For the first time, Mesopotamians began looking at their lives in a regional sense, rather than just a local one. City-states had become members of a larger enterprise, rather than being individual actors themselves—and this was because Hammurabi had brought so many of them into his orbit through naked force and intimidation. His reward was the elevation of Babylon into a capital unlike any other.

Kingship itself was to be associated with Babylon long after Hammurabi was dead. Moreover, Babylon captured the region's religious fervor, becoming—virtually overnight—the spiritual capital of the land between the rivers. This was Hammurabi's legacy—his personal achievements vaulted the city he loved into a class by itself. Babylon became the jewel of the Euphrates, the capital of kings, the god-ordained. No wonder the Hittites went out of their way to sack the place—it instantly made them the Near East's terror *du jour*.

## THE CHALDAEANS

Like all great cities, Babylon underwent severe turns of fortune. The whole region of Babylonia, at times an independent kingdom, at others a dependent province, became a sort of melting pot of migrating peoples. One of these was the Chaldaeans, a people who became associated with the southern reaches of the Tigris and Euphrates as they converged in the swamps bordering the Persian Gulf.

Records attest to a large Chaldaean presence in southern Mesopotamia by the ninth century BC. Though they were herders living in large groups in a tribal society, they seem to have embraced the local urban culture and formed close ties to the cities. It was not long before they inserted themselves into mainstream society, becoming one of a number of ethnicities with a vested interest in the affairs of the region. They gradually worked their way into centers of power, and by the eighth century BC they were as influential in Babylonia as any other group; by the following century, they were dominating events, especially in the south.

In fact, it was they who agitated so effectively against Assyrian rule when that great empire, seemingly at its zenith in the seventh century, found nothing but trouble in southern Mesopotamia. "Chaldaean" and "Babylonian" had become all but synonymous—the great city of Hammurabi chafed at the restrictions placed upon it by the conquerors in the north, and the Chaldaeans were the ones who rode this wave of resistance into greatness.

Around 625 BC, a Chaldaean leader named Nabopolassar assumed the throne of Babylon. By this time the last great king of Assyria, Ashurbanipal, was dead, and tremors were already being felt on the empire's frontiers. Nabopolassar spent nearly a decade securing his position against rival claimants as all of Mesopotamia surged with uncertainty and internecine violence. Despite Babylonia's troubles, Nabopolassar could smell the death of Assyria as the Medes marched on Nimrud and Ashur from the east. All-out war now raged between the desperate Assyrians and their foes, who included the Babylonians, Medes, and Scythians. Nineveh fell in 612 BC, destroying Assyrian might forever.

## NEBUCHADNEZZAR

Though the sack of Nineveh is traditionally considered the final nail in the Assyrian coffin, the Assyrians, hard-bitten to the end, continued to fight on. Nabopolassar was busy conquering in the north, while his son Nebuchadnezzar was campaigning in the west. And it was there, in the old arena along the Mediterranean, that Chaldaean expansion faced its greatest challenge.

The Egyptians, though no friends of the Assyrians, had made common cause with them, so acute was their fear of a resurgent Babylon. Pharaoh Necho II swept into Syria, linking up with the remnants of Assyria's once-great army at Carchemish. In 605 BC Nebuchadnezzar struck their combined forces, dealing them a resounding defeat in a battle that seems to have been a grisly bloodbath. He then displayed some of the relentlessness that would earn him so much renown in coming years. Having

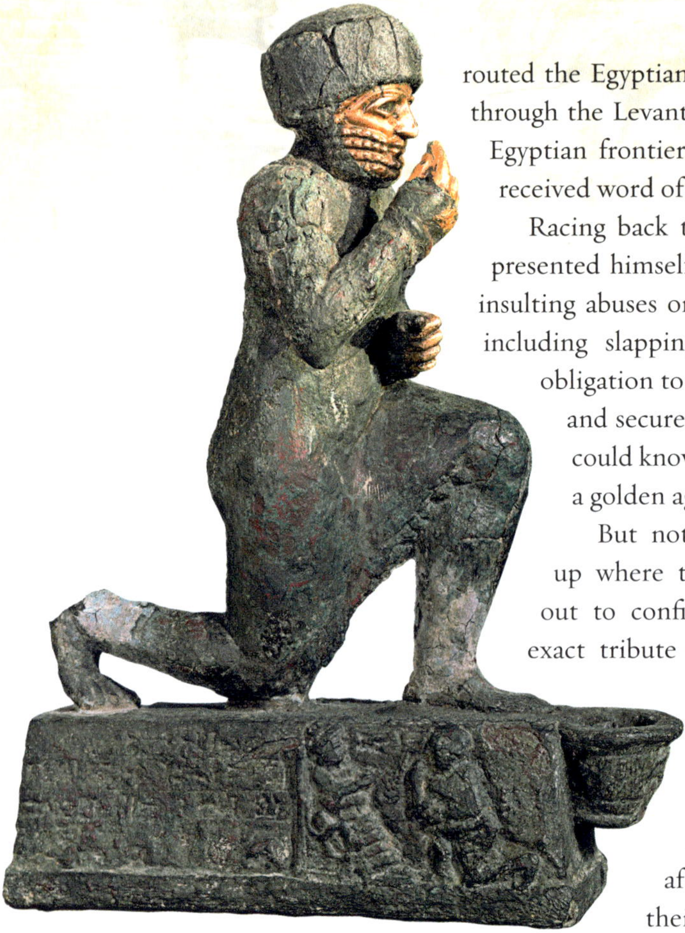

routed the Egyptians and Assyrians, he hounded them south through the Levant, nipping at their heels all the way to the Egyptian frontier. He would have kept going had he not received word of his father's death.

Racing back to Babylon, the vanquisher of Necho II presented himself to the priests of the city, endured their insulting abuses on behalf of the gods (ancient indignities, including slapping, that reminded the monarch of his obligation to the deity and his earthly representatives), and secured their sanction as the next king. Nobody could know it at the time, but it was the beginning of a golden age.

But not for everybody. The new king, picking up where the Assyrians had left off, led his army out to confirm the new borders of Babylonia and exact tribute from subject states, particularly in the recalcitrant west. Nebuchadnezzar even marched against Egypt, eager to put that nation's constant scheming in Syria and Palestine to an end. Fierce fighting ensued on the Egyptian frontier, after which the two empires retreated to lick their wounds.

It was around this time, in the first years of the sixth century BC, that the king of Judah famously ran afoul of Babylonia. Jehoiakim had originally submitted willingly to the new power from the east, offering Nebuchadnezzar a host of hostages to live in Babylon as a sign of goodwill, but with the Egyptian Twenty-Sixth Dynasty having rejuvenated its standing on the world stage, Jehoiakim started having second thoughts. Located at the center of the Near Eastern cockpit of squabbling empires, the Jewish kingdom had always to balance self-interest against the shifting sands of fate to ensure its own security. Jeremiah, prophet and advisor, warned the king not to stop payments of tribute to Babylon, but to no avail. Jehoiakim bet on Egypt's ability to thwart Babylonian ambitions in the region and dared to defy Nebuchadnezzar.

It was a bet he lost. The new Babylonian dynast came from a world in which such flagrant acts of defiance could have only one response. Around 597 BC Nebuchadnezzar sent an army to punish the king, whose hope of Egyptian intervention was in vain. Jehoiakim did not live to see the consequences of his folly, probably having died before

*Above: Votive bronze statuette of a praying man, perhaps Hammurabi. The face, beard, and hands are covered with gold foil.*

the Babylonians showed up. Ten thousand of his subjects were sent into exile, including his son and his family, and treasures from the Temple of Solomon were carried east as prizes.

Jerusalem had been spared, however, and its people were placed under a pro-Babylonian named Zedekiah. But Zedekiah, too, flirted with the Egyptians and broke with his masters. Nebuchadnezzar could only assume that he had reckoned on the wrong puppet, an error in judgment that reflected poorly on his reputation. His wrath soon spilled into Judah like a plague.

The Babylonians marched west and invested Jerusalem, their siege engineers proceeding without the expectation of the sort of surrender that had occurred the first time. Eighteen months passed before a breach was made in the city's formidable walls—a development made possible mostly by the famine that ravaged the isolated populace within. In 586 BC the besiegers took the city and caught Zedekiah himself trying to escape in the night with a coterie of defenders. He soon discovered that dying on the city walls would have been preferable.

Zedekiah was taken to the headquarters of Nebuchadnezzar on the Orontes River, where he was made to look upon his sons as they were slaughtered. That done, his captors gouged his eyes out and packed him off to Babylon as a prisoner. Then Nebuchadnezzar sent the captain of his personal bodyguard, Nebuzaradan, to deal with Jerusalem in a manner befitting its perfidious behavior.

Nebuzaradan directed one of the most thorough and systematic destructions of a city ever to have been recorded in the ancient world. Jerusalem's walls were razed, its houses smashed and gutted. The temple was burned to the ground. With their city in ashes, Jerusalem's citizens were marched east into captivity, where many of them would remain until the end of their days. Not all of them would make it, however: priests, military leaders, royal officials—all those deemed responsible for the kingdom's act of defiance—were executed outright on Nebuchadnezzar's command.

## BUILDING A LEGACY

Acts of subjugation and mass deportations were old Mesopotamian tactics, but the empire's security would require something else, too: walls. In 573 BC Nebuchadnezzar learned firsthand about the value of defensive works when, in one of his most celebrated exploits, he captured the island-city of Tyre after a thirteen-year siege. His own most famous military structure—running from Sippar on the Euphrates to Opis on the Tigris—actually spanned the distance between Mesopotamia's two fabled rivers. It was called the Median Wall, after the great civilization it was meant to keep at bay, and it is supposed to have been as high as a hundred feet in some places. It stood for centuries, a testament to Babylonia's reemergence as ruler of the Near East.

Nebuchadnezzar's most impressive project, however, involved his beloved capital. Babylon was girded with defenses intended to thwart, once and for all, any future attempts to ravage its beauty. They relied on three principal elements: an outer series of walls, an inner circuit, and a moat between them. The outer walls alone were simply awesome, consisting of three barriers in succession—the innermost of the three, built of stout mud bricks to a depth of twenty feet, made a formidable barrier on its own. Should attackers be lucky enough to breach it, they would stumble into the watery trench of the moat, only to be met by the inner circuit, its broad face studded with towers for raining

## HANGING GARDENS?

"Vaults had been constructed under the ascending terraces which carried the entire weight of the planted garden; the uppermost vault, which was seventy-five feet high, was the highest part of the garden, which, at this point, was on the same level as the city walls." So wrote the Greek historian Diodorus in his description of the Hanging Gardens of Babylon. Allegedly built by Nebuchadnezzar for his Median wife, who missed the lush greenery of her homeland, the Hanging Gardens were included in the Seven Wonders of the Ancient World for their beauty and ingenious engineering. "The approach to the Garden sloped like a hillside," Diodorus went on, "and the several parts of the structure rose from one another tier on tier." He also mentions "water machines" that brought water up from the Euphrates by some brilliant artifice, out of sight of visitors. Rather than "hanging," the gardens probably seemed "suspended" on their terraces, producing a stunning amalgam of verdant growth and architecture.

But did they actually exist? Neither Diodorus nor any of the other authors (such as Strabo) who wrote about the Hanging Gardens actually set eyes on them. As for the Babylonian sources, no mention of the gardens has been found—a curious silence indeed, given all the royal records that have turned up. It certainly would have been a spectacle in its time, especially given the mysterious "water machines," which, some have speculated, may have employed the same principle as Archimedes's screw.

Interestingly enough, recent excavations have turned up what could be the foundations of the Hanging Gardens. One possibility, a series of thick walls with vaulted construction, is near the king's southern palace. Another possible site, where massively thick walls have been discovered, lies along the river's banks, making it a more realistic possibility. Despite these tantalizing developments, however, the existence of this legendary construction remains open to question.

punishment upon all comers. Once the areas between the outer three barriers had been filled and paved over, they formed the foundation of a veritable road around the city—broad enough to allow the passage of a four-horse chariot. Nor did Nebuchadnezzar forget the Euphrates River, whose course through the middle of the city offered an entirely different avenue of attack. The king placed two sets of grates, one at either end of the great river's course through the city, to prevent the passage of uninvited guests but still allow the passage of water.

The building that Nebuchadnezzar was probably most proud of, however, had little to do with defense. At the heart of Babylon lay Entemenanki, the massive ziggurat that had been started and abandoned by earlier regimes. With a three hundred square foot foundation, the colossal multi-story structure would have been visible for miles. This was the biblical Tower of Babel—an arresting achievement, circumscribed by its own enclosure, that awed the ancient world and was finished during Nebuchadnezzar's reign. Just outside the ziggurat's enclosure to the south lay the city's most important religious structure, the Temple of Marduk, known as Esagila. This was the house of Mesopotamia's most revered deity.

## A DYNASTY'S DECLINE

Nebuchadnezzar (who died in 562 BC) had the unfortunate fate of being his dynasty's greatest ruler—unfortunate because he was only the second in his line, and the Neo-Babylonian Empire would last only forty-five years after his death. What followed his epoch-making reign was a dissipation of talent through unworthy heirs, a theme so common in ancient history that its mere mention seems redundant.

Nebuchadnezzar's son Awil-Marduk proved either too incompetent or too dissolute for the Babylonian elite, who seem to have disposed of him in disgust. They put on the throne Nebuchadnezzar's son-in-law, a general named Neriglissar, who campaigned vigorously on the empire's borders before dying in mysterious circumstances. Next came Labashi-Marduk, the young son of Neriglissar, whose reign was cut short by a rebellion that vaulted an eccentric named Nabonidus into the kingship.

Nabonidus, an enigmatic figure, was a scholar first and a ruler second. "I am Nabonidus," he proclaimed, "who have not the honor of being a somebody—kingship is not within me." Perhaps a man to whom supreme authority came uneasily, Nabonidus wrestled with his own demons and came up short. He was the son of the longest-lived queen mother in antiquity, Addagoppe, a priestess of the god Sin of the city of Harran. When she died in 547 BC, she was around 103 years old (!)—her wide experience was either a bane or a boon to Nabonidus, but we may never know which.

Her piety, however, pointed to the heart of Babylonia's weakness. Unlike the Assyrian kings, on whose methods they based much of their imperial policy, the Neo-Babylonians were not wholly in control of their state. They had to deal with the priests, whose authority in Babylonia had been entirely out of proportion to their numbers since well before the Chaldaeans came to power. Indeed, the priests controlled literally enormous tracts of cultivable land, backing their ideological gravitas with tons of pure, beautiful grain.

The Assyrian kings had been like divinely ordained masters of the earth, but in Babylon the king was only as good as his backing from the priesthood—a fact that was acted out every year when the Babylonian king had to subject himself to the ritual indignities of the city's priests, eager to remind him of their infallible influence. Babylon's uniquely transcendent spirituality, the quality that had preserved the city for so long, had become its special frailty.

Nabonidus proceeded to do what every historian since has dubbed bizarre, but what anyone who has suffered from severe self-doubt or depression would recognize as inevitable. He retired with his army to an oasis in the Arabian desert, there to wage a conveniently endless war with Jewish mercenaries against nomads whose elusiveness made them ideal enemies. In the desert he built an outpost of civilization that would last well into the Roman period, but his house was clearly not in order. Back in Babylon, his own people were growing uneasy about his self-imposed exile.

Nabonidus may well have made history as just another eccentric leader in a Mesopotamian world that produced no shortage of them, but his ambivalent reign coincided with the rise in the east of a perfect storm—a warrior people whose appearance on the scene would have been difficult for a dynasty in complete control, much less one that now seemed hobbled by both a brooding king and an overweening priesthood. Babylonia's days as an independent power were numbered.

## ENTER CYRUS

The vast highlands of Iran had always been a bane to Mesopotamian empire builders, who seemed to see enemies whenever they looked in that direction. There were the Elamites, who had constantly meddled in Mesopotamian affairs, and the Medes, who actually burned Assyria's cities to the ground. Now a new people were on the rise in the east, and they would make the Elamites and Medes look innocuous by comparison.

The Persians were a sturdy warrior race of Indo-European origin who lived on the Iranian plateau. They thrived in the shadow of the Medes, their cousins and fellow Indo-Europeans, who were too busy building an empire of their own to notice.

Then along came Cyrus II, indisputably one of the greatest conquerors in human history. Forging his fellow Persians, virtually overnight, into an expansionist nation of the first order, he relied on cunning, charisma, personal courage, and a host of other elusive qualities to take his people on one of the most spectacular adventures in antiquity. After devouring the Medes, whose relatively new empire now became a Persian enterprise, he set his sights on the fulsome prize of Mesopotamia, under the absent leadership of Nabonidus.

When he returned to Babylon in 542 BC, Nabonidus found a city that was all but ready to rebel against him. The priests of Marduk were particularly disgusted, especially after the king formally backed the old Sumerian god Sin by making his own daughter one of the deity's priestesses. Babylon's powerful priests sent word to Cyrus, who hovered over Mesopotamia like a snake ready to strike, that they would welcome his rule. He obliged them.

Cyrus, the sort of conqueror who was happy to rely on subtler means of expansion than force, had been busy filling the Chaldaean Empire with propaganda about his liberal religious policies. This effort was clearly paying off, aided by the bumbling of Nabonidus and the strife that characterized his relationship with the priesthood. In 39 BC Cyrus struck, marching the massive Persian army into northern Babylonia. Nabonidus fled, overwhelmed by the absurdity of his position. This was fortunate for Babylon, whose gates were thrown wide for the Persian conqueror, sparing the populace and its treasures from the usual bout of plundering. And so the Chaldaean dynasty passed into memory.

It is worth considering how different our modern perception of these events is from that of the people who lived through it. To many Mesopotamians, this was merely the exchange of one master for another, regardless of race or nationality. Cyrus's perceived equity and potency as a leader trumped his identity as a barbarian outsider.

We see it, on the other hand, as the end of a long era. Mesopotamia, birthplace of cities, had seen its last native dynasty come and go. The "land between the rivers" had become too important and too accessible for foreign aggressors not to hunger after. And now it belonged to them.

*Following pages: Cyrus entered the city without a fight, but this has not prevented the "fall of Babylon" being viewed as an apocalyptic event.*

CHAPTER SIX

# KUSH

## LEFT BEHIND BY THE MARCH OF HISTORY

IN January 2003, a team of Swiss archaeologists working in northern Sudan made the discovery of a lifetime. Near the ancient city of Karmah, they found the dismembered remains of seven life-sized statues, their granite torsos and limbs heaped in a ditch and covered with sand. Though carved in Egyptian monumental style, they bore the likenesses of five Nubian kings, two of whom had reigned over Egypt as pharaohs of the Twenty-Fifth Dynasty.

Reassembling the destroyed statues proved a daunting task. Without access to heavy machinery, the archaeologists had to employ the most basic of hoists to lift the pieces out of their cache. Preparation for this was painstaking: removal of the dirt, sand, and other debris that filled the pit and surrounded the broken statuary required the utmost dexterity to avoid moving the carved pieces, even a little, lest they scratch each other. Once this was done, the team had to make a difficult decision. Would the pieces be reassembled off site, or on? Given the extraordinary state of preservation of the statuary's polish, which had been buried far from the elements since the sixth century BC, the team opted to do the work on site so as to avoid any damage from transportation.

Once reconstructed in their original forms, the figures made an awesome sight. Standing with the left foot forward and arms rigidly straight at their sides, they stare confidently from faces majestic and serene, in classic Egyptian fashion. But a few elements are unique. For one, these kings wear a double uraeus on their crowns—two arching serpents, side by side, as opposed to the one usually worn by Egyptian pharaohs. Moreover, unlike other pharaonic statues, these figures are clearly dark-skinned.

Each statue is supported from behind by a column on which identifying inscriptions have been carved, but even without the identifying hieroglyphs, Professor Charles Bonnet and his team knew whom they were dealing with. These were rulers of the Twenty-Fifth Dynasty of Egypt and their Nubian successors—kings of Kush, from the mysterious land south of Egypt.

*Previous pages: Capital from the "kiosk" at Naga.*
*Above: Sandstone statue from the temple of Isis at Meroe shows the unique style developed by Kushite artists.*

Underpinning the triumph of Bonnet's find was the fact that so little is known of the land from which these men came—a land known to the Egyptians as "Kush." And the demise of their kingdom is equally mysterious.

## OUT OF AFRICA

In 730 BC Piy (also known as Piankhi), a king of Nubia who ruled from the city of Napata, undertook a crusade. Sailing his army down the Nile, he stopped at the temple complex of Karnak, where he made sacrifices to Amon while his troops ritually bathed themselves in the river. Such acts of purification served to anoint Piy's enterprise as a holy one—an armed intervention into Egypt to restore the ancient order and banish chaos from the land. And there was plenty of chaos to banish—Egypt, to put it simply, was a mess. Libyan warlords had assumed control of the Delta, petty kings ruled throughout the land from regional centers of power, and strong pharaonic leadership was fast becoming a distant memory.

Piy was coming north to sort things out. His armies captured Hermopolis and then moved down the Nile, occupying towns as they went. Memphis, which refused to capitulate, was stormed and sacked, though Piy was insistent that the temples not be touched. Before long the Nubian had vanquished every army that came against him and received homage from the whole of Egypt. Tefnakhte, the most powerful of the Delta's warlords, begged for mercy: "Be gracious! I cannot see your face in the days of shame, I cannot stand before your flame, I dread your grandeur." It was a striking military achievement. Egypt had been united once again—by a Nubian prince.

His task completed, Piy went south again to rule from Nubia until the end of his days. Although Shabaka, Piy's successor, was obliged in 716 BC to renew operations in the north to subdue the last remnants of resistance in the Delta, the Twenty-Fifth Dynasty—Egypt's period of Nubian control—had well and truly begun.

Military power underpinned the dynasty's authority, but these were kings who earnestly believed that they were guardians of Egypt's most sacred institutions. Centuries of contact with—and occupation by—their northern neighbors had turned the Nubians into purists of the Egyptian tradition. In the process of their enculturation, they had become more Egyptian than the Egyptians themselves, adhering to an idealized version of pharaonic essence that harkened back to earlier days. Seeing the mighty empire of Ramses the Great sundered into squabbling little principalities was as much a scandal to them as an opportunity.

Though pharaohs had traditionally been rulers of the two lands of Upper and Lower Egypt, the Kushite pharaohs now assumed control of the two lands of Egypt and Nubia.

A double uraeus adorned their headdresses to emphasize this. For the Twenty-Fifth Dynasty, the Old Kingdom was the model—the world of iconic megalomaniacs who built the Great Pyramids and set the pattern for pharaonic majesty. The Nubian pharaohs now ruled from Memphis, ancient capital of Upper Egypt, deliberately connecting their era with the origins of Egyptian greatness. They drew on archaic models to emphasize their legitimacy and to bring back the stability of an age that they had romanticized.

Perhaps feeling a bit overstretched, in Egypt the Nubian pharaohs depended on a decentralized administration to handle day-to-day affairs while Kush remained under tight control. Whatever the scheme's weaknesses, Egypt underwent a renaissance of sorts, repeating the cultural achievements of long-gone eras. Rigid adherence to traditional methods of governance and religious observance allowed the empire to grow—and to reassert itself beyond the frontier.

The Twenty-Fifth Dynasty's efforts to win Syria and Lebanon back from under the boot of Assyrian rule drew the unwanted attention of the formidable Assyrian war machine. Taharqa (690–664), second-to-last of the dynasty's pharaohs, found his Egyptian realm invaded by irresistible Assyrian armies, who chased him all the way back to Nubia.

*Egyptian sources provide much of our evidence about early Nubia. In this relief of Amenhotep III, Nubians are shown as bound captives.*

Taharqa was hardly finished with Egypt, however. The great kingdom had become too much of an obsession with Nubian kings not to fight for it. Having left behind an inadequate force, the Assyrians found their Egyptian prize stolen once again by Kushite forces. Taharqa, sensing weakness, boldly led his army north again to take Egypt—and so the seesaw between Kush and Assyria continued. Taharqa was kicked out once again in 667 BC, but his successor, Tanutamon, led an invasion to subdue and punish all the dynasts who had pledged obedience to Assyria, once again drawing out an army from Nineveh. The Assyrians conquered and ravaged nearly all of Egypt and sent Tanutamon packing for the last time. This marked the end of an era—never again would the rulers of Kush hold sway over Egypt.

## IN THE SHADOW OF THE PHARAOHS

Who were these people who had managed to control the Egyptian Empire for the better part of a century? Sadly, the Twenty-Fifth Dynasty of Egypt is better understood than any other period in Nubian history. For the rest of Kush's story, evidence is quite sketchy.

By the beginning of the Egyptian Old Kingdom, during the third millennium BC, the Nubian state was known as Ta-Sety, or "the Land of the Bow," by its northern neighbors, who clearly had developed a respect for Nubian archers. The Nubians thrived as cattle-herders and farmers along the Nile, ultimately posing a threat to the security of Egypt itself. Fortresses appeared during the Middle Kingdom around the Second Cataract of the Nile, built by the Egyptians to secure local gold mines and guard the border against the possibility of Nubian incursion.

From about 1700, a mighty kingdom known as Kush thrived south of the Third Cataract with its capital at Karmah. Grown rich from trade with Egypt, which relied on Kush for luxury items like ivory from the African interior, the kings in Karmah were buried in lavishly appointed tombs, often with hundreds of servants. Now a power to be reckoned with, Kush was able to dominate the fortified border with Egypt, whose leadership gradually lost control during the Second Intermediate Period around the middle of the second millennium. It was during this period that the kings of Kush assumed mastery of the Nile trade and formed an alliance with the Hyksos in the north, threatening a teetering Egypt from both directions.

The vice was soon broken by the dynamic Theban dynasty that ushered in Egypt's New Kingdom. After crushing the Hyksos, Egyptian armies swept south around 1550 BC, reclaiming the old fortresses and pushing deep into Nubia. In the decades that followed war raged between the two lands, until Karmah itself was destroyed and all of Nubia annexed by a militarized Egypt. The pharaohs moved their new southern border all the way to the Fourth Cataract and created a viceroyalty known as the "King's Son of Kush" to rule these new possessions. Filled by high-ranking Egyptian aristocrats, this office reported directly to the pharaoh and ruled in his name.

The region, dotted with colonists and officials from the north, soon became thoroughly Egyptianized. The imperialism of the New Kingdom and its warrior pharaohs ensured tight control over Nubia, its gold, and its trade routes to the interior. Epic building projects, especially Ramses's magnificent temple at Abu Simbel, offered palpable proof of Egyptian greatness to a Nubian people who revered Egyptian gods, embraced Egyptian institutions, and ultimately accepted Egyptian culture as an ideal.

They also came to look upon themselves, in the eighth century, as guardians of a civilization that seemed in danger of collapse—a situation they would correct with armed invasion.

## THE CONQUEROR CONQUERED

King Piy's historic campaign in Egypt and the Twenty-Fifth Dynasty that it spawned ushered in a spirit of archaism that brought the Egyptian elite back to its roots. But the Kushites had aroused the ire of the Assyrians, who sent their armies in to bring Kushite rule to an end after less than a century. Egypt would fall to an Egyptian named Psamtik, founder of the Twenty-Sixth Dynasty, who would exploit the tumultuous situation of his country to become pharaoh. Tanutamon retired to his ancestral capital at Napata.

Egypt was lost to the Kushites forever, but a curious thing seems to have happened: the kings of Kush went on as if they did not realize it. The Napatan rulers who continued in Tanutamon's wake never discarded the double uraeus on their headgear, a clear and rather bizarre symbol of their alleged claim to Egypt. Even stranger, they rarely referred to themselves as rulers of Kush, preferring to style themselves as "kings of Upper and Lower Egypt." Defiant in their capital at Napata, the Kushites buried their rulers in Egyptian style, wrote in hieroglyphs, and bided their time until some effort could be made to conquer Egypt once again.

In fact, the next invasion would be *from* the north rather than *to* it. During the first decade of the sixth century BC, Pharaoh Psamtik II led a large army into Nubia, its ranks swollen with mercenaries from as far away as Greece and Phoenicia. The nature of the relationship between Kush and Egypt in the years since Tanutamon had been evicted remains unclear. Trade there certainly was, but how much and for whose benefit is largely unknown. Nevertheless, peace had reigned along the Nile.

That is, until Psamtik II ascended the throne. At some point during his reign, a formal rejection of the Twenty-Fifth Dynasty went into effect. Judged to have been illegitimate, the Kushite kings became *persona non grata*, their images violated and chiseled away (smashing a statue's nose was a favorite tactic of vandals, who believed they were magically preventing the victim from breathing). Before long Psamtik was marching south, where he clashed with Nubian armies in a series of bloody campaigns. It was during this time that the statues found in 2003 by Professor Bonnet and his team were broken and, upon being discovered by Nubians after the Egyptian army retired, given a respectful burial.

Though Psamtik's invasion humbled his Nubian neighbors and extended Egyptian control into Lower Nubia, Kush remained an independent power, its kings still reigning from Napata, near the Fourth Cataract. But with an unpredictable, predatory Egypt to the north, the center of Kushite civilization gradually shifted further up the Nile, well

## THE TRUEST FORM OF FLATTERY

Those looking to find the greatest concentration of ancient pyramids must travel not to Egypt, but to the Sudan. The remains of over two hundred Kushite pyramids bear solemn testament to the fact that the ancient Nubians found Egypt's pyramids just as entrancing as we do today.

The first Nubian pyramids were built just west of the Fourth Cataract, at a cemetery called el-Kurru, site of the most ancient royal tombs in Nubia. Taharqa, penultimate pharaoh of the Twenty-Fifth Dynasty, broke with tradition and built his pyramid at Nuri, across the Nile from el-Kurru, near the majestic butte of Gebel Barkal. It was at Nuri and Gebel Barkal that the royalty and aristocracy of Kush continued to be interred beneath their pyramids until well into the third century BC, when royal burials also began to appear outside the new capital complex of Meroe. When Italian explorer Giuseppe Ferlini came to Meroe in search of treasure during the 1820s, he recklessly smashed the tops off forty pyramids to peer inside. Some of the items he found ended up in European museums, where they remain today.

Kushite pyramids were considerably smaller than their northern prototypes, and the interred was placed in a tomb beneath the pyramid rather than inside it. Though the pyramids were clearly inspired by Egyptian examples, one Kushite burial practice was distinctly homegrown. Entombed near the necropolis at el-Kurru are the remains of twenty-four horses belonging to rulers of the Twenty-Fifth Dynasty. Apparently favored by their owners, the animals were interred with supports so that the corpses would stand up for eternity in their narrow graves. The Kushite respect for horses was well known to the ancients, and it is borne out by a victory stele left by Piy at Gebel Barkal. This records his successful siege of Heliopolis and the fury he felt upon seeing the poor state of the city's stables: "As true as I live and as Re loves [me] ... that my horses were made to hunger pains me more than any other crime you committed in your recklessness ..."

beyond the Fifth Cataract, to a city called Meroe. It was there that ancient Nubia would experience its final flowering.

## A BLEND OF CULTURES

Probably in the sixth century BC, the Kushite court moved upriver from Napata to Meroe, about 124 miles north of the modern Sudanese capital of Khartoum. Certainly by the fourth century the Kushites were burying their kings there rather than in the traditional region around Napata.

Having distanced themselves from the Egyptian frontier while maintaining control over the upper and middle Nile trade, Kush embarked on a period of robust prosperity. Archaeologists have discovered the foundations of a massive royal palace at Meroe, as well as evidence of extensive ironworking facilities, the heaps of slag attesting to feverish activity. Kush grew rich from its industry and river commerce as it continued to funnel exotic goods from sub-Saharan Africa into Egypt and received in return the bounty of the Hellenistic and Roman worlds. With firm control over an empire that stretched from Lower Nubia to well south of Khartoum, the kings at Meroe became the most important powerbrokers in Africa. A native script evolved, based on twenty-three Egyptian hieroglyphs, and temples to the god Amon gradually lost precedence to those dedicated to local Meroitic deities, evidence of how Kush had moved beyond the attachment to Egypt without abandoning it entirely. There evolved a thriving, distinctly Kushite civilization that incorporated Greek and Roman artistic influences with the Egyptian and African heritage that had defined it for centuries.

But by the third century AD, Meroitic Kush seemed to be in decline. Signs of this are scant and sometimes confused, leading scholars to debate the issue to this day. Royal tombs, for instance, became decreasingly indulgent, pointing to a monarchy with fewer resources at its disposal—or an aristocracy that had acquired increasing control at the expense of a decentralizing court. However gradual this change was, by the dawn of the fifth century AD it had run its course: Meroitic literacy and monumental architecture had disappeared, and Nubia, though inhabited and prosperous in some areas, had become a backwater.

Though nothing about this situation or its causes is absolutely verifiable, scholars have zeroed in on a select group of circumstances that, taken together, offer a plausible explanation for the passing of Kushite greatness. To begin with, much—if not all—of Nubia's wealth and success depended on control of the Nile traffic that took goods north into Egypt and to other nations of the wider Mediterranean world. By the time of the Meroitic decline, however, an alternative trade route established by the Egyptians was up and running, gradually stealing business from the Nile. This route, running through the Red Sea and along the African coast, made it possible to bring the luxury goods of inner Africa and elsewhere up to the Mediterranean without having to navigate the Nile, with its cataracts and political instability. In time this must have sapped Kush of the commercial activity that had sustained it since the days of the ancient pharaohs.

Exacerbating this problem was the condition of Egypt, Kush's primary conduit to the rest of the ancient world. During the first centuries AD Egypt, the breadbasket of the Roman Empire, remained a cherished possession, but the demands of more troubled areas—such as Europe and Mesopotamia—forced the emperors to pull the defensible border back to the First Cataract, shrinking the territory of Roman Egypt, constricting its once-great economy, and drawing it further away from the Nubians who depended upon it for their livelihood.

However, it was probably incursions by foreign peoples that delivered the final blow to Kushite supremacy. Chief among these peoples were the Aksumites, an Ethiopian people named for their capital, Aksum, whose operations in the Nile valley, though controversial, are widely believed to have taken advantage of a weakened Kush. The Blemmyes, a collection of desert tribes whose martial prowess with the help of the camel had become legendary, also made inroads that Kush was ultimately powerless to stop. Though few of these campaigns qualified as "invasions," the sporadic raids ate away at Kushite sovereignty over the course of years and Kushite control was eventually extinguished as greater numbers of the outsiders settled in the Nile valley.

A clearer picture of Kush's collapse awaits the appearance of more evidence, but clearly Kush found itself falling away from a changing world—and falling prey to aggressive peoples eager to take advantage of a state in decline.

*The pyramids at Meroe, just north of Khartoum. Kushite rulers used this Egyptian form of burial for many centuries.*

CHAPTER SEVEN

# ACHAEMENID PERSIA

## SPARKING A FIRE IN THE WEST

AT around 500 BC, according to the Greek historian Herodotus, the tyrant of Miletus came to Sparta for help. Aristagoras was hoping to enlist the aid of Greece's most respected warrior state in a fight to free his native Miletus and the rest of Ionia from Persian rule.

The Ionian cities of Anatolia shared a long Greek heritage with Sparta. Originally settled by Greek colonists, Miletus and its fellow Ionian communities were thriving centers of Greece's Classical Age. But unlike Sparta or the other cities of mainland Greece, they were possessions of the Persian Great King in Susa. It was this burden that Aristagoras hoped to throw off with Spartan muscle.

He had quite a task before him. Known for their peculiar dual kingship, their unsparing militarism, and their suspicion of foreign lands, the conservative Spartans were unlikely to look favorably upon a distant venture on behalf of strangers, even Greek ones, but Cleomenes, one of Sparta's two kings, was proud and honor-bound to receive ingratiating emissaries. He gave the Milesian an audience.

Aristagoras carried with him a magnificent curiosity: a great bronze tablet on which lay a map of the world. Cleomenes had certainly never seen the like of this creation of Ionian intellectualism and probably gazed upon it with a blend of wonder and suspicion as his clever visitor made his pitch.

The Milesian tyrant softened up his mark by regaling him with images of Persian weakness: "They wear trousers in the field, and cover their heads with turbans." Can you imagine? Creampuffs! Moreover, the treasure that surrounded their king in Susa was beyond reckoning—"more good things than all the rest of the world put together."

Then Aristagoras directed the Spartan's attention to his marvelous map, introducing him to the enemy by pointing out the various regions that lay within the Persian realm. Nearest to the Aegean, of course, were the Ionians, of whom Aristagoras was a prominent member. Then came the Lydians, rich in silver and gold, and the Phrygians, and the Cappadocians, each farther east than the people before, the finger of Aristagoras slowly tracing a path across Anatolia toward the center of Asia. Next came the Cilicians, "who pay [the Great King] a tribute of five hundred talents." Even further were the Armenians, then the Matieni, and finally the province of Cissia, wherein lay the city of Susa, where the Great King sat on his throne surrounded by goodness knows how much treasure.

All the Spartans had to do was lead a victorious army that far to make themselves richer than Zeus himself.

Cleomenes was duly impressed by the presentation and promised to offer a response in three days' time. But at the appointed date, Cleomenes confronted Aristagoras with

*Previous pages: Bull capital from the Hall of 100 Columns at the Apadana Palace at Persepolis.*

a question rather than an answer: How long was the journey from Ionia to the Persian king's residence in Susa?

Aristagoras, who had personally made the trip on missions of tribute to his Persian overlords, had a ready answer: three months.

*Three months!*

"Milesian stranger," grumbled an irate Cleomenes, "quit Sparta before sunset."

## THE MATTER OF SIZE

Few Greeks, much less the Spartans, were eager to embark on a journey that took them three months from the sea. Indeed, most Greeks had trouble imagining such a place. But the three-month trek from the Aegean Sea to the heart of the Persian Empire as described by Aristagoras covered *just half* of the Great King's possessions. There were satrapies of the empire stretching as far east as Bactria, Sattagydia and the Indus—places that, as far as King Cleomenes was concerned, might as well have lain beyond the stars.

At its greatest extent the Achaemenid Empire was the largest empire of antiquity in terms of square miles—larger even than the Roman Empire, which came well after it. The product of military and organizational genius, this realm would achieve a level of centralization entirely out of proportion to its vast, ungainly size, taking the ancient Near Eastern practice of empire building to new heights. Few of the enemies who opposed it had any idea how many people paid homage and tribute to its Great King.

All of which begs the question: How could such a goliath fall? Achaemenid Persia's weakness lay not in its scale or government, but in its choice of enemies. Aristagoras of

*Stone relief in the palace at Persepolis, showing tribute bearers arriving from all parts of the empire.*

Miletus represented a culture—Ionian Greece—that proved more trouble to Persia than its conquest was worth. Persia could not have known this when it swept across Anatolia in the mid-sixth century BC, gobbling up the Ionian cities as it had so many other regions. But the Ionians were just the eastern outpost of a vast and complex Greek world that would prove the undoing of Persian dreams. Diverse, competitive, restless, the Hellenic world represented more than just the far western extreme of Persian expansion—it was the fertile ground in which the seeds of Achaemenid collapse were sown by the Persians themselves. The Greek world under the yoke of Macedon, schooled in the lessons taught them by the wars with Persia, would eventually go east in search of vengeance against the Great King, and it would succeed spectacularly.

This, in other words, is a simple story of conquest from without.

## HARD PEOPLE OF THE HIGH PLATEAU

According to Herodotus, all Persians between the ages of five and twenty were taught three things: to ride a horse, use a bow, and tell the truth. In addition to giving us an image of the Persians as noble, anti-intellectual, spirited, and martial, this reminds us of our reliance on Greek sources, for scholars are still obliged to base much of their knowledge about the Persians on information gleaned from their enemies, the Greeks. This is at once ironic and appropriate. Ironic, of course, because sources such as Herodotus wrote about the Persians so that their fellow Greeks could understand why so much Greek blood was spilled in fighting them. But it is also appropriate, for the Greeks and the Persians were actually distant cousins—a fact we all too often forget today in our rush to divide the world into East and West.

Both peoples were Indo-European in origin, emerging out of the same greater cultural group somewhere in southern Eurasia. The Greeks, one of the splinter sections of this mass movement, trickled westward and down into the Greek mainland. The Persians, by contrast, were members of the vast group that migrated south, settling in the highlands of what is today Iran. By the time these two peoples were facing off in the fifth century BC, they had acquired distinctive cultures, formed during the centuries of separation, but they shared a linguistic heritage that set them apart from the Semitic peoples of the Near East with whom both traded, settled, and fought. Modern Iranian languages, including Persian (Farsi), are closer to English than they are to Arabic or Hebrew.

Despite their relationship with the Greeks, the Persians embraced an equestrian way of life that their western cousins had long abandoned. The bow, ubiquitous tool of the steppe, was as revered in the Persian world as it was dismissed in the Greek, and the ability of Persian nobles to loose arrows from the saddle was a subject of fascination in the West. Persia was a horse culture of the vast plains and valleys, which were punctuated by small settlements that never lost touch with the windswept wilderness.

That changed in the sixth century BC. The Persians' neighbors and overlords, the Medes, with whom they shared a cavalry tradition, had carved out an empire of their own after helping to destroy the Assyrians. In their southern Iranian homeland, the upland Persians paid tribute to the Medes just like other subject nations. Then a man named Cyrus came along and turned the old order upside down.

## A MAN FOR THE AGES

Cyrus the Great is a man scholars approach with caution. Sifting truth from legend is difficult with this hallowed figure, not least because the greatest empire of the ancient world traced its founding directly to him. Cyrus could do no wrong: the Babylonians welcomed him as an enlightened conqueror and the Jews, freed by him from their captivity in the east begun by Nebuchadnezzar, remembered him as a veritable savior.

The Achaemenids took their name from a legendary founder named Achaemenes. Cyrus, however, represents the true wellspring of Persian culture, the nexus of history and legend that gave the empire its genesis. With both Persian and Median blood in his veins, he represented at once a merging of peoples and a break with the past.

According to legend, his life was very nearly cut short before it had a chance to begin. Astyages, his grandfather and king of the Medes, ordered him exposed when he was still an infant. The old king had heard a prophecy that the boy threatened his reign, and Astyages was not taking any chances. Fate intervened, however, and the boy fell into the hands of common shepherds, who raised him as their own, allowing him eventually to win his way back into court life and pursue his destiny. Of course, such folktales are a requirement for great leaders, and it seems more likely that Cyrus came to the throne directly from his father's line. In 559 BC he inherited the title "king of Anshan," the primary city of *Parsa*, or Persia, which paid tribute to the Median Empire.

Within six years he was leading his people in open revolt. After several battles with the Medes, in 549 BC Cyrus captured Astyages's capital at Ecbatana. In just four years, he had turned his fellow Persians from subjects of the Median Empire into masters of it, easily seizing control of a realm that stretched from the heart of Anatolia to the shores of the Arabian Sea. And he was just getting started.

The vast kingdom bequeathed to Cyrus by the vanquished Medes offered the perfect base from which to launch his growing armies against other realms, most of which had been allies of Astyages. Lydia fell first. Its king, Croesus, famous in legend for the gold that made his western Anatolian kingdom so desirable, led a substantial army out to invade Persian territory. At the battle of Pteria, the two armies fought each other to a bloody draw, compelling Croesus to retire to his capital at Sardis. Cyrus followed, laid siege to the great city, and took it in 546 BC. Lydia, with all its gold and its populous Ionian cities, was now under Persian control.

Babylon fell in 539, its disaffected populace welcoming Cyrus as a just liberator from the aloof and neurotic leadership of Nabonidus. Like the Median Empire before it, the Neo-Babylonian establishment—in Mesopotamia, Syria, Judea, and elsewhere—was absorbed by Cyrus, and its people and aristocrats were pacified by Persian tolerance for local ways and religions. Indeed, the Persians were henotheists: while their god, Ahura Mazda—a deity of light and fire who represented all that was good in the world—was considered unique and supreme, the Persians accepted the preference of other peoples for their own gods. Nothing exemplified this more clearly than Cyrus's decision to free the Jews from the "Babylonian Captivity." At Persian expense, he resettled them in their homeland and rebuilt their temple in Jerusalem. Persians could certainly be as brutal as any conquering people, but tactics like this ensured they rarely needed to be.

## FROM HIGHLAND TOUGHS TO MASTERS OF THE WORLD

Cyrus died in 530 BC while campaigning in the far east of his new empire. Upon his tomb, according to Plutarch, was inscribed a simple epitaph: "Oh man, whoever you are and wherever you come from, for I know you will come, I am Cyrus who founded the empire of the Persians. Do not therefore grudge me this little earth that covers my body."

Few conquerors had achieved as much in so brief a time. The expanse of territory Cyrus entrusted to his son and heir Cambyses verged on the stupefying, challenging as never before the tolerances of imperial administration. The Persians, elevated virtually overnight into the overlords of kings, managed to step lithely into history. Peace, more often than not, would be the order of the day in their far-flung lands.

By what means were they able to achieve this? To begin with, they had precedents to guide them. From the days of the Assyrians, Mesopotamia and its surrounding territories had comprised a massive laboratory for the development of effective imperial governance. The Neo-Babylonians, for instance, had essentially coopted the Assyrian infrastructure—a system of tribute and layered overlordships with which everyone in the Near East was by now quite familiar. The more things changed, the more they remained the same. When the Persians showed up as the new top men, a tradition of stability through acceptance eased a transition that might otherwise have been occasion for grisly acts of repression and terror. The Persians were not welcomed everywhere, of course, but the relative stability that characterized their assumption of authority stood in stark contrast to previous conquerors, most notably the Assyrians.

Another factor, already alluded to in reference to religion, was the absence in Persian society of cultural exclusivity. The empire eventually comprised just over a score of provinces, or "satrapies," each with its own satrap—a governor who ruled as a local overlord. Satraps were usually of royal blood or favor, but locals could ascend to the ranks through ability and loyalty. Moreover, the institutions that defined local culture were usually unaffected by Persian dominance; as long as tribute kept flowing and nobody rose up in armed rebellion, life could go on as usual. In exchange for this the Persians ensured peace within the empire, no small thing for peoples who had grown tired of watching out for aggressors.

Communication throughout a realm as vast as this was crucial. To ensure it did not fail, the Persians expanded the old Assyrian royal roads, maintaining them as arteries of empire for the exclusive use of messengers, armies, and imperial envoys. Assiduously kept and policed by royal troops, these highways—particularly the "Royal Road" that ran a daunting 1,600 miles from Sardis in the west to Susa in the heart of the empire (the route that Spartan King Cleomenes would dismiss as way too long for Greeks)—carried only those with imperial business, all of whom had to provide evidence of their station or mission. Couriers carrying messages to the capital were the most common sight along these lonely highways, and all of them were capable of driving a horse to its limits in the quest for haste. Outposts along the routes provided all the necessary supplies, fueling a network as efficient as any at the time for carrying information.

## EGYPT, CHAOS, AND THE END OF AN ERA

Cyrus fathered an heir who ended up being nearly as fascinating as himself, though for different reasons. Cambyses is reviled and beloved in turn in the sources, emerging as a blasphemous eccentric with an outsized ego. Certainly there are biases in the record, though he clearly was not the charismatic superman that Cyrus had been. Nevertheless, Cambyses's chief accomplishment was remarkable indeed.

In 525 BC he invaded Egypt, the last great independent kingdom outside the Persian sphere of influence and still the most treasured prize of the Near East. Cambyses displayed characteristic Persian thoroughness in his plans, carefully forging alliances with the Bedouins of the desert, who provided water to his army as it crossed the Sinai. Once across, the Persians routed the Egyptians at the battle of Pelusium—a victory, according to myth, that Cambyses secured chiefly by fronting his forces with an army of cats, whose significance as sacred beings to the Egyptians stayed their bow strings.

Though it would prove difficult to rule, Egypt had finally been absorbed by a power that would not let go of it. The days of the pharaohs—at least, of the homegrown variety—were essentially over.

But so was the rule of Cambyses. If this new titanic empire had an obvious weakness, it was about to show itself: sheer size, combined with the ambitions of nobles at the court, served to undermine Cambyses while he was busy adding Egypt to his inheritance. When the emperor's away, the relations will play. Smerdis, Cambyses's brother, took advantage of the absence of his sibling to snatch the throne for himself. Before Cambyses could react decisively from his military camp in remote Egypt, his brother managed to secure legitimacy throughout much of Asia. Or so it seemed, anyway. At least one prominent aristocrat was willing to dispute that fact. According to Smerdis's brother-in-law, Darius, "Smerdis" was not Smerdis at all, but an imposter who had murdered the emperor's brother and assumed his identity in a brazen coup. Darius, incensed, murdered the pretender and assumed the throne himself.

The truth behind all this skullduggery will probably never be known, as our primary source is Darius himself. It is not at all improbable that he simply murdered the real Smerdis and seized the Persian crown, hoping to conceal his ruthless usurpation behind a fanciful tale. Who knows?

As for Cambyses, somebody else was still sitting on *his* throne. He organized resistance to Darius, but it seems to have been ill conceived and half-hearted, and by 522 BC he, too, was dead under circumstances that continue to be debated. Darius, quite possibly the murderer of Cyrus the Great's sons, was now the new King of Kings.

## CONSOLIDATION

Not for the blood on his hands would Darius go down in history as "the Great," though the dubious nature of his succession spawned revolts clear across the empire, and he was obliged to quash them quickly and thoroughly. That done, however, this infamous crown-thief set about building a golden age.

High on the list of priorities was a new capital. The Persians, horse-warriors used to the rarefied air of the Iranian plateau, had yet to overcome their innate aversion to lowland cities with their suspect largesse, confining walls, and stinking, bustling humanity. In the days of Cyrus the best they could do by way of a capital was Pasargadae, a ceremonial center in the heart of Persia named for Cyrus's tribe, where he was interred. As the empire exploded outwards, it remained a hallowed place of pilgrimage and little more.

Imperium demanded administrative centers, and Darius responded with the construction of Persepolis. Built with materials from across the empire and containing the best artistry that Persia could summon, the magisterial buildings of Persepolis became a marvel of the age. Magnificent pillars crowned with mythological beasts, high platforms on which to perform the theater of power, and colonnaded porticos all came together in a relatively small piece of regal real estate. Persepolis was the gathering place of empire, where all those bearing tribute, from Ionia to India, would converge in the grand ceremony of submission while gazing at the grandeur of Persia made manifest.

Though beautiful, awe-inspiring, and an archaeological attraction to this day, Persepolis proved unequal to the task of running so massive a realm. Persia's court and bureaucracy ultimately moved to Susa, a city at least as old as the Elamites and strategically located at the center of the empire.

Persepolis was merely the most attractive of Darius's many accomplishments. He reformed the military, introducing conscription, training, and regular pay; he standardized the empire's weights and measures, spurring trade throughout his possessions; he expanded and improved the extensive road network, making it the envy

*The magnificent palace built by Darius I at Persepolis was designed to reflect the grandeur of his achievements.*

## CLIFF NOTES AT BEHISTUN

Though ancient Greek sources are invaluable to scholars studying the Achaemenid Empire, they are not the only material at hand. In fact, there is plenty of Persian documentation, as well—and the reason that scholars can read it today is down to a man named Sir Henry Rawlinson.

Along the road between Babylon and Ecbatana, on a mountain in what is today far western Iran, is an astonishing sight known as the Behistun monument. Carved into the cliff face over three hundred feet off the ground, it presents a majestic scene in relief: thirteen figures in royal garb, one of whom, at the center, holds a bow and rests his foot upon a vanquished opponent. Above them hovers a winged deity, while blocks of cuneiform script surround the figures, telling the same story in three languages: Old Persian, Elamite, and Babylonian.

For centuries after the fall of the Achaemenids, travelers along the road would look up in wonder at the figures and the strange writing that accompanied them, but nobody knew for sure what the monument commemorated. In 1835, Rawlinson made it his mission to understand its lost message. A young officer with the British East India Company in Persia, he had more than just a keen mind—he also had guts and a strong physique, enabling him to scale the cliff to stare at the inscriptions face to face.

Through a lot of hard work and exertion, Rawlinson—aided by the earlier writings of the German scholar Georg Friedrich Grotefend, who had made some inroads into Old Persian—managed to crack the cuneiform code, allowing all three languages on the rock to be understood. Behistun, in effect, became the Rosetta Stone of the ancient Mesopotamian world, allowing carvings, tablets, and other records to be understood on their own terms.

As for the scene itself, Rawlinson soon discovered that it was a depiction of Darius I receiving defeated rebel leaders. The king had had the monument carved after usurping the throne to emphasize the legitimacy of his reign. The presence hovering above Darius is none other than Ahura Mazda himself, sanctifying the new ruler.

of the world; he sponsored missions of exploration to the Indian Ocean; and he ordered a canal built to connect the Nile with the Red Sea.

And, of course, he waged war against the Greeks. Of the many revolts that Darius had to cope with, Ionia's was the most onerous. There was no reason to assume so at the time; indeed, being on the far western edge of the empire, the Ionians could almost be expected to raise a little hell at the first opportunity. What made the rebelliousness of the Ionian cities so dangerous was their capacity to draw mainland Greece into the fray.

And that is precisely what happened.

## AUDACITY

The Athenians, swept up in the fervor of adventure and an inchoate pan-Hellenism, agreed to aid the rebellious Ionians when the Spartans would not. In 499 BC their efforts came to naught in a botched military operation against Sardis. Ionia, abandoned to its fate, fell to Persian retribution.

The whole affair could have ended there, but Darius the Great decided, not irrationally, to punish those who had aided his Ionian subjects in their treacherous enterprise—and to add the considerable population and resources of European Greece to his burgeoning empire. It is not too much to say that the seeds of Persia's demise were sown at this moment.

Darius made two attempts to humiliate the Athenians, in 492 and 490 BC, both of which failed from a combination of bad luck, Greek resourcefulness, and Persian overconfidence. Darius planned a third attempt but died before bringing it to fruition. It fell to his heir, Xerxes, to finish the job.

Xerxes inherited a grudge, but lived to see it morph into a colossal nightmare. Apparently more vainglorious than his father but with just as much ambition, Xerxes embarked on a crusade against Greece that would assume historic proportions and fix in the world's imagination a boundary between his own empire and the lands to the west that would endure, incredibly, into our own era as "East" and "West." The nightmare was not the fault of Xerxes alone, but the obsession and drive with which he willed his great forces westward set the stage for a struggle that could brook no quarter—a struggle with resurgent European militarism that his own empire would ultimately lose, and badly.

Such dark happenings as these were still in the future when the Persians proved to the world just what they were capable of. Xerxes invaded Greece with a force meant to awe its foes—hundreds of thousands of troops supported by hundreds of warships and transport vessels, an instrument of aggression that only Persia was capable of fielding in the fifth century BC. The engineers, however, stole the show.

To cross the Hellespont, the fabled channel that separated Europe from Asia, Xerxes insisted on something novel. His engineers constructed a bridge the like of which no one had ever seen. Requisitioning some six hundred ships of various sizes, Egyptian and Phoenician workers fashioned two massive pontoons. The ships were lashed together with great cables of papyrus and flax that were in turn anchored on both shores by wooden posts. Upon the ships' decks the laborers affixed wooden planks, creating two broad avenues across the mile-wide stretch of water. Wicker barriers were erected along either side of both bridges to conceal the surrounding water and prevent horses panicking. The Great King's engineers even found a way to allow sailing vessels to pass

unimpeded, though nobody is sure how this was done.

Bridging the Hellespont was impressive, to be sure, but an even greater project was underway on the Athos Peninsula in northern Greece. One of Darius's attempts at invading Greece had been foiled along the shores of this peninsula when a storm blew off Mount Athos and ravaged his fleet. It was in the hope of averting a repeat of this disaster that Xerxes had ordered the construction of a canal to cut across the neck of the peninsula. Taking three years to build, the final channel could accommodate two vessels abreast and featured massive breakwaters at either end to thwart silting. It was an awe-inspiring accomplishment.

## FORTUNES DASHED

Xerxes may have been able to master nature, but the Greeks would prove a bit harder to overcome. Despite the size of his army and navy, the resources at his command, and the thoroughness of his preparations, Xerxes would never take Greece. This had much to do with the strength of the Greeks themselves, whose martial tradition was the equal of any in the ancient world. Fractious by nature, Greeks dwelt in an atmosphere of competitiveness conducive to matters of war and combat, and their shared cultural institutions allowed them to put provincial concerns on hold when a united defense was needed to drive off the invader. This the Greek city-states did smartly in a series of sea and land engagements, often relying on familiarity with local terrain, duplicity and misinformation, and a refusal to join combat until ideal conditions were attained.

At first Persian might and prestige had seemed more than enough. Many Greek city-states, such as Thebes, simply welcomed the Persians with open arms to avoid unnecessary destruction, a process derided by defiant Greeks as "Medizing." But the initial successes concealed Persian vulnerabilities. The Great King's forces were drawn from every satrapy in his empire, producing a host that, though of unprecedented size, was of dubious cohesion. Moreover, support for such a multitude—effectively a kind

*Above: Darius I sits enthroned in this relief from the Treasury, part of the palace complex at Persepolis.*

of mass migration—could never be maintained in a sea-girt land like Greece without mastery of the water, making this the first occasion in their history when the Persians were forced to rely heavily on the performance of their subject navies. The Greeks exploited this when, at the battle of Salamis in 480 BC, they dealt the Persian fleet a decisive defeat. Though Xerxes had already conquered Athens and torched its acropolis, the effective loss of his fleet crippled his plans to conquer the Peloponnese, where resistance continued. The approach of winter only made things worse, and Xerxes left Greece with most of his army to avoid a logistical catastrophe. Further defeats followed as the Greek alliance maintained its momentum, and the dream of turning Greece into a Persian satrapy slipped away forever.

The failure of his Greek enterprise was a blow to Xerxes, mostly because of its implications for his reputation. Having failed to supersede (or even match, for that matter) the deeds of his forebears, the great king was vulnerable back at court—another reason for his hasty retreat after Salamis.

Nevertheless, it should be borne in mind that Persia had suffered a humiliating reverse, not a calamitous defeat. The empire was still the largest the planet had ever seen, Persian arms were tarnished but still feared throughout the Near East, and Xerxes himself would reign for another fifteen years.

And yet, when the Persian tide receded, it left behind a changed Greek world. Xerxes had overreached, taking on a remote and dangerous people who had given him more trouble than they were worth but, his lesson learned, the Great King turned his attention to matters over which he had greater control. The Greeks, by contrast, would never forget and many of them, transformed by the cauldron of war, began imagining an empire of their own and the annihilation of Persian power.

## TEN THOUSAND CAUSES FOR ALARM

The immediate effect of the Persian debacle in Greece in 480–479 BC was the loss to the empire of the Balkan regions, the Ionian cities, and Cyprus. But longer term effects had been set in motion, not least a seething acrimony on the part of the Greek world.

The Greeks decided not to rest on their laurels and enjoy the fruits of survival. Formed to carry the war eastward in perpetual vengeance, the Athens-led Delian League pooled resources from around the Aegean to hit Persia along the Mediterranean periphery of its empire. Despite its ability to discomfit Persians from Egypt to the Black Sea, however, the league was hard-pressed to do anything more than singe the Great King's beard. Greece may have been beyond Persian reach but, conversely, the Persian Empire could not be undermined merely by amphibious operations in the eastern Mediterranean.

Besides, Athens, increasingly looking over its shoulder to keep an eye on Sparta, began turning the anti-Persian "league" into an Athenian Empire.

What emerged around the middle of the fifth century was a peculiar three-way stalemate between the principal actors of the Aegean: Athens and its maritime subjects, Sparta and its fellow Peloponnesian allies, and a Persian Empire that was willing to buy off either of the other two in order to keep the Greek world and its formidable hoplite armies in continual strife.

In 431 BC Sparta and Corinth orchestrated a war with Athens to deprive it of its empire. Known as the Peloponnesian War, it would end in 404 BC with a decisive Athenian defeat—a conclusion reached partly with Persian funding. By this time the Persian Empire and the Greek world on its western doorstep had become strangely dependent on one another. While Persian kings and satraps steadily grew addicted to hoplite mercenaries for quashing rebellions or staging royal coups, no Greek city-state could hope to become *hegemon* (first among equals) without backing from Persian coffers. An economy of chaos had arisen in the Aegean and eastern Mediterranean, fed by, on the one hand, waspish Greek city-states and their soldiers of fortune and, on the other, a titanic empire whose prodigious military requirements rapidly absorbed the eager hoplites-for-hire.

The round-robin of power plays continued. After funding the demise of Athens in the fifth century BC, Persia sponsored the destruction of Sparta during the initial decades of the fourth by funding the Athenian power it had once helped to destroy. And so it went. Under the reign of Artaxerxes II (r. 404–358 BC) Persia experienced a cultural flowering, with the widespread adoption of Zoroastrianism as the state religion, the streamlining of the bureaucracy, and decades of relative peace made possible by an overflowing treasury. By 386 BC, Artaxerxes had arranged the humiliation of Sparta and the containment of Athens, and had even managed to reassert Persian authority over the Ionian cities, which promptly underwent an urban flowering—all while the Greek city-states continued to lash each other in their arena of forlorn ambitions. By the 370s Thebes had become the latest contender for hegemony, smashing Spartan power forever at the battle of Leuctra.

Despite this picture of strength and stability, a page from the story of Artaxerxes's rise to supremacy offered a lesson in potential Persian vulnerability. Artaxerxes was challenged upon his succession by Cyrus, his brother, who raised an army to seize the empire by force. At the battle of Cunaxa in 401 BC, the two armies clashed near Babylon in a furious fight that claimed the life of Cyrus. Artaxerxes's triumph, however, came with an embarrassing addendum: the most formidable element of his late brother's army, a corps of some ten thousand heavily armed Greek hoplite mercenaries, stood undefeated on the field, the death of their employer ensuring only that they now lacked a purpose beyond survival. Demands for the Greeks to surrender were gruffly turned down, and at any rate Artaxerxes had no means to enforce it. Though technically victorious, he had little choice but to allow these implacable foreigners to march themselves out of his empire to the safety of the Black Sea, shadowed all the way by Persian forces that were capable of doing little more than harassing them.

The "March of the Ten Thousand," as the event came to be celebrated in Greece, put two Persian weaknesses in bold relief. The first of these involved the satrapies, whose semi-autonomy hindered cooperation, allowing the Greeks to escape the attentions of one merely by entering the territory of another, one after the other, until they reached their goal. This is an oversimplification, of course, but the failure to coordinate efforts to trap the hoplites during their quest for succor emphasized the political and logistical limits of the empire's checkerboard organization.

The second weakness was more significant, at least in the minds of Greek apologists who would harken back to it for generations. Like an epic experiment in cultural disparity, the awkward inability of King Artaxerxes to extinguish a corps of irreverent hoplites in the heart of his very own empire seemed to prove beyond the shadow of a doubt the superiority of Greek arms. All that remained was for someone in Greece to find a way out of the cycle of perpetual city-state warfare, and the Hellenic world could do more than just embarrass the King of Kings: it could conquer his vast realm altogether.

Now *that* would be something, but who could pull off such a feat?

## BACKDRAFT

No one in the heart of the Greek world, that was certain. Athens, Sparta, Thebes, and Corinth, along with the cloud of fickle allies that crowded about them, had all dissipated their strength in a long fight back to parity. The notion of any one of them acquiring the status to force through a unified Greece was patently ludicrous.

Nevertheless, the question hung in the air with palpable anticipation. Despite the unscrupulous ties that bound them to Persia, many Greeks yearned for a day when the old fires could be avenged and the hauteur of Persia laid low. In the end it fell to those on the periphery of the Hellenic world to show them the way—for better or worse.

By the reign of Darius III (r. 336–330 BC), the Persian Empire had weathered revolts throughout its territories, most infamously in Egypt, and come through politically and financially intact. Uprisings throughout Anatolia between 366 and 359 BC had caused tremendous problems in the west of the empire, but they were all eventually overcome without ever posing a genuine threat to central authority. Persian rule was a delicate

*The epic battle of Gaugamela, in which Alexander the Great (on white horse at left) defeated Darius III, was the end of the Achaemenid Empire.*

balance: stability gained by allowing the satraps local autonomy had always to be measured against the threat of regional uprisings. In a government as personal and clannish as it was regimented, the Great King's relationships with far-flung aristocrats were always as important as the maintenance of the royal roads that afforded swift communication between them, and the imperial troops that made it possible. By giving elites at the local level a significant degree of cultural and political autonomy, the King of Kings courted opportunism as often as loyalty. But if this quasi-feudal power structure, based on controlling the flow of tribute, had its drawbacks, they were not acutely obvious in the time of Darius III. Persia was strong, vibrant, and secure.

Destruction would come from without. Persia had lit a fire in the West that, until now, had merely smoldered. After the middle of the fourth century BC it erupted into a conflagration that very quickly engulfed the whole of the Achaemenid enterprise.

The agent of that destruction was Macedon. On the northern frontier of the greater Greek world, the Macedonians were at once separate from and very like the Greeks who argued, built, wrote, pondered, destroyed, and squabbled to the south in a cultural melee both dazzling and stupefying. In 336 BC Alexander III of Macedon, soon to be known as Alexander the Great, inherited from his visionary, megalomaniac father, Philip II, a war machine like no other. Its creation could be traced to Macedon's martial heritage and abundant resources, as well as the region's proximity to both Greek and Persian military innovations. But its inspiration came from Philip's consuming quest for empire—an empire he knew he could get the Greek world to build at the expense of the civilization that had been its evil genius for a century: Persia.

The fifth-century expeditions of Xerxes that had destroyed Athens and united the Greek world in defiance, however briefly, had birthed their final offspring. Defining themselves against the Persian example for so many generations, Greece was ready for Philip and Alexander when they came with their imperial message. Philip had to drag his southern cousins kicking and screaming into this program, but once Greece had been conquered he turned his attention east before succumbing to an assassin's knife. It fell to Alexander to actually carry out Philip's vision.

Persia's reaction to the initial Macedonian invasion was telling, shedding light on the chinks in the empire's armor. Before his death in 336 BC, Philip of Macedon had sent an advance force across the Hellespont into Asia as a kind of reconnaissance-in-force. That this vanguard of Macedonian invasion had made little headway was due primarily to one man: Memnon of Rhodes, a Greek general in Persian pay and a wily opponent. Persia's military fortunes were now openly and unabashedly placed in the hands of Hellenic soldiers of fortune, an indication of the empire's inability to keep pace with martial developments to the west. Nevertheless, neither Memnon nor his Persian colleagues were able to destroy this initial foray, allowing Alexander, in 334 BC, to enter Asia by way of a Macedonian bridgehead.

What happened next proved disastrous for the Persians. Faced with an all-out invasion by Alexander's professional army, Memnon cautioned his employers against a head-on collision and suggested a scorched-earth policy. Destroy the countryside, he urged, to deny the Macedonians any hope of local supply. This, at least, would slow their advance considerably. But the local satraps in charge of defending this part of the empire, and in whose hands the ultimate decisions lay until the Great King himself showed up, blanched at the prospect of torching their own sources of revenue. Fatefully, they opted to give battle instead, and at the Granicus River Alexander smashed them to pieces.

These unfortunate idiosyncrasies of the Persian political scene certainly highlight the empire's structure at its most inefficient, but one wonders if Memnon's advice, or the presence of Persian nobles with broader vision and better priorities, could really have saved the empire from what was breaking in upon it. The Persians and their subjects fell before new tactics that, in all fairness, were unstoppable at the time. The Macedonian phalanx was built on the Greek system of heavily armed, close-ranked infantry, but adopted new weapons—particularly the eighteen-foot-long pike—that made it a revolutionary, war-winning formation. Alexander also employed cavalry that was more heavily armed than anything the Persians fielded. These new developments, combined with Alexander's awesome leadership, doomed the Achaemenids to destruction before the ponderous system of their empire could adapt. At the battles of Granicus (334), Issus (333), and Gaugamela (331), the Macedonians and their subjects/allies decisively defeated Darius's forces, confirming the arrival of a new military order and, virtually overnight, bringing the Persian Empire to its knees. Darius III, last ruler of the Achaemenid dynasty, was murdered in 330 BC by one of his own satraps and left in the road as a grisly curiosity to slow Alexander's advance.

Rarely had a great and robust empire fallen so quickly from foreign invasion. While they rarely had trouble on their eastern borders, the Persians had the misfortune of engaging to the west a civilization that they could neither destroy nor contain—a civilization that would ultimately win the brutally simple test of military superiority.

CHAPTER EIGHT

# ATHENS

## THE BURDEN OF SUCCESS

OF all the historical sites in Greece, there is one that invariably remains off the itinerary of tourists. It is hardly surprising. Located in the far south of Attica, some thirty-seven miles from Athens, the vent holes and galleries of Mount Laurium are unremarkable in their own right, leading visitors into a gloomy and claustrophobic underworld. Chambers scoured out of the hills are the only evidence here of ancient engineering, offering nothing like the Temple of Poseidon or the Parthenon to dazzle modern eyes. But these pits, once the site of massive and dehumanizing slave labor, may well be the most important ancient ruins most people have never heard of. In fact, the mines of Laurium played a role so pivotal to the outcome of ancient history that their significance is impossible to exaggerate.

By the late sixth century BC, the mines had been a fundamental source of wealth for the citizens of Athens for generations. Silver, all of it hacked out of the rock by slaves who were literally worked to death in horrifying conditions, was minted into coins featuring the goddess Athena on one side and an owl, symbol of her wisdom, on the other—the famous Athenian "owls" that became standard currency throughout the Greek world.

In 483 BC, however, a new and enormous vein of silver ore was struck at Laurium, sparking an emotional debate about what to do with the unprecedented wealth. Many Athenians believed it should be distributed among the people, enriching the citizens and giving a substantial, if short-lived, jolt to the local economy, but one man had a rather different idea.

A minor aristocrat of humble origins, Themistocles was hardly one of the city's richest or most accomplished citizens—but he was ambitious, cunning, and far-sighted. In a move that would profoundly influence the course of his civilization, he boldly stood up at the Athenian assembly and made a suggestion: use the windfall to build a fleet. His fellow citizens concurred.

Themistocles was envisioning a means to intimidate the city's Greek neighbors, particularly the nearby island of Aegina, but it was a foe of infinitely greater power and status that ultimately felt the effects of his proposition that day in the assembly. In one of the singular coincidences of antiquity, 483 BC was also the year that Xerxes, ruler of the incomparably huge

*Previous pages: Doric column from the Parthenon in Athens.*
*Above: A silver "owl" made from Laurium silver.*

Persian Empire, decided on an invasion of Greece—an invasion that would run afoul of the very fleet whose origins lay with Themistocles and the precious silver of Laurium.

Such were the unlikely origins of Athenian greatness: democracy, slaves, silver, ships, visionary thinking, and a stroke of luck. Athens would use these to thwart Persian might and build an empire—one that the idiosyncrasies of Greek culture ironically doomed to destruction.

## A CITY OF EXTREMES

Like many city-states in Classical Greece, Athens had once been the home of a Bronze Age dynasty, its acropolis crowned by a Mycenaean citadel. In the dark age that followed, it continued as a place of settlement, entering the Archaic period of the eighth, seventh, and sixth centuries BC as one of many Greek societies struggling to find order in chaos. The long saga of its emergence as a great city is filled with extraordinary personalities, but several stand out.

In 594 BC Solon, statesman and poet (in that order), became leader of Athens, charged by the people with establishing peace. Aristocratic factions had been vying for control of the city since time immemorial, locking the community in a perpetual state of *stasis*, or civil strife. Solon met the crisis head on by overhauling the city's social structure, replacing the power of the old factions with a new standard of community leadership: from now on wealth, rather than birth, would be the basis of voting power in Athens and its countryside. He also shook up the economy, freeing debtors from slavery and breaking the deadlock over land ownership that had put so much power in the hands of so few.

Solon's "new deal" was ambitious—too ambitious, in fact, as subsequent events made clear. After the conclusion of his archonship Athens descended once again into chaos, the old factions—some representing the hill country, some the urban center, still others the agricultural countryside or the seaside fishermen—battling it out in the streets for control of the city. It was rule by mob. Into this maelstrom strode a character named Pisistratus, a swaggering, devious strongman who would not rest until he had become sole ruler—tyrant—of Athens. In 546 BC he achieved just that, crushing all opposition with his private army after infamously entering the city in the company of a six-foot-tall local girl who had been pressed into dressing like the goddess Athena.

The nature of his entrance into Athenian history may have been asinine, but Pisistratus was no fool. He ruled not unlike an enlightened despot—established laws were enforced and elections were held. Pisistratus built temples and improved the city's infrastructure, and he expanded the mining operations at Laurium. More than anything else, however, he brought order to the city and a sense of identity. Athens was a coherent community by the end of his reign, having come to appreciate its true potential.

Unfortunately, even good tyrants have descendants, and none of Pisistratus's could hold a candle to him. The Athenians came to look at the dynasty as an oppressive scourge and threw the Pisistratids out in 510 BC. Tyrants needed no longer apply in Athens.

That very year marked the rise of the most influential leader in the evolution of Athens to full democracy. With the tyrants gone, there was an opportunity to fill the vacancy for leader, a fact not lost on the aristocrats who continued to jockey for supremacy. Cleisthenes, leader of a prominent Athenian faction, managed to force his principal opponent, Isagoras, into exile, not least because Cleisthenes assumed the role of demagogue—he played to the needs of the *demos*, or ordinary people. With their backing he remade Athens into a radically new city-state.

## TRIUMPH OF THE *DEMOS*

Having achieved supremacy within the frenzied, patchwork political scene of Athens, Cleisthenes was in a position to build a bulwark against his foes and ensure his own political survival through sheer force. But that is not what he did. Instead, Cleisthenes masterminded one of the greatest revolutions in history. Though a shameless aristocrat, he empathized with the mass of ordinary Athenian humanity, with whom he forged an enduring and sincere relationship. They, the *demos*, would rule Athens, banishing their fear of *stasis* by universal participation in government.

Cleisthenes was a man of tremendous charisma and tenacity, and he had to be—for he pushed through a radical re-imagining of Athenian demographics. When he came to power, every Athenian owed allegiance to one of four tribes. Cleisthenes broke this four-way stalemate with a single stroke, replacing it with ten new "tribes," some of which seemed entirely arbitrary. But there was a method to his madness. Each tribe, according to his program, was divided into thirds, each of which corresponded to one of the three regions of Attica: city, farmland, and coast. Each of these thirds was in turn divided into "demes" that could vary widely in number and size depending on the region and tribe in question. All told, the people of Athens were divided into 140 demes.

Creating new axes of loyalty and influence was just the beginning. Cleisthenes imagined a whole city-state of self-governors who would never have cause to rely on tyrants again. He created a council of five hundred, whose purpose was to direct the agenda of the popular assembly and whose members were chosen by lot every year from the ten tribes. The result was a government in which virtually everyone who considered himself an Athenian was required to serve at one point or another. (And "himself" should be taken literally, as only men were considered citizens—a fact throughout the Greek world.)

Incredibly, despite its complexity and intrusiveness, the grand scheme of Cleisthenes took. Every Greek city-state, from the south of Spain to the island of Cyprus, considered itself a community in which the Hellenic virtues of competition and opportunity were enshrined. Athens, however, took the notion of popular rule to a unique extreme, laying the groundwork for a future revolution in which the power would be shifted even further to the people.

## DEFYING THE GREAT KING

By the dawn of the fifth century BC, the Greek world had undergone immense changes. Since the eighth century, intrepid Greek settlers had struck out to the remote limits of the Mediterranean, establishing colonies that were both trading posts and conduits for foreign influences to enrich the Greek diaspora. Of these diverse and far-flung colonies, none was as influential as the cities of Ionia, strung out along the west coast of Anatolia (modern-day Turkey). Numerous, densely populated, wealthy, and cosmopolitan, the Greeks of Ionia had wrested cultural preeminence from their homeland cousins, producing an explosion of artistic and philosophical expression that eventually pulled the axis of the Greek world further east.

But they were not the masters of their own fate. Standing on the far western fringe of the Near East, where empires had been displacing each other in an endless parade of aggression, the Ionian Greeks were as much subjects of the East as they were descendants of the West. The latest landlords of Anatolia, the Persians, were happy to let the Greek culture of their Ionian subjects thrive as long as local Persian governors (satraps) were obeyed and the tribute kept coming.

Around 500 BC, tired of living under Persian rule, the Ionians staged a revolt. All too aware of the long odds, they sent an emissary named Aristagoras of Miletus to seek help from Greece. Sparta, the usual destination for those seeking military muscle, rebuffed Aristagoras, who promptly went to Athens and got a warmer reception. There, before the Athenian assembly, the Ionian struck a chord, getting the city's impassioned citizens to make a commitment of ships and men for the great revolt across the Aegean.

In 499 BC the Athenians, aided by a smaller force of Eretrians, landed twenty-six ships at Ephesus and sent a small hoplite army marching to Sardis, capital of Persian power in the Anatolian region of Lydia. Sardis fell, but the city garrison held out in the citadel, defying all attempts at dislodging it. Whether by accident or design, the city itself burned to the ground, the Greeks leaving a scene of smoking desolation in their wake as they gave up on the citadel and retired toward Ephesus. Attacked on the march by a punitive force of Persians, the hoplites suffered dreadful casualties. They staggered into Ephesus, boarded their ships and sailed away, bitterly determined to leave the Ionians to their fate.

The Athenians' next clash with Persia turned out quite differently. Darius, Great King of the Persians, crushed the Ionian revolt by 494 BC but he never forgot those brazen Athenians and Eretrians who had scorched Sardis. And he certainly could not forgive them. It was more than just pride that drove him—the temple of Cybele, the great mother goddess, had been consumed by the fires that ravaged Sardis, a desecration demanding justice.

His first attempt to smite the Athenians, in 493 BC, had mixed results. Darius sent an army across the Hellespont into Europe where it made its way toward Athens via Thrace and Macedonia. The army's supporting fleet, however, was broken and scattered by a ferocious storm off Mount Athos, dashing Darius's plans.

In 490 BC, he tried a different route, sending an invasion force straight across the Aegean to launch an amphibious invasion near Athens itself. This expedition ended up making history—but not for the Persians.

At a place called Marathon, twenty-five miles or so northeast of Athens, nine thousand Athenians and one thousand Plataeans dealt a stunning defeat to an invading Persian army perhaps twice their number. After five days of inactivity, the two armies facing each other in a tense waiting game, the Greeks under Miltiades acted on intelligence from Ionian defectors in the Persian army that the dreaded Persian cavalry was away, having boarded the nearby ships, gone off on a raid, or done something else forever lost to history. The Greeks ran forward, their phalanxes driving the Persians into a rout. At a cost of fewer than two hundred of their own, the Athenians slew six thousand of the enemy. Marathon endured in legend as Athens's finest hour.

## CHILDREN OF HOMER

At Marathon the Persians came up against a type of warrior that would forever confound them. The hoplite had become ubiquitous in Greece, representing a conservative approach to warfare that relied on limited engagements between city-states to settle disputes. He was heavily armored, carrying a large wooden shield sheathed in bronze, as well as wearing greaves, breastplate, and a menacing "Corinthian" helmet that enclosed the head. Though a sword hung at his side, the hoplite relied more than anything on his spear, a thick, nine-foot hardwood shaft tipped with a deadly iron point for thrusting into the vitals of an opponent.

All this equipment cost money, meaning that hoplites were at least modestly well-off—middle-class landowners whose ability to afford a hoplite's kit depended on the farms for which they, in turn, were willing to fight. Such men could also afford a slave, who might accompany his master on campaign as a load-bearer or retainer. Aside from the Spartans, however, Greek hoplites were not professional fighting men. When they donned their armor and took up the spear, it was usually with the assumption that the conflict that had compelled them to do so would be over by harvest, at which time they could return to the business of life.

Nevertheless, the Greek way of war was unique. Packed close in a phalanx, eight ranks deep, their shields presenting a wall over which heavy spear points could slaughter at will, hoplite warfare produced maximum punishment with minimal effort. Nearly everyone else in the known world fielded armies that relied on speed, maneuvering, and sheer numbers to win battles, forgoing heavy armor and weapons for fear of their cost and burden. Hoplites, on the other hand, evolved out of a Greek desire to join combat immediately and fiercely with metal-clad men whose lack of endurance was offset by their ability to take and dish out tremendous damage—to grapple decisively and force a resolution.

Such tactics proved valuable throughout the Mediterranean world. During the Classical period, Greek mercenaries would turn up literally everywhere, leveraging their outstanding martial tradition for treasure and travel. Even the Persians employed them, gleefully paying top dollar for those willing to look past cultural distinctions. It is no exaggeration to say that soldiers of fortune were one of the Greek world's leading exports. These were people, for all their fervent belief in debate and knowledge, who ruminated deeply and often on issues of war. Not for nothing were Homer's blood-soaked epics revered by Greeks as the greatest works of their cultural heritage.

## SALAMIS

With their ancient cavalry tradition and their reliance on light infantry and archers from throughout their vast empire, the Persians found fighting the hoplites frustrating. But if they considered Greek soldiers an infuriating curiosity, they would come to dread Greek ships with an abiding and totally justified terror.

As landlocked nations of warrior horsemen, the Persians and their Median cousins never truly took to the sea. In the empire they created through military expansion, however, these Iranian hill people came to dominate some of the Mediterranean's most legendary mariners, including the Phoenicians, the Cilicians, the Egyptians and, of course, the Ionians. Now the Persians relied heavily on the naval ability of their Ionian subjects to quell the Greeks, but like their Ionian cousins, the free Greek states had long cultivated the tactics and technology of naval warfare, and none more so than the Athenians.

This was the legacy of Themistocles and his gambit to turn the bounty of Laurium into a force to rule the waves. The Athenian hoplites had already defeated the Persians at Marathon in 490 BC when, seven years later, Themistocles made his historic suggestion. With the Asiatic enemy humbled at Marathon, he had his sights set on dominating trade and colonization in the Aegean and beyond.

The two hundred ships that Athens built at the urging of Themistocles were triremes, three-tiered ships of war featuring naval architecture that was relatively new at the dawn of the fifth century. In addition to a modest complement of "marines," each typically carried a crew of 170 rowers, all of whom, contrary to popular belief, were free citizens drawing a wage. In other words, large navies were the exclusive purview of wealthy states—Athens had nearly forty thousand seamen on the books in times of war, another testament to the vital importance of Laurium and the owls that flew from its mines.

In September 480 BC this great fleet, purchased with Athenian silver and foresight, waited off the island of Salamis, within sight of the acropolis of Athens. They formed the heart of an allied Greek navy of perhaps 380 triremes in all, representing the last hope of Greek defiance against the Persian invader.

It had not been a good year. When the invasion of Greece that Xerxes had been planning for three years finally came, it was a show of awesome, unprecedented imperial power. Numbers from ancient sources, which almost certainly exaggerate, put the Persian land army at something like a million and a half men. Though this seems impossible, the true numbers—nearly 400,000 is more likely—were still big enough to make this the greatest invasion of continental Europe until the twentieth century. Shadowing the army along the coast was the Great King's fleet, numbering around a thousand vessels that had been mustered from Persia's maritime subjects along the Mediterranean coasts.

The Greeks had managed to check the Persian fleet at the battle of Artemisium, where the narrow channel between the island of Euboea and the mainland worked against the invaders' superior numbers, preventing them maneuvering against the more skillful Greek crews. But this fight was the only success in a string of grim setbacks. Three hundred Spartan heroes and their Thespian allies had been wiped out to a man at Thermopylae, the head of their leader, King Leonidas, ending up at the end of a Persian pike to be mocked and spat upon. City-states throughout Greece were "Medizing," deciding to submit to the Persians as subjects rather than suffer the consequences. And Athens, co-leader with Sparta of Greek defiance, had been conquered, its population having fled to nearby Salamis to dwell in exile while Xerxes garrisoned his troops in their homes and set the acropolis ablaze.

By September the ships huddling in the strait between Salamis and Attica were all that stood between Xerxes and complete victory. Though officially commanded by a Spartan named Eurybiades, the fleet's true leader was none other than Themistocles, whose two hundred Athenian triremes formed the cadre around which ships from throughout the Aegean had come to fight. Themistocles, exhibiting a revered quality that the Greeks called *metis*, or cleverness, sent a multilingual messenger in a boat to the Persian fleet, moored near Athens, beyond the eastern entrance to the strait. The messenger, a man of learning who tutored Themistocles's large brood of children when he was not engaging in wartime acts of disinformation, shouted a message in the nighttime darkness to the Persians in their native language. The Greek fleet, so he claimed, was demoralized and about to break apart, its numerous contingents eager to return to their respective homes. Athens, infuriated at this mass desertion, was willing to teach their erstwhile allies a lesson by striking a deal with the Persians. All they had to do, went the message, was sail into the Strait of Salamis, and virtually the whole Greek fleet would be theirs to destroy.

The ruse worked. Xerxes, too close to complete victory to turn down what appeared to be a juicy opportunity, took the bait and ordered his fleet into the strait. After all, he reasoned, the Greek world was torn asunder by his invasion, with many having decided that Persia represented the coming world order. Medizing Greeks had been flocking to his standard and offering him assistance since the invasion began. Against this background the message from Athens seemed entirely believable.

*The naval battle of Salamis, in September 480 BC, was a turning point in the Greeks' struggle against the invading Persians.*

It was a poor decision. When morning broke the Persians found themselves in a trap, the confining strait having all but negated their vast superiority in numbers. Out of the sheltering harbors of Salamis came the Greek triremes, their victory hymn to Apollo, the *paian*, carrying ominously over the water. The Phoenicians and their fellow Persian subjects heard the war chorus in the dawn and despaired. Drawn up in three ranks against the coast of Attica, they could only engage the oncoming Greeks with the first line. The second and third, eager to perform heroically before their king, who sat watching the battle from the heights above the strait, shoved forward, dooming the frontline in the press. The Greeks swung onto the flanks and slowly crushed their enemies in a furious, day-long battle of careening ships and frenzied boarding actions.

All Xerxes could do on his perch was watch the fiasco and tear his robe. He boarded his chariot and stormed back to Athens with his brooding retainers in tow. Greece, it seemed, had been saved.

## WATERY DEATH

The principal tool of Athenian force, the trireme, was typically 120 feet long and twenty feet in the beam. Arranged in two columns of three tiers, 170 oarsmen powered the vessel into battle, the rhythm of their strokes coordinated by a piper's music. Featuring sleek lines and a 500-pound, bronze-girded ram at the prow, a trireme's principal mission was to acquire tremendous speed and launch itself like a torpedo into the bowels of an enemy ship.

Naval battles were confusing and terrifying, but more so for those in the lowest of a trireme's three tiers. Known as *thalamites,* these fifty-four rowers performed their duty in absolute ignorance of events beyond their sweaty, claustrophobic cloister over the bilge. Despite warnings from those on the top tiers, who could see what was happening, thalamites were the most vulnerable to incoming rams, which would have smashed some of them outright before unleashing hellish, watery bedlam. Drowning would have quickly claimed most of them.

Rowers were trained to reverse quickly after ramming in the hopes of disengaging from their impaled victim. It was during these times that a ship's marines, numbering a score or more, were crucial. Including hoplites, slingers, and archers, these combatants could oppose enemy boarders or board an enemy ship themselves should it prove necessary. Oarsmen, barely clothed and usually unarmed, were helpless on their own, relying utterly on their marines to fend off boarding actions. Nor did the sea offer any sanctuary: those attempting to swim to safety were routinely shot, impaled, or even struck by oars. Little wonder ancient sea battles incurred such ghastly mortality.

## VICTORY AND AN UNCERTAIN FUTURE

Salamis, one of the legendary victories in Western history, was Greece's finest hour. Nevertheless, though they had been outnumbered by around two-to-one, the Greeks' success was not so very surprising after all.

Why?

To begin with, the "Persian" fleet was not truly Persian, a variation on a theme that every conquering empire in history has had to deal with. Subject peoples are just that—vanquished populations who have been coerced into fighting for a power they may or may not find palatable. The Phoenicians, Cilicians, Cypriots, and Egyptians all had proud seafaring traditions, but they were not fighting for themselves at Salamis. As for the Ionians, whom the Phoenicians accused of treason during the battle, they were of very suspect loyalty indeed. Many of them fought like lions that day for the Great King. Others, however ...

The Greeks, by contrast, were fighting for their cultural autonomy. Add to that their naval tradition, which emphasized hard hoplite-like fighting in addition to aggressive seamanship, and you had a force to be reckoned with. Nevertheless, Themistocles's *metis* had played a decisive role, as had the uniquely massive Athenian fleet. Sparta would remain the official leader of the pan-Greek alliance but Athens was clearly a power on the rise—even as the city lay in ruins.

Xerxes left for home in a huff in the wake of Salamis, but he left an army in mainland Greece under his principal commander, Mardonius. The Persian navy, humiliated and shaken, retired to the coast of southern Anatolia. The Greek alliance managed to defeat both in 479 BC: while a hoplite army some thirty-eight thousand strong (and supported by some seventy thousand light troops) defeated Mardonius at the battle of Plataea, Greek triremes sailed across the Aegean and smashed Xerxes's remaining naval forces at the battle of Mycale.

So ended the third and final Persian invasion of Greece. The greatest empire the world had ever seen had been defeated by a dramatically smaller nation of squabbling rabble-rousers. Greece's accomplishment was singular, if only because (most of) its divisive city-states had been able to overcome their differences. Persia had given them the perfect foil to achieve this, threatening to extinguish their treasured freedom and replace it with something far more uniform and threatening.

But how long could this unnatural collusion last? The Greeks enjoyed cultural unity in their sacred games at Olympia, their shared reverence for the same pantheon of gods, and their universal respect for oracles, most notably at Delphi, but central to the Greek psyche was *agon*, the love of competition. This obsession with struggle, which they considered so natural and healthy, produced a Greek population predisposed to local loyalties. One's "nationalism," to borrow an anachronism, ended at the borders of one's city-state. Only self-preservation had allowed them to emphasize their similarities rather than their differences.

Now, with the Asiatic foe in retreat, these fractious Greeks had some decisions to make. Would they remain united? And if so, why? To retaliate against Persia? Or to achieve some other end?

## ALLIES IN VENGEANCE

Out of this profound moment in history, pregnant with significance and fraught with danger, emerged an opportunity for Athens to become a power of the first order. Up to now all those in the Greek world willing to engage in coordinated efforts had looked to Sparta as *hegemon*—the first among equals who would direct operations in wartime. It was Sparta that had dominated the councils and led the armies and navies.

This was quite natural for the Greeks, who looked on Sparta as a sort of ideal society. The Spartans dominated a very peculiar kingdom that had come into being during the Archaic period. Having defeated the neighboring Messenians in a series of brutal wars, the Spartans made them into a permanent underclass of laborers (helots) whose sole purpose was to toil for Sparta. A whole people had been damned to serfdom in perpetuity so that the relatively small population of Spartans could concentrate on other things—namely, the creation of perfect hoplite soldiers. To maintain order, the Spartans codified a system of terror and absolute repression to subdue the helots, creating one of the first and most ruthless police states in history.

To the aristocrats of the other city-states, this harshly stratified society, unique in the Greek world, offered up a lesson in order and the nobility of simple militarism. They found many Spartan habits unpalatable—the repulsively tasteless food, the communal life in barracks, the rejection of commerce, the absence of creative subtleties—but admired the uncompromising Spartan spirit and the devotion to *polis* (city-state) that it engendered. As for the Messenians, slavery was their fate—a perfect example of weakness and its consequences.

In the wake of the Persian wars, however, with the soldiers of the Great King everywhere in retreat, Sparta stumbled. The Ionians, wishing to ensure their freedom from future Persian predations, asked Sparta to become their official protector and leader. But the Spartans, deeply conservative and xenophobic, merely advised the Ionians to abandon their beautiful cities in Anatolia and move to Greece—to take over those cities that had submitted to the Persians—or flee to some other place, such as Italy, any place as long as it was far from those relentless Persians. The Spartans went home to Sparta, where the questions were not so complicated and the people listened to their betters.

The Athenians were ready to lead. Themistocles was a hero, his fleet had proved invaluable, and the Athenians were feeling pretty important. And why not? Had they not defeated the Persians back in 490 BC at Marathon all by themselves? Having been turned down by Sparta, the Ionians approached the Athenians, who jumped at the chance. It was soon resolved that Athens would be *hegemon* of a new league of allies from throughout the Aegean and Ionia, a league formed to maintain the war against the barbarians from the east. The Persians may have been in retreat but the war, it seemed, was anything but over.

Although today we refer to this association as the Delian League, after the island of Delos where the alliance was formalized and sanctified in 477 BC—its 150 or so members solemnizing the occasion by dropping ingots of iron into the sea—to the ancient Greeks this new and formidable partnership of states ringing the Aegean was always referred to as "Athens and her allies."

It would eventually become Athens and her subjects.

## GOING ON THE OFFENSIVE

The Delian League envisioned an unending war against the Persians. To avenge the assault on Greece, to keep the Persian goliath off balance, and to gain by the Great King's losses, this band of brothers would set the Aegean alight with their maritime strikes—*forever*. Hardened by war, the Greeks of the league saw the future stretching out before them in blood and adventure.

Had he been able to go back in time, Winston Churchill, ardent promoter of commando operations, would have been impressed. The ships of the league's navy became the bogeymen of the Aegean, rowing to the far-flung limits of the Persian Empire and its Medized periphery and launching amphibious operations with speed and skill. Satraps on the frontiers of Persia's empire came to loathe and respect the league in equal measure, losing income and prestige to its operations.

The Athenian behind it all was Cimon, the wealthy son of Miltiades, who had led the Athenian forces at Marathon. With an expansive charisma and a crop of red hair, Cimon led the league forces through their daring heyday—and through their most famous triumph. In 466 BC at the Eurymedon River in southern Anatolia, Cimon and the league forces managed to rout their naval opponents, make landfall to smash the local Persian land forces, and then dupe a contingent of Phoenician ships sent as reinforcements into a perfect ambush.

Cimon's most important campaigns, however, were made back home in Athens. A great admirer of Sparta, Cimon strove to do to his beloved city what the Spartans had done to theirs—only instead of militarizing it, he would make it a completely naval society. Everyone, high and low, was involved. He had the city enlist every wealthy Athenian in a rotating duty roster of ship command and pass a law requiring all the city's poorest to take their turn at the oars. Before Cimon and the days of the league, serving in the navy had been a civic responsibility—now it was a requirement. Athens became the first compulsory-service naval power in history, its considerable financial and human resources harnessed to sustain a naval juggernaut of potentially irresistible size and efficiency.

Where would it lead Athens? Cimon, like Themistocles, foresaw nothing but Greek glory and Athenian power.

## TO PEACE

By 460 BC both men had fallen from authority and been driven into exile. Brilliant and enterprising, they had unleashed forces too vast to control with the traditional power structure in Athens. Themistocles gradually infuriated his fellow citizens with his ego and grasping nature. Offended by his constant attempts to cash in on his glory days, the Athenians ostracized him in 471 BC.

Cimon's downfall was more spectacular. In 462 BC the city's *thetes*—lower-class citizens—staged a revolt to seize power from the aristocratic leaders. The enormous manpower requirements of naval warfare had elevated Athens's landless to a position of immense importance in the city's affairs. Now they demanded equal representation in government and a say in the city's agenda, which had always been restricted to the middle and upper classes. Among those who opposed this sweeping radicalization was the man who had unwittingly set it in motion: Cimon. Like an unstoppable tide, the people swept him aside, formally ostracizing him.

Athens had now become a strange beast indeed. History is replete with examples of wartime tyranny, but in Athens mobilization and constant campaigning had led to a revolutionary democratization of power. The Athenians were now a sort of thalassocracy whose plebeian state was created by—and depended upon—constant trireme warfare and the economy of munitions, expansion, and booty that resulted from it.

Swept up in their peculiar crusade, the Athenians led the league with renewed gusto against an embattled Persia. From Phoenicia to the Hellespont, Greek forces raided and plundered. They even answered an Egyptian call to help throw off Persian occupation, sending a large army and navy to the Delta. After aiding the locals in their war of independence, they governed Egypt jointly until the Persians returned in 454 BC to throw them out again in a long and ugly fight.

Permanently adding the land of the pharaohs to Athens's widening sphere of influence may have been a dream, but peace with Persia was not. In 449 BC the league, many of its members weary after decades of conflict, sent the Athenian Callias to negotiate with King Artaxerxes of Persia at his capital in Susa.

The peace treaty that resulted not only ensured the freedom of the Ionian cities whose condition had started the wars so long ago, it also recognized Athenian supremacy at sea. In exchange, the Persians demanded that no further attacks be made on their possessions. In effect, the document confirmed the existence of two neighboring realms: a Greek one, dominated by Athens and encompassing the entire Aegean and its periphery, and a landlocked empire under Persian rule. Peace, after three decades of fighting, had come at last. Athens now faced a new reality, and the path it ended up taking both gave the city a golden age and guaranteed its fiery destruction.

## THE INTOXICATION OF DOMINANCE

Those visiting Athens today will find their gaze inexorably drawn to the white marble ruin overlooking the modern city from its lofty perch on the acropolis. Though the victim of weathering, vandalism, earthquakes, and even a huge explosion, the 2,500-year-old structure still has a classic perfection that is at once magisterial and organic—and unmistakable, even at a considerable distance.

It is, of course, the Parthenon, possibly the greatest architectural achievement of the ancient West. Built between 447 and 431 BC, it completely eschews straight lines to create the illusion of looming grandiosity. Its columns bulge slightly in the center; its stylobate, or base, exhibits a subtle curvature; and the whole mass leans almost imperceptibly inward, drawing one's view up to the capitals. It is the quintessential Doric temple.

As if the Parthenon were not overwhelming enough on its own, it is surrounded by other great buildings from the same period: the Temple of Athena Nike, the Erechtheum, the Propylaea. How did Athens manage to pull off this singular display of artistic and engineering genius? With lots of money. Other people's money. The acropolis of Athens is a massive badge of empire—the glorious statement of a city that had become used to an inflow of money and refused to have it cut off once peace arrived.

Tribute had become the drug of choice in Athens. Unlike traditional Greek land warfare, with its reliance on self-supporting hoplites, navies required legions of technocrats and countless hours of labor. Since the founding of the Delian League, Athens, as its leader, had regularly collected tribute from member states. Some provided ships and men, others money. All were part of the massive requirements of a trireme fleet and its facilities. But the peace made with the Persians raised a very important question: Was there any further need for the league?

By this time a new leader had emerged in Athens, and he had an unambiguous answer to that question. Pericles, one of the leaders of the revolution that had given power to the masses in 462–461 BC, was a populist, a nationalist, an imperialist, and probably a genius. Under his direction, Athens would gradually transform itself from league leader into empire builder. As he saw it, peace was equivalent to vigilance. The Persians might be defeated for now, but the lessons of the past instructed caution: let the tribute to Athens from its allies continue to ensure future security.

It does not take a leap of imagination to understand why Athens's allies increasingly saw their duty as onerous. In 454 BC the league's treasury, a massive concentration of wealth built with booty and tribute, had been moved from its original location on the island of Delos to Athens, a sign of things to come. Indeed, it would ultimately end up in the Parthenon, which was more a treasury than a temple—and a building constructed with league funds. Athens no longer pretended to make a clear distinction between league and empire.

As suspicious as this was, other actions by Athens gave even greater cause for concern. With the Persian wars over, many allies saw no further need to hand over treasure.

## WHATEVER HAPPENED TO THEMISTOCLES?

The man who was so fundamental to Athens's rise as a naval power came to an ironic end. In the wake of the war with Persia, Themistocles, ever on the lookout for opportunities to increase his modest personal fortune, involved himself in a series of shady business dealings that eventually sullied his reputation beyond hope of repair. The Athenians sent him into exile, where he found himself in a very uncomfortable predicament: with Athens's influence now so vast thanks to the navy he helped to procure for it, finding a place in Greece where his enemies could not ruin things for him had become all but impossible.

So he went to Persia, where he offered his services to the Great King. Recognizing the coup this represented, Xerxes gave him three cities in Ionia to govern—Lampsacus, Magnesia on the Meander, and Myus—all of which considered him a very just ruler.

Those members of the league who stopped payment of tribute as assessed by Athens, however, were invaded and their lands absorbed as Athenian possessions, to be governed not as independent colonies but as actual extensions of Athens itself. The rejection of imperialism served only to feed the imperialist agenda.

By the 440s Pericles and his fellow Athenians were officially done with moral introspection, freely engaging in the heady consumption that would occasion one of the greatest flowerings of intellectual brilliance in recorded history. Schools of philosophy were established. Seekers of knowledge gravitated to Athens, where they gathered in the agora to speak, instruct, and debate. Architects, playwrights, historians, and military theorists all shared ideas as they mingled in this stimulating milieu, their stomachs filled with grain that came from as far away as Russia, thanks to Athenian trade and naval supremacy. There were craftsmen, smiths, armorers, shipbuilders, all made busy by their city's newly minted imperium.

This is the Athens immortalized in the history books. It was the flowering of a way of life unique to time and place, a robust assertion of creativity and the radical democracy that gave birth to it, made possible by an influx of cash the likes of which the Greek world had never seen.

The Athenian Golden Age rolled on, secure in the naval strength that had made it possible. Pericles saw to the completion of the fortifications at Piraeus, four miles from Athens and the great city's link to the sea. Piraeus was the Athenian port and naval base, connected to Athens by the "long walls"—a pair of fortified walls that joined the two communities like an umbilical cord.

While Athens blossomed, her "allies," still forced to make payments, seethed. Perhaps most galling of all, most league cities paid the same tribute to Athens that they had been forced to give the Persians—a consistency that now, in peacetime, seemed utterly insulting. And just like the Persians, the Athenians wasted no time in punishing rebellious states with fire and sword, exiling their wealthiest citizens, and coopting their territory.

The irony of a democratic state behaving tyrannically abroad was not lost on the Athenians. Nevertheless, they now accepted conquest as a destiny they could not avoid—empire had made them great, and greatness could do naught but further feed the imperial impulse.

In his history of the Peloponnesian War Thucydides recounts a moment that sums up the Athenian mindset neatly. Threatened with destruction by an Athenian army on their doorstep, the people of Melos protest by citing the insignificance of their little island, only to receive a reply that has echoed down the violent ages: "The strong do what they will and the weak suffer what they must."

*An idealized view of the Acropolis at Athens, with the Parthenon on the right. Tribute from across the empire paid for the architectural Golden Age of Athens.*

## ENDGAME

In 430 BC, as Thucydides recounts, Pericles was called upon to give a funeral oration for all those Athenians who had died the previous year. In it he made a famous reference to the empire and its significance: "To recede is no longer possible, if indeed any of you in the alarm of the moment has become enamored of the honesty of such an unambitious part. For what you hold is, to speak somewhat plainly, a tyranny; to take it perhaps was wrong, but to let it go is unsafe." Pericles, who gave this speech in the second year of the war that would topple Athens, died the following year in a ghastly plague that brought his ambivalent city to its knees. To "let the empire go" may have been unsafe, but holding on to it turned out to be much worse.

The Peloponnesian War of 431–404 BC, a calamity of breathtaking proportions for the Greek world, spelled the end of the Athenian Empire. Its roots can be found in Athenian domination and the spirit of aggression that perpetuated it. Corinth, a powerful maritime city-state in its own right, grew increasingly wary of Athenian attempts at expansion into what the Corinthians considered their trading sphere in the waters west of Greece. The Corinthians chastised Sparta, their ally and the traditional foil of Athens, for not taking a hard enough line against the Athenians. It was against this background of tension that Athens slapped nearby Megara, a strategic city near Corinth, with an embargo meant to bully its citizens into joining the empire. Corinth, incredulous, shot a furious glance at Sparta, who finally sat up and took action—not least because Megara was considered a Spartan ally.

Happy to play the heavy, the Spartans gave Athens an ultimatum: lift the Megarian decrees or suffer the consequences. The Athenians, goaded and assured by Pericles, essentially laughed. The war was on.

The obsession with competitive independence that permeated Greek culture had prevented leagues of cities joining in common cause against each other—until now. By the mid-fifth century a loose alliance of city-states had emerged in response to the Aegean empire created by Athens. Led by Sparta, the principal city of the Peloponnese, this council of Athenian antagonists included such heavyweights as Corinth, on its isthmus, and Thebes, to the north of Athens in Boeotia. Forming a broad arch that threatened Athens from the southwest to the north, these cities had nothing in common beyond jealousy of Athenian power and a primordial, typically Greek longing to ruin it.

*Above: Marble bust of Pericles, the Athenian politician who led Athens during its dominance of the Greek world.*

Their success was anything but assured. Athens had access to outrageous amounts of treasure and manpower, thanks in large part to its ruthlessness. Those in doubt of this fact had only to look at the operation against Samos. In 440 BC the Samians rebelled against their Athenian masters with the assistance of the Persians (who preferred by this time to wage war by proxy), inviting a siege that lasted nine months and that cost the Athenians, according to historian Victor Davis Hanson, the equivalent of eight million days of man labor—this while they were conducting operations elsewhere *and* funding the construction of the Parthenon.

Nevertheless, in the coming conflict Sparta would prevail for four main reasons: first, the plague that struck down so many Athenians, including the irreplaceable Pericles, in the early years of the war; second, the existence throughout the Athenian Empire of disaffected subjects just waiting for an opportunity to rebel (an all too familiar theme in this book); third, Sparta's exemplary ability to adopt new tactics; and fourth, the Athenian operation against Syracuse—a devastating folly of stupefying senselessness.

## THE PELOPONNESIAN WAR

These two mutually exclusive camps led by Athens and Sparta had already sparred during the 450s, finally concluding their differences in the Thirty Years' Peace of 446 BC. Needless to say, the peace did not last thirty years—and the second war would utterly eclipse the first in sheer suffering and violence.

In the first stage of the war that began in 431 BC, Spartan hoplites annually marched into Attica to destroy everything of worth they came across, especially olive groves and wheat fields. Such tactics served to highlight the strangeness of this conflict between a land-locked power and its maritime enemy, as the Athenians merely retreated before the Spartans inside the walls of Athens, where they patiently awaited the enemy's departure before reoccupying the countryside. Sparta could control the rich Attic farmland only as long as the campaign season lasted, at the conclusion of which they were forced by the onset of winter to retire to Sparta. As for Athens, the maritime trade networks could easily bring grain from Egypt or the Black Sea to offset any destruction wrought by rampaging Spartans. Sparta lacked the siege craft to breach Athens's walls, and the Athenians lacked the hoplites to defeat the Spartan invaders. A sort of stalemate ensued.

Unfortunately for Athens, the Periclean strategy of huddling within the walls spawned an awful side effect: plague. Thucydides is unsparing in his recollection of the pestilence, which broke out in the second year of the war and brought terrible, widespread suffering. Inflammation of the eyes, sneezing and hoarse coughing, spasms in the stomach, the spread of ulcers and pustules, restlessness and weakness by turns, debilitating diarrhea—all of these tormented the afflicted to varying degrees, overwhelming the city's already strained wartime infrastructure. Physicians, confused by the scale of the sickness and as vulnerable as their patients, fell in droves. The dead soon filled the streets, where they dammed up the gutters and filled the air with the stink of putrefaction. To this day scholars debate the precise identity of the epidemic that laid Athens low during the Peloponnesian War. Not even the vivid descriptions by Thucydides have provided a conclusive answer.

It is a testament to human endurance and Athens's resilience that the city recovered from this nightmare. Fighting against Sparta continued, particularly amphibious operations around the Peloponnese, where Athens's naval mobility could keep the enemy on the defensive. But the plague had sapped a significant portion of the city's strength, and a new generation of leaders jumped into the void left by the death of Pericles.

One of them was Nicias, an aristocrat who saw his role in the war as a champion of moderation against the radical democrats. In 421 BC he sponsored a truce with Sparta that came to be named for him. Rather than a peace treaty, it resembled a lag in the action between two frustrated goliaths who needed to catch their breath. No one in Greece expected the hiatus to last long.

It was during this period that emissaries from Segesta, a city on the island of Sicily, arrived in Athens to plead for help with their war against Selinus and her ally, Syracuse. In the contentious debate that ensued over whether to become involved in Sicily, Nicias grappled for the hearts of the Athenian assembly with Alcibiades, a young firebrand who was as romantic and impetuous as his older rival was sober and methodical. For Nicias an operation to the central Mediterranean against a great city like Syracuse while an ongoing fight against Sparta was still unfinished at Athens's very doorstep was tantamount to insanity.

For Alcibiades, however, the invitation from Segesta was a golden opportunity—literally. Sending an army to help Segesta would be just the beginning. By exerting direct influence over an island as large and as rich as Sicily, the Athenians would be able to double at a stroke the resources and treasure available to them in the war against Sparta. All Greece might soon be theirs! Athens had not arrived where it was by acting timidly—it was time to up the stakes once again, to do what came naturally to all good Athenians.

Carried by the rhetoric of Alcibiades, the Athenians, seemingly heedless of all danger, plunged into the largest, most ambitious operation of the Peloponnesian War.

They probably should have listened to Nicias.

## COMING TO RUIN ON THE EPIPOLAE

The greatest amphibious operation ever organized by a single Greek city-state ran into trouble right from the start. Alcibiades, the campaign's most important supporter, was recalled by Athens to answer allegations that he had committed sacrilegious crimes before departing. This outstanding bit of bad timing was rewarded with disaster when Alcibiades, refusing to let his Athenian enemies destroy him, defected to Sparta. Command of the force sent to Sicily in 415 BC—including 134 triremes and over five thousand hoplites—now fell to other generals, one of the most senior of whom was Nicias.

Such beginnings hardly augured well for the Athenians and their allies as they decided how to proceed once they had landed on Sicily. Their principal target was Syracuse, a fellow democratic state and arguably the strongest power in the greater Hellenic world. Founded by colonists from Corinth, the city had grown steadily to become a commercial and cultural powerhouse that clearly dominated the entire island. This was not going to be a walkover—especially when the Athenians found a dearth of willing allies on the island. Local support was one of the factors that Alcibiades had relied on to build a case for invasion. Now, it appeared, they were quite alone.

What followed was a confused race for control of a plateau called the Epipolae—a stretch of high ground above Syracuse and on which any successful siege would have to be anchored. Without catapults and other siege engines, the Athenians were restricted to the classic stratagem of circumvallation—literally cutting the Syracusans off from the outside world by building walls around them while Athenian ships blockaded the harbor.

The Syracusans responded in kind, attempting to prevent completion of the Athenian walls by flanking them with their own *counter*vallation, commencing a bizarre building race that, due largely to inexplicable Athenian complacency, the Syracusans ultimately won, effectively rendering the Athenian siege itself untenable.

This was bad enough, but the arrival of Alcibiades in the Spartan camp back home had produced results. Alerted to the situation on Sicily, the Spartans sent a tiny flotilla of ships that managed to penetrate the Athenian blockade and deliver their dangerous cargo: Gylippus, a brilliant and resourceful Spartan general who would inject the city's defenses with formidable energy.

Gylippus did everything right: he galvanized the Syracusans with his confidence and knowledge, recruited reinforcements from inland communities, and constantly exerted pressure on the Athenian lines with opportunistic strikes—strikes that were soon made even more effective with the arrival of Corinthian reinforcements who slipped through the blockade. (Clearly the Athenians were bungling even the naval part of this fiasco.)

By the end of 414 BC the Athenian situation was dire. After receiving a letter saying so from Nicias, the Athenian assembly actually reinforced the operation the following year, ignoring Nicias's thinly veiled plea for extraction. This exercise in egregious judgment merely compounded the scale of the catastrophe; Sicily had officially become an insatiable devourer of Athenian men and treasure. A final push to retake the Epipolae in 413 BC was staged during the night—a rare tactic in antiquity for reasons that became all too clear to the Athenians and their allies as they ran into each other in the darkness and the attack descended into bedlam. The assault produced only casualties, many of which were incurred when frantic Athenians, disoriented in the darkness, ran off a cliff.

Withdrawal had become the only sane option for the Athenians, but there was one more needless tragedy to be played out. On a clear night in August 413 BC a lunar eclipse interrupted the course of events. As a result Nicias, deeply religious, insisted that no action be taken for a period of twenty-seven days.

The last opportunity to get out while the getting was good had passed. Enemy naval units struck, routing the Athenian fleet outside the harbor. Abandoned to their fate on a hostile island, the Athenian hoplites—the cream of Athens's agrarian middle class—were hunted down like game by enemies from throughout Sicily who were eager to profit by the destruction of these illustrious invaders from afar. Nicias, the man who had once struggled so manfully to thwart the bellicosity of his city, met a grisly fate. After retreating for days in the hot wilderness, he and his parched soldiers came upon a river. Mad in their thirst, they drank even as a force of Syracusans descended on them, the

*The hoplites' helmet, round shield and greaves portrayed on this vase from c. 600 BC are much the same as those used during the Peloponnesian War.*

waters running red with gore. Most were struck down as they cupped the fouled water to their lips. Those who survived this phantasmagoric spectacle were penned up in a local quarry and allowed to die slowly from months of exposure in the Mediterranean sun. Nicias and his fellow general, Demosthenes, were simply butchered.

## PASSING

The crushing Sicilian debacle may have played center stage in the downfall of Athens (it certainly did in Thucydides's mind), but it would take Sparta another nine years to ruin the city. While Athens marched doggedly ahead, Sparta, traditionally the ossified conservative, adapted impressively. The Spartans built a permanent fortified base in Attica to make the region's spoliation more systematic and to cut off shipments of silver from Mount Laurium, they amassed a fleet to hit Athens in its own element, and they accepted Persian funds to sow rebellion against Athenian rule throughout the Aegean. The result was a collapse of Athenian hegemony on all fronts.

In 404 BC a Spartan fleet sailed into the Piraeus to secure the surrender of Athens. Afterward, the "long walls" were gleefully torn down by Athens's enemies—to the music of pipes, no less. The time had come for maximum humiliation.

This was the essence of ancient Greek culture: the ever-present dimension of strife between competing city-states that made peace an exception rather than a rule. Greek communities lived in a perpetual scrum, constantly jostling for a supremacy that, it was understood, was fleeting by its very nature. If the city-states of Greece shared a common pantheon, they also shared the fundamentally accepted fate of never-ending competition. This, they believed, is what gave their societies vitality and energized their citizens, who knew that if you did not have any enemies, you must not have been getting ahead.

More specifically, the Athenian Empire was a product of war—and therefore inherently vulnerable to war's vicissitudes. Nothing electrified Greek passions and enterprise quite like the invasion by Persia, an epochal event that transformed parochial Greece by fire. In defeating the Great King the Athenians dared to see wholly new possibilities, and in realizing them they pushed beyond the limits of city-state politics, fortifying their adversaries even as they embarked on an adventure for which they were ill prepared. Brazen overconfidence ensured their destruction.

Was it all merely a crazy escapade by greedy revolutionaries caught up in the moment? Perhaps. But the Parthenon is something to behold.

CHAPTER NINE

# MACEDONIA

## THE LIMITS OF GREAT MEN

IN 1977 archaeologists made a remarkable discovery near the town of Vergina, Macedonia, in what is now northern Greece. Not far beneath the surface, they uncovered a regal-looking tomb. Inside rested two golden *larnakes*, or square chests that were used as receptacles for the ashes of the dead in ancient Greece. One of them contained the remains of a man between forty and fifty years of age whose charred bones bore certain distinctive marks.

The excavation team was elated. Given the location of the tomb, the evidence uncovered around it, the grave goods within it, and the condition of the bones themselves, they made the sensational announcement that they had stumbled across the final resting place of Philip II, legendary king of Macedonia and father of Alexander the Great.

The claim remains disputed to this day. Whatever the truth may be, it is worth noting why the archaeologists were confident of their claim in the first place. Among other signs that point to the famous king is the skull, which bears evidence of trauma in the right eye socket. Then there are the greaves, or bronze shin guards, which were placed in the tomb along with other grave goods. Strangely, they are of different lengths, suggesting an owner with a seriously gammy leg.

Little wonder the excavators thought of Philip, who is known to have suffered at least three terrible wounds in his long, violent career. During a siege in 354 BC, a missile deprived him of his right eye. Nine or so years later, an attacker's blow shattered his shinbone. And in 339 BC he endured yet more agony when a well-aimed spear passed through his leg and into his horse, fixing the king's ruined limb to the dead animal until it could be freed—a process that must have induced otherworldly pain. By the time he had conquered Greece and was preparing for the invasion of Asia, this icon of European dynamism was truly a sight to behold: a one-eyed, limping, disfigured totem of battlefield brutality.

This is perhaps appropriate, as the empire that he and his son created was built largely on revolutionary methods of killing people. But more to the point, Philip and Alexander in a very real sense

*Previous pages: Ionian capital from Temple of Athena Polias at Priene, dedicated to Alexander the Great c. 334 BC.*
*Above: Gold casket, or larnax, found in the tomb of Philip II of Macedon at Vergina.*

*were* the Macedonian Empire. As a result of their brilliance it sprang into existence like Athena from the head of Zeus. Tied intimately to their unique abilities, it would not survive their passing.

## MILITARY EVOLUTION

In 371 BC, a Spartan army marched into the region of Boeotia with the intent of settling, once and for all, its longstanding power struggle with Thebes. It was led by King Cleombrotus and numbered around eleven thousand combatants, with a core of heavily armored hoplites. In three hundred years, no army of Spartans had ever suffered a major defeat in mainland Greece. Confidence, to the say the least, was high.

To meet this invasion of what they considered their backyard, the Thebans could muster some 7,500 warriors, but their inferior numbers were more than offset by revolutionary training and tactics. Epaminondas, their general, was the most extraordinary Greek of his time, and he was about to reverse three hundred years of history.

When the two armies clashed at Leuctra, it represented a contest between old and new. Epaminondas was an astute collator of current events, both military and political, and the actions of his army that fateful day represented the culmination of years of Greek innovation in the art of war. Drawn up into two massed lines facing each other, the opposing armies must have looked quite similar to a distant observer, but closer inspection would have revealed profound differences.

Epaminondas meant to turn Greek military tradition on its ear so as to spoil every convention on which his Spartan foes relied. To begin with, he ordered the Theban line to angle itself obliquely to the Spartans, with the far right of the line back-pedaling while the left advanced. Such a maneuver militated against the linear, head-on clash with which hoplite battles usually climaxed and forced the Spartans to cope with an opposing army at an awkward angle. The real surprise, however, remained a secret until it was too late for the Spartans to do anything about it.

Ancient convention stipulated that a hoplite army's best troops form up on the right wing, resulting in a clash that inevitably saw decisive struggles on both flanks as the opposing elites sought to turn each other's left. Epaminondas, however, insisted not only on putting his finest men on the left, where they would clash immediately with the cream of Spartan manhood, but also on buttressing their advance with an unprecedented concentration of numbers. Most hoplite armies stood eight to twelve ranks deep, but at Leuctra the Theban left wing stood a breathtaking *fifty* shields in depth—a staggering accretion of manpower of which the Spartans, capable of seeing only the first few ranks, were completely unaware.

As Epaminondas's left-wing hammer maneuvered for the blow, three hundred Thebans of the "Sacred Band" screened its advance as elite skirmishers. Consisting of 150 handpicked pairs of homosexual lovers trained and maintained at state expense, the band contained the most respected warriors in Greece. When the time came to deliver the decisive assault, these men spearheaded the charge.

The Spartans had no idea what hit them. Crushed on their right by the massed weight of fifty ranks of Theban hoplites, the best Spartan warriors—including King Cleombrotus—fell like blades of grass beneath a rolling boulder. Before long the rest of the Spartan line, comprising clients and allies who were not accustomed to seeing Spartan warriors cut down in such numbers, broke and fled. Sparta's uncanny winning streak had been brought to an end. And Epaminondas, whose bold synthesis of imaginative tactics had decided the new order in Greece, was the man of the hour and the most important leader of his civilization.

Thebes started widening its sphere of influence. Not long after the triumph of Leuctra, the city became involved in a tussle over Thessaly with a barbarian people to the north known as the Macedonians. Alexander II, king of Macedonia, attempted to conquer Thessaly, only to be thwarted by Theban intervention. An uneasy peace ensued, followed by the usual exchange of hostages. To honor his end of the bargain, King Alexander sent his brother to live in Thebes.

The prince was just twelve years old. His name was Philip, and as a hostage he would dwell in the household of none other than Epaminondas.

## TOOLS OF POWER

The great Theban general must have played a crucial role in honing Philip's skill as a future conqueror. An impressionable young man of aristocratic blood, the young Macedonian must have devoured every little lesson in tactics and strategy offered to him. But Epaminondas was not the only innovative thinker of the age to make an impact on Philip's education.

The fourth century BC was one of constant conflict and instability as the great city-states of Greece warred with each other in the quest for a supremacy that none of them would ever achieve for very long, but Greece's culture during this period was as dynamic as its political arena was chaotic.

Philosophy, sculpture, poetry, theater, and science all underwent exciting changes in an environment of experimentation and debate. From Syracuse to Byzantium, the Greek world was undergoing an intellectual shake-up that made almost anything seem possible.

War, forever a topic of enormous significance to Hellenic communities, was also undergoing change. The age of the hoplite was slowly drawing to a close as thinkers attempted to refine new, more decisive methods of deciding battles. One of these thinkers was a man named Iphicrates. A brilliant Athenian general, Iphicrates put forth a number of new ideas intended to replace the traditional bifurcation of Greek infantry into heavy warriors (hoplites) and light skirmishers (peltasts). Though peltasts had always been important in Greek armies as slingers, archers, and light auxiliaries, their numbers and availability had made them even more important as the fourth century gave way to the third. The costly hoplite "panoply" of heavy shield and armor restricted its use to those middle-class landowners who could afford it, while almost anyone could be a peltast. It was against this background that Iphicrates sponsored the creation of a kind of hoplite-peltast hybrid—a soldier whose smaller shield and lighter armor freed both hands to deploy a spear of unprecedented length. Such warriors had greater mobility and longer striking power.

There is no conclusive evidence that Iphicrates had a direct impact on Philip, but ideas such as his and Epaminondas's informed a steady change in equipment and tactics that were readily proven or discredited in the endemic conflicts of the period. Conflicts, incidentally, that Macedonia was happy to watch from the sidelines up north. While Thebes, Sparta, Athens, and Corinth maintained their march of folly, Philip—ruler by 359 BC—oversaw the completion of Macedonia's military revolution.

The result was an army like no other. The phalanx, the traditional formation of hoplite infantry for centuries, was turned by Philip into something that Leonidas or Pericles would not have recognized. To begin with, hoplites were nowhere in sight. Philip's phalangites, in fact, looked a lot like those of the Iphicratid reforms. Rather than heavy Corinthian helmets, they wore open-faced headgear that afforded greater awareness and communication on the battlefield. Their small shields were slung from the neck and shoulder, freeing both hands to wield a pike of *eighteen feet or more* in length. This extraordinary weapon, the *sarissa*, soon became the bane of the known world, allowing the Macedonian phalanx, twelve thousand men strong, to behave like a tremendous hedgehog. Sixteen rows deep, with the first five rows thrusting their *sarissai* forward, the phalanx had the momentum and killing reach to make resistance all but hopeless.

In battle the infantry phalanxes were intended to be the anvil on which enemies were ground to dust. Philip's corresponding hammer, the cavalry, incorporated innovations that were just as revolutionary as those in the phalanx. Unlike traditional Greek horsemen, who played a secondary role in battle, Macedonian cavalry were instrumental to Philip's tactics. Wearing armor and weapons similar to those of the phalangites, they were trained, not to skirmish and harass, but to charge and kill, performing the role of heavy horsemen, stabbing with their shorter *sarissai* tucked under the arm. Known as the "Companion Cavalry," these hard, mounted warriors were recruited primarily from the nobility, forming an elite who enjoyed an easy familiarity with Philip and, later, Alexander.

Nearest the king on the battlefield were the hypaspists, or "shield-bearers." Around three thousand strong, these specially trained, highly adaptable infantry could be deployed wherever the king needed them most, either to reverse a crisis or drive home a victorious breach of the enemy line. The core of them formed Philip's Royal Guard.

The result of all these reforms was an army that improved on the best ideas from West and East—a force that brought the Greek phalanx together with Persian-type mobility, enhancing both and coordinating them in new ways. Moreover, these were not feudal levies or civic-minded yeomen inspired by love of *polis* to don a breastplate for a few weeks every summer. Philip's warriors were paid professionals, recruited in regional units from their various rugged Macedonian neighborhoods and drilled relentlessly to be full-time slayers. They drew a wage from the king himself, who thereby eliminated all loyalties except to him and created an army-to-hand that required only his word to form up and move, at any time of the year. Soldiering was the new career in Macedonia, and business was going to get very brisk indeed.

## CHAMPION OR TYRANT?

Philip's army was merely the most spectacular of the tools with which he intended to build an empire. A man consumed with territorial expansion for its own sake, he was far too shrewd to use his soldiers when he did not need to. Diplomacy, bribery, bluff, and marriage—he had a modest bevy of wives who assured peace with clients at home and abroad—would also feature in Philip's efforts to turn a rural kingdom on the periphery of the Mediterranean into the most powerful state of the ancient world.

That he was one of the most extraordinary leaders in history cannot be doubted. Macedonia, a wild land whose mountains only grudgingly gave way to plains and river valleys nearer the Aegean Sea, was as rich in fractious warlords as it was in timber and ore. For generations beyond reckoning, Macedonian kings had ruled by consent. They were "first among equals" more than absolute monarchs, always careful to avoid actions that could jeopardize their support among the nobility. To have centralized

*Marble statue of Philip II, whose conquests in Greece formed the basis of the Macedonian empire.*

power in the kingdom to such a degree must have required tremendous charisma, energy, imagination, and ruthlessness.

Once his power base was assured in Macedonia proper, Philip began to expand. He neutralized Macedonia's traditional foes to the north and west, and then moved on the coastal regions to his east, adding their gold and other resources to his realm. He intervened in a civil war in Thessaly, his fertile neighbor to the south, having himself appointed *tagos*, or military commander, of the Thessalian League, and he swept the Aegean coast with his armies, adding Thrace to his kingdom. By the middle of the 340s BC he had formed an empire stretching from the shores of the Black Sea to the pass at Thermopylae, and he was poised to move south on the heart of Greece itself.

The prospect was not unpalatable to all Greeks. Philip was no longer a barbarian—the assumption of leadership over Thessaly, a region within the accepted Greek world, had made that official. But more importantly, the dynamic king of Macedonia bent over backwards to drape his country in the raiment of Greek culture. Not surprisingly, he succeeded. Macedonia had long been under the cultural influence of Athens, whose colonial mining interests had operated just beyond Macedonia's border on the northern Aegean coast (until they were annexed by Philip).

Philip came to the throne as a man who looked to Athens as a capital of enlightenment and peopled his court with intellectuals and artists from that city-state as well as others in its orbit. The effect was not entirely forced—plenty of Greeks from the south, despite a disdain for Macedonian customs, were happy to flock north to become part of Philip's entourage.

Within the wider Greek world, a debate raged over whether Philip was a savior or a destroyer. Isocrates, Greece's passionate advocate of pan-Hellenism, became spokesman for a movement that saw Greece crumbling under its own endemic recalcitrance and wondered angrily at what it might be capable of under the right management. To Isocrates, at least, that "management" meant Macedonia, whose power could unite the Greek world in a crusade against the Persians.

Philip was happy to let the Greeks dither and discuss while he plotted, husbanding his resources for a push south and stalling for time by engaging Athenian diplomats in ceaseless negotiations. By the time it became obvious to everyone that the Macedonian king intended to put an end to Greece's independence, it was too late, and all the city-states could do was attempt to defeat his army as it marched into their midst.

They failed spectacularly. In 338 BC, Athens and Sparta fielded the last great hoplite army in Greek history and met the Macedonians at Chaeronea. Philip, with his eighteen-year-old son Alexander in command of the Companion Cavalry, broke the enemy phalanx and slaughtered much of it in pursuit, offering a stunning display of the efficacy of his new tactics. The Theban Sacred Band, defiant to the last, were slaughtered to a man. Greece lay all but defenseless before him.

The battle of Chaeronea was a watershed in European history. Greece had at last been unified—by its conqueror. It would not be free again until the nineteenth century.

Philip, whose purpose in all this was to facilitate his upcoming war against Persia, needed peace and stability in Greece. Dusting off the old Greek idea of confederation in time of war, the king created the League of Corinth, comprising all the city-states of Greece save Sparta. Regional distinctions in government and social norms were maintained, and city-states were welcomed as "members" in a noble enterprise of cooperation against the usual barbarian of choice, Persia.

Greek autonomy, of course, was a sham. Making himself commander-in-chief of the league's forces, Philip meant to take as many levies as possible with him into Asia, both to augment his own armies and to deprive a potentially rebellious Greece of its finest soldiers.

The time of retaliation against Persia, dreamt of for so long but hardly attainable, was finally at hand. For all those in Greece who grumbled about Macedonian aggression and duplicity, there was no shortage of pan-Hellenists who saw their civilization's destiny in the person of Philip. If this was the only way to move against the Persians, they thought, so be it.

Let the adventure begin.

## VENGEANCE COMES OF AGE

It is hard to know where Philip's outsized ambition ended and the Greek world's desire for retaliation against Persia began. Was the Macedonian king merely using entrenched anti-Persian sentiments to suit his own visceral need for expansion? Or was it the other way around—was the wave of anti-Persian sentiment in the Hellenic world at last breaking upon Asia and taking Philip along with it?

Probably both. The need to define themselves against the perpetual enemy in Persia was a real and formidable element in the public life of Greeks, even as countless young men took up the spear to serve as mercenaries in that distant empire. On the other hand, Philip of Macedon is a perfect example of the "great man" theory of history. His kingdom rose to greatness solely because of his own efforts, which were unprecedented and sweeping. The effect was a synchronicity rare in history—a segue of man and moment.

Nevertheless, Greece and Macedonia would prove strange bedfellows. To the rough men of Macedonia, Greece—though wellspring of the arts and philosophy—was a ridiculous land of effete, high-minded dissidents. Macedonians, by contrast,

were considered uncouth, backward, and banal by their neighbors to the south. The great orator Demosthenes once dismissed Philip himself as "not even a barbarian from a place that can be named with honor, but a pestilent knave from Macedonia, whence it was never yet possible to buy a decent slave." To the xenophobic urbanites of the city-states, Macedonia was a place of brutish excess—it is worth noting, for instance, that the Greeks, hardly a bunch of teetotalers, regarded Macedonian drinking habits with genuine alarm. Only a man with Philip's skills could make such an uneasy "partnership" work—and he was murdered only two years after the battle of Chaeronea.

It is impossible to know the precise facts behind Philip's assassination, as they are debated to this day. The Macedonian court was a viper pit of intrigue and skullduggery, and the assassin—a member of Philip's bodyguard named Pausanius, who stabbed the king in broad daylight during a royal marriage celebration—was slain within moments of performing the act for which he has become a fixture in the history books. Variously written off as a spurned lover, a vengeful opportunist, or a creature of Philip's son Alexander, Pausanius took the truth with him when he was slaughtered.

Like all new Macedonian kings before him, Philip's son and designated heir, twenty-year-old Alexander III, now scrambled to ensure his succession by ruthless force. Alexander, whose relationship with his father had been uneasy at best, would be the one to realize Philip's grandiose dream of conquering Asia. But his first vital task lay closer to home.

The flies had barely begun to gather over Philip's corpse by the time Greek agitators to the south started severing their relationship with Macedon. The *hegemon* had been Philip, not his beardless pup. As far as they were concerned, Philip's role in the Corinthian League died with him.

Alexander soon showed just how nasty the bite of a beardless pup could be. In his eyes Greece was a Macedonian protectorate, and that was not open to discussion or interpretation. After securing his position at home with an assertiveness that would have made his father beam with pride, the new king of Macedon went south, laid siege to the rebellious Thebans, breached their walls, and razed their glorious city to the

*Above: Alexander the Great conquered the greatest empire the world had seen.*

ground. He left standing the temples, their marble capitals hovering like ghosts over the smoldering waste that had once been a *polis* of the first rank.

Dissent in Greece disappeared.

## GOD OF WAR

The annihilation of Thebes was a sign of things to come. Alexander now took the practice of war in the ancient Mediterranean world to a new level of uncompromising severity. It was to become a grisly hallmark of this man in whom so many extremes were manifested.

Given the people who shaped his upbringing, it is perhaps not surprising that Alexander became "the Great." His father, the most accomplished general of his time, was a man of insatiable physical and psychological appetites who forced a warrior kingdom to his will and launched a new age. His mother, Olympias, was a princess of Epirus in what is today Albania. As intelligent and fiercely passionate as her husband, with whom she carried on a bitter feud, she was a devout follower of the god Dionysus and a dabbler in snake cults, practices that gave her an air of the exotic and sinister amid the Macedonian nobility.

Alexander's tutors were just as extraordinary. In addition to the great Athenian philosopher Aristotle, in whose care Philip had placed his son's intellectual development, there was Alexander's physical instructor, a tough brute named Leonidas, while Philip's generals, especially the invaluable Parmenio, passed on their military wisdom. In such esteemed company, it is little wonder that Alexander grew to expect and achieve great things.

With Greece pacified, Alexander completed his preparations for a campaign against Persia. Though Philip had sent an advance force across the Hellespont before his death to "soften up" initial Persian resistance, it had met with little success and now awaited the bulk of the Macedonian army to get things rolling properly.

Alexander crossed into Asia in 334 BC with an army forty-five thousand strong, including five thousand cavalry from Macedon, Thrace, and Thessaly (these last being considered the finest horsemen in Greece), more than fifteen thousand Macedonian infantry, and a host of hoplites and other auxiliaries from throughout the Greek world. To meet this force the satraps of northwest Anatolia amassed an army of typically impressive Persian size: twenty thousand cavalry, perhaps twenty thousand Greek mercenaries, and a vast complement of infantry mustered from throughout the region.

The two armies clashed at the Granicus River. Arriving late in the day to see the Persian army arrayed on the opposite side of the watercourse, whose relatively steep banks presented a formidable barrier, Alexander—impetuous, exuberant, confident—prepared to attack over the protests of Parmenio and the other old hands. He had his army form up with the great Macedonian phalanx in the middle and the hypaspists to its right. Cavalry stood on the wings, with the Companions, led from the front by Alexander himself, on the right, and Parmenio, with the allied cavalry, on the left.

Into the teeth of the Persian horse, whose enormous numbers formed the bulk of the Persian front line, rode Parmenio and the cavalry of Thessaly and Thrace, their formations incurring frightful punishment as they splashed through the river and up the far bank. Their situation was about to become critical when Alexander struck, leading the Companions on the right across to charge into the enemy flank as the Persians busied themselves with Parmenio on the left. Now pushed and battered on both ends, the Persians fought to right themselves and hold the line, keeping faith in their superior numbers.

Then, in the center, the river disgorged a terrifying sight. Marching up the bank with their long pikes probing, the men of the Macedonian phalanx came on slowly and inexorably like a great beast sporting a throng of undulating appendages. There was no hope that the Persians could resist such an onslaught from the front while they struggled on the flanks. Attacked from three directions, the Persian horse hesitated, floundered, and then broke altogether. Alexander, very nearly killed in the melee, led his cavalry in a relentless charge against the right, herding the enemy to slaughter. Fighting without quarter, the Macedonians claimed crowds of victims, and soon all that remained of the opposition was the great host of Greek mercenaries.

Having stood behind the Persian cavalry in reserve throughout the battle, this phalanx had watched Alexander's machine grind Persian might into powder and now had no stomach for resistance. After all, they were Greeks—perhaps Alexander, as self-proclaimed *hegemon* of their homeland, would accept their surrender and recruit the best of them for his crusade.

It was not to be. Unyielding in his chauvinism, Alexander detested Greeks who fought for a Persian lord. Either his Greek cousins were with him, or they were against him. This was West versus East, and he was going to make everyone understand that point.

With what must have been nervous rage fueled by the adrenaline of combat, the young king ordered an attack. The Macedonian army crowded onto the enemy hoplites and cut them to ribbons, carpeting the earth with corpses. The battle at Granicus had descended into naked butchery. Those who survived this sanguinary exhibition, most of whom were found cowering beneath piles of bodies, were publicly humiliated and sent back to Macedonia as slaves, where they lived out the rest of their horrible lives as laborers in the mines.

*The battle on the banks of the Granicus River in May 334 BC showed the Persians just what a formidable opponent Alexander was.*

## THE SIEGE OF TYRE

In addition to innovations in battlefield tactics, the Macedonians employed the very latest developments in siege warfare. Sophisticated siege engines such as catapults emerged in the Mediterranean world at the end of the fifth century BC and underwent significant advances during the following century. By the time Philip of Macedon was crushing his foes, the technology existed to take a city in a matter of weeks, rather than the months or years that had characterized sieges during the Peloponnesian War.

Of all the sieges conducted by Alexander in his sweep through the Near East, none was more spectacular than his attack on Tyre in 332 BC. Tyre was one of the glorious and ancient Phoenician cities on the Levantine coast that had grown rich from trade, and it boasted some of the most impressive defenses of any city in antiquity. Settled on an island separated from the mainland by a swift-running channel, the city featured high, massive walls built right up to the water, denying an attacker any firm ground on which to conduct a siege. A large population, bursting treasury, and formidable navy serviced by two harbors all but assured that any effort against it would fail.

It is easy to understand, then, why the Tyrians felt safe in turning down a request by Alexander to worship at their temple to Melkarth, the local god. They were only acting out of respect for their deity and a suspicion of conquerors looking for ways to get fortified cities to open their doors. Alexander quickly settled down to do the impossible task of conquering Tyre.

Served by the best military engineers of the age, who seem to have developed a heavier form of catapult based on torsion, Alexander embarked on a chess match with his defiant Tyrian foes that tested his patience and leadership as never before. Shipping in grain from recently conquered cities to feed his troops as they labored to build siege works, Alexander was aided significantly by warships sent by newly won allies/subjects in Phoenicia and Cyprus. With these he gradually won control of the waters surrounding the city. To bridge the strait he ordered the building of a causeway—a huge project requiring countless hours of labor and the construction of two defensive siege towers, each 150 feet in height. The Macedonians fashioned seaborne siege engines—rams and catapults mounted on ships that could sail around the island and deliver punishment to the walls. Employing this strategy, the Macedonians eventually made a breach. When the time came to storm the breach, Alexander chose an elite force of hypaspists and other tough infantry, and led them personally off the ships, over the gangplanks, and into the city, where savage fighting ensued.

The city was taken amid a frightful slaughter of its inhabitants. Most of those who survived—men, women, and children—were sold into slavery. Alexander eventually had his moment in the temple of Melkarth, where he quietly worshipped. And outside the city, along the beaches that stood at the foot of its impressive walls, Alexander had two thousand Tyrians crucified as a warning to the world.

## STEALING AN EMPIRE

Granicus was emblematic of Alexander's *modus operandi*. Cavalry actions on the flanks, phalangite advances in the center, a preference for battlefields coursed by rivers, reckless personal courage, and utter remorselessness all featured prominently in the battles by which he trounced his enemies and subjugated the world's greatest empire.

Once Great King Darius III realized that he was facing an opponent of uncanny ability and resourcefulness, he moved with an alacrity that stood in inverse proportion to his empire's lethargic mass. Alas, it availed him little. Alexander marched south, liberating the Greek cities of Ionia and ultimately passing into Syria. At the battle of Issus in 333 BC, he unleashed his usual bag of tricks, shattering the Persians with professionalism and tactics that they simply were not capable of matching. The Macedonian even managed to capture Darius's personal train, complete with his wife and mother.

In the coming months Darius appealed to his opposite for reason and offered Alexander essentially half of the Persian Empire. But the Macedonian responded with the sort of hubris that would have made him a criminal in the history books had his enterprise turned out differently. Convinced that he had already set himself up as Great King of Persia and was merely taking by force what belonged to him by divine right, Alexander, increasingly vainglorious and unmanageable, told Darius that *all* of Persia was already his—who was Darius to offer any of it in negotiation? Stunned and resolved to muster his empire's strength in defiance of this headstrong warmonger, Darius prepared for the future.

Alexander, by contrast, played demigod. With Persia's armies everywhere in retreat, he led his army into Palestine, Sinai, and Egypt itself, adding the most ancient and glorious realms of the Near East to his exploding empire.

Egypt held a special place in Alexander's plans. Timeless proving ground of conquerors, its inclusion in his enterprise anchored his ambition in something more tangible than youthful élan. He journeyed through the desert in 331 BC to the oasis of Siwa, where an oracle had been dispensing prophecies for centuries. There he was recognized as a son of the god Amon-Re, reinforcing the spirit animus within him that whispered of immortal prowess. Everywhere he went, it seemed, Alexander acquired proof of his godhood.

He visited seers, sacrificed at temples, and founded cities—most notably Alexandria, which remains a jewel of the Mediterranean to this day—but his arch-enemy, Darius, still dominated Asia, and Alexander would have to destroy him to realize his dream. Fortunately, destroying things was Alexander's strong suit.

To make his final stand against the invaders from the west, Darius had two years to amass a daunting force while his opponent added territory along the coast. The new Persian army represented the empire's adaptation to new developments, particularly the heavy infantry that had always confounded Asian generals. Also present in Darius's army were heavily armored cavalry that mirrored Macedon's formidable horsemen. The Persians, it seemed, were weaning themselves from the need for hoplite mercenaries.

The battle of Gaugamela in 331 BC, in what is today northern Iraq, pitted the best that Persia had to offer against a weakened Macedonian army that had marched clear across the Near East to meet the challenge. When the two armies formed up to face each other, the Persian line was a mile longer than the Macedonian. Moreover, it boasted elephants and a corps of chariots with scythes attached to their wheels. But none of these factors could help the Persians, who, once again, failed to cope with the pike-wielding infantry and intensely aggressive, hard-hitting cavalry of Alexander's army.

Victory at Gaugamela ensured that the immense Persian Empire would pass into the hands of young Alexander. The dream of Isocrates—and of Philip—had been realized.

## TO THE ENDS OF THE EARTH

Alexander had already accomplished much, and he was about to build upon it. Persia was now his. Adding it to his homeland of Macedonia and the hegemony of Greece, he now presided over the largest empire the world had ever seen. He had exceeded the deeds of Nebuchadnezzar and Cyrus the Great.

It was not enough. Alexander, still in his twenties, presents the image of a man whose insistence on *more* matched his father's but who was galvanized by a heroic yearning that the calculating Philip would have considered reckless. This was conquest for the sake of conquest, rather than for the imperium it could build.

Pushing east with armies swollen by peoples now paying homage to him as the new Great King, Alexander swept like a hurricane into regions at the very limits of Greek awareness and beyond: Arachosia, Bactria, Scythia. By 326 BC he was campaigning in northwest India as far as the Indus River, engaging in a series of ferocious battles and sieges against peoples, especially the Allacenians, who stubbornly refused to recognize his authority. He smashed their armies, chased them into the mountains, and systematically reduced their strongholds. Countless numbers of those who surrendered were either murdered or sold into slavery. Crossing the Indus, Alexander fought the armies of Prince Porus at the epic battle of Hydaspes, where his hard-pressed infantry barely survived a charge by the enemy's war elephants. Some twenty thousand of Porus's soldiers were butchered in fighting that was exceedingly vicious even by Macedonian standards.

*By the time they reached India, Alexander's men were used to confronting elephants. They won the battle of Hydaspes but refused to march further east.*

Here, beyond the edge of the world they had once known, Alexander's men had given the last measure of their strength after years of constant, costly campaigning. They had waded through the blood and gore of enemies beyond number. And here they stopped.

Plutarch later wrote, "When Alexander saw the breadth of his domain, he wept for there were no more worlds to conquer." Alexander probably did weep, but not because he had run out of "worlds" to subjugate; rather, it was because his men had mutinied. No amount of cajoling or threatening or begging on his part could move them from their decision to say "enough," and the greatest conqueror the world had ever seen stormed off to his tent and sulked for days. India was as far as his men were going to go. It was time to go home and live like ordinary people once again.

## THE HARDER THEY FALL

Alexander, of course, could never be ordinary. Whatever chemistry of charisma, vision, tenacity, and nerve had allowed him to pull off a Herculean journey of conquest also denied him the privilege of having simple problems. If he thought big and acted on a grand scale, his passions and failings were writ just as large. His decision to return to Babylon from India via the southern route, for instance, seems like an epic act of vengeance on his men as it took them through the infernal, waterless expanse of the Gedrosian Desert. Huge numbers of them perished.

Holding Alexander's vast possessions proved a great deal tougher than winning them. Many of the men he hastily chose to govern his satrapies proved either unreliable or *potentially* unreliable. Both varieties were summarily executed.

Death, in fact, had been walking freely in the Great King's presence since he came to the throne. In 324 BC Hephaestion—Alexander's lifelong friend, second-in-command, and probable lover—died from fever. Others close to Alexander were not usually fortunate enough to die from natural causes. Back in 330 BC, the king had ordered the assassination of Parmenio on suspicion of his participation in a regicidal plot. Two years later Alexander, in a drunken rage, killed Cleitus the Black, an officer who had actually saved his life during the fighting at Granicus.

One of the issues that drove Cleitus and his king to quarrel that night was Alexander's increasing insistence on the adoption of Persian customs at his court. This became a defining issue of Alexander's brief reign, and it is easy to overlook its significance. A man straddling two cultures as Macedonian king and Persian *shahanshah*, or "king of kings," he needed to represent two sets of customs without insulting either. The matter was of immense importance. After all, the Macedonians and their Greek allies were a tiny minority in a vast foreign land, and peace had to be maintained. By assuming the titles and mantle of a Persian king, he sustained the notion that his new subjects could look on him as the rightful heir, thereby promoting stability.

But that meant doing things that were repugnant to any good Greek or Macedonian—things like prostrating oneself before the Great King and kissing his hand. To Macedonians especially—men who prided themselves on the affinity they shared with their king as brothers-in-arms—such customs were not only effete and disgusting, they were sacrilegious. Only gods deserved such devotion. And there was the rub, for Alexander, in his heart of hearts, understood himself to be a god.

Issues such as this continued to fester in a court atmosphere made listless and indulgent by the absence of military campaigning. If Alexander was a god, he was a crapulent one. Drinking to excess was literally a pastime in Macedonia, and the higher up the social ladder you were, the more you were expected to consume. By 323 BC Alexander had incurred several dreadful wounds and his body had been battered by the constant privations of campaigning. He had also contracted malaria. But the incalculable volumes of wine that drowned his nights in bleary oblivion had also taken their toll. It is worth noting that, according to some sources, the last noteworthy accomplishment of Alexander's life was the chugging of a colossal cup of wine dubbed the "bowl of Heracles." Immediately after emptying the vessel to the last drop, he was struck with a pain in his back and took to his bed. Several feverish days later, on June 11, 323 BC, he died. He was just thirty-two years old.

## A NEW ORDER FOR AN ANCIENT WORLD

There was little chance that the military acquisitions made by Philip and Alexander would survive as a single "empire" upon the latter's death. The irony is that Alexander seems genuinely to have worked toward a blending of cultures, particularly through intermarriage—toward the obliteration, in other words—of the very East–West antagonism that floated his epic enterprise in the first place. With his exit from the stage, the tension over cultural ambivalence, the agonistic nature of Alexander's generals, and the lack of an obvious heir (Alexander's only legitimate son had yet to be born) all combined to sunder the vast empire. Having been created by the will of extraordinary men in a matter of a few years, it required extraordinary men to hold it together. And while there were plenty of those gathered around the king's corpse, they were not exactly on a par with Philip or Alexander.

In response to the question of who should succeed him, the dying Alexander is supposed to have said "the strongest." Such a proclamation set the tone for things to come. In the coming decades the most powerful generals/satraps built up local power and influence, and one by one started calling themselves kings, dispensing with the illusion of imperial cohesion. Ambitious, warlike, they clashed and gradually shaped the new political order. In Egypt, Ptolemy, one of the late king's most trusted and esteemed generals, set himself up as a Hellenistic pharaoh. The last of his line, Cleopatra, would figure prominently in the struggles of Rome. Macedon and Greece fell to the heirs of Antigonus the One-Eyed. And Seleucus, perhaps the most ruthless of Alexander's *diadochi*, or generals, carved out the largest of the Hellenistic successor states, the Seleucid Empire, incorporating all of the Levant, Mesopotamia, Persia, and the eastern regions of the empire to the borders of India. There were many lesser kingdoms as well, including a Greco-Bactrian state in distant middle Asia.

*Detail of the Alexander Sarcophagus, showing a battle between Greeks and Persians. It was made for King Abdalonymos of Sidon, in Phoenicia.*

Alexander's legacy, however, went far beyond a few squabbling dynasties. The young king pulled a carpet of Greek culture across western and southern Asia, planting Western ideas that would find fertile ground in new cities stretching in a great arc across the known world. Indeed, the Greek language would survive in many of these places for centuries as the lingua franca of the elite. The Hellenistic Age, one of stupendous artistic and intellectual achievement, had begun.

Philip and Alexander left another legacy, as well. War of the Macedonian variety involved not just victory, but the destruction of opponents en masse. Literally hundreds of thousands of people had been killed by Alexander's aggression. A new chapter in military affairs had begun, with Macedon's geniuses having showed the Mediterranean world the rewards of absolute victory by concentrated violence. The petty tussles of city-states, the constraints of feudal obligation, the limited aims of amateur warriors, all were now of the past, rendered obsolete by professional armies and tactics that could destroy an enemy power rather than merely defeat it. It is vital to remember how Alexander won his gargantuan prize—with ceaseless, methodical butchery on a scale that historians have been trying to define and comprehend ever since. His brilliance and historical centrality cannot be divorced from the blood on his hands.

CHAPTER TEN

# CARTHAGE

## STAR-CROSSED TARGET OF THE ROMAN JUGGERNAUT

IN 153 BC Cato the Elder, a senior senator of Rome, returned to Italy from Africa, where he had been part of a diplomatic mission charged with helping the city of Carthage reach a peaceful accord with its Numidian neighbors. Carthage, which had suffered two decisive defeats over the previous century at the hands of Rome, had become a shadow of its former self, stripped of its empire and its navy. As a humbled power, it now found its affairs overseen by the very Romans who had risen to preeminence at Carthage's expense.

But Cato had not seen a defeated city-state during his visit. Self-appointed champion of Rome's most conservative faction, Cato was a man who had fought against Carthage in his youth, who bemoaned the encroachment of Greek sophistry into Roman culture, and who embodied his city's traditional reverence for martial virtues. While in Africa, he was shocked to see a Carthage that bore no resemblance to the savage den of shame that everyone back in the Senate seemed to think it was. The markets were bustling and the harbor was full of vessels bringing goods from throughout the Mediterranean world.

In fact, visitors to Carthage today can see the remnants of that harbor—a rough approximation of two bodies of water connected by a narrow channel. In ancient times, the first of these, rectangular in shape, served as the maritime hub of the city, where merchant vessels from around the ancient world docked to offload their wares.

Only Carthaginian warships were allowed to pass into the second body of water, a circular harbor that was the home of the city's navy. Dominated by a circle of land (upon which the commander's administrative buildings bustled with activity) in its center, this protected ring of water housed berths on both its inner and outer circuits—enough to shelter around two hundred warships.

This harbor, so cleverly designed and—in 153 BC—still so lavishly maintained, even after a series of enervating defeats, was too much for a brooding old patriot like Cato to stomach. He knew what Carthage was capable of—that its mariners had gone far beyond the Pillars of Hercules to colonize western Africa and trade with Britons, and that its soldiers under Hannibal had once menaced Rome itself. Now, even after its colonies had been seized, Carthage seemed once again in charge of its commanding position at the confluence of Mediterranean trade routes.

By the time he was back home, Cato had acquired an appreciation of Rome's old enemy that brooked no compromise. Henceforth, every one of his speeches, whatever its subject, ended with the same line: *Carthago delenda est* ("Carthage must be destroyed"). On one occasion he even resorted to theater, letting fall from the folds of his toga figs

*Previous pages: Detail from the Mausoleum of Bes at Sabratha in Lybia.*

that, he proclaimed to his fellow senators, had come from Carthage—a city merely three days' journey from Italy. Though some historians maintain that he had merely brought them from his own farm, Cato's efforts were on the side of history; many of his fellow Romans did not need a couple of plump figs to goad them into crushing the great city across the Mediterranean.

Within a few years, they would do just that, capturing and razing to the ground the metropolis that had once been the heart of a vast commercial empire. This was what came of crossing the Romans.

## MARINERS WITHOUT EQUAL

So complete was the destruction of Carthage, in fact, that none of its records have survived to help historians fully understand the city. Apart from archaeological evidence, scholars have had to piece together the story of Carthage by relying overwhelmingly on the literary sources of the Greeks and Romans—two peoples with whom the Carthaginians waged long and costly wars.

However, much is known of the civilization that founded the city. The Phoenicians—firmly established by the sixteenth century BC along the coast of modern-day Syria, Lebanon, and Israel—were the finest navigators and traders of their day. According to Herodotus, the Pharaoh Necho II (r. 610–595 BC) directed an expedition of Phoenician mariners to circumnavigate Africa, proceeding from the Red Sea and returning via the Pillars of Hercules. Though no conclusive proof of the astounding voyage exists, belief in it persists to this day precisely because the Phoenicians were capable of it.

Organized into city-states that were as fiercely independent as their Greek counterparts, the Phoenicians enriched themselves by leveraging their maritime skills into dominance of the Mediterranean's carrying trade. Their accomplishments were numerous and profoundly significant.

At the beginning of the seventh century BC, the Assyrian emperor Sennacherib launched a seaborne invasion of Elam, in southwestern Iran, a formidable undertaking requiring the leadership of Phoenician naval experts. Many historians credit the Phoenicians with the first bireme and trireme warships, and the crucial role Phoenicia played in maintaining seaborne links between the ancient Near East and the wider Mediterranean world was fundamental in the formation of Western culture. Take the Greek alphabet, for instance. Appearing in Greece after the illiterate Dark Age that followed the loss of Linear B script during the ravages of the Sea Peoples, the Greek alphabet was borrowed directly from the Phoenicians—a new alphabet using Semitic-inspired symbols to write an Indo-European tongue.

For such a thing to occur, the Phoenicians had to have been in Greece. And they were—as well as everywhere else in the Mediterranean. Like the Greeks, who undertook an explosion of colonization during the eighth and seventh centuries BC, the Phoenicians sent out colonizing expeditions. But unlike the Greeks, for whom colonizing efforts were principally a means of dispersing population to avoid confrontation over arable land, the Phoenicians looked to their far-flung outposts as havens for distant trading fleets and as strong points for the collection and control of local resources—whether ore, produce, grain, or timber—that could be channeled into the trading network for profit. Also, Phoenician colonies seem to have maintained a closer allegiance to their founding cities than Greek colonies did to theirs.

Carthage was a perfect example. Established in the ninth or eighth century BC by settlers from Tyre, Carthage was intended from the beginning to take advantage—on Tyre's behalf—of its marvelous location on the northernmost tip of Africa, where it stood guard over the western approaches to Sicily at the heart of the Mediterranean. According to legend, a bold Tyrian princess named Dido fled with her followers after

*A legendary Punic–Roman encounter: Queen Dido of Carthage meets Aeneas, who fled from the fall of Troy to settle in Rome.*

her brother, King Pygmalion, murdered her husband. Arriving on the North African coast, she bargained with locals to take only as much land as she could cover with a single oxhide. After cutting the hide into very slender strips, she laid out the circumference of her future capital: Carthage, or "New City."

Though much of the story is impossible to separate from myth, it seems entirely likely that there was a Dido, Queen of Carthage, whose origins lay in the great Phoenician city of Tyre. And while the details are vague, one thing is certain: a new city was born, perfectly situated to become the dominant force of the western Mediterranean.

## CUT LOOSE

In 575 BC the great city of Tyre accepted absorption into the Babylonian Empire under Nebuchadnezzar, effectively ending its history as an independent power. Along with the other great Phoenician cities, Sidon and Byblos, it had helped to spread Phoenician culture across the Mediterranean. Now its colonies, including Carthage, were on their own.

By this time Carthage, which had regularly sent tokens of tribute to Tyre, had grown to prominence among the Phoenician communities in the western Mediterranean. Mixing Semitic and local North African elements, it had established a civilization all its own—known to us, via the Romans, as "Punic"—that would continue to flourish in the wake of its severance from Tyre. By establishing colonies of its own as well as gradually assuming control over those that had once paid tribute to a now-occupied Phoenicia, over the ensuing centuries the Carthaginians amassed a trading empire that left it in virtual control of the western Mediterranean's mercantile activity. Much of the North African coast, Sardinia, Corsica, the Balearic Islands, and southern Spain ultimately fell under the control of Carthage's "thalassocracy," or extended maritime network.

Though as deeply religious as any ancient Mediterranean culture, the Carthaginians were driven to their mission through the commercial impulse. Profit trumped all other concerns. They would ultimately develop a very rich agricultural hinterland in Africa, but their burgeoning empire was defined by coastlines—ports of call connected by well-defended sea lanes. As their Phoenician forebears had done, the Carthaginians meant not only to control access to as broad a variety of goods as possible, but also to assume the sort of maritime sovereignty that allowed them to collect duties from other commercial fleets that wished to do business. A host of methods were employed to advance this agenda, including treaties and overseas settlement. War was always an option, as long as its long-term rewards outweighed its costs. The Carthaginians did not value war for its own sake as a calling to great men, but rather a necessity in cruel times—a last resort whose risks required careful consideration. And they did not tolerate failure: defeated Carthaginian generals were typically crucified, an extremely rare policy in antiquity (perhaps for good reason).

In no theater were the Carthaginians willing to employ force for as long or on such a grand scale as they were in Sicily. Here their competitors were not scattered islanders or Iberian tribesmen, but Greeks—a settled Hellenic populace dominated by city-states such as Syracuse that were as populous, well organized, ambitious, and militarily powerful as the Carthaginians. Despite the hot competition, Sicily drew great powers to its shores like bees to honey. A vast bulwark at the heart of the Mediterranean, Sicily was the greatest of prizes, and the Carthaginians, separated from the large island by less than 150 miles of ocean, could not afford to let it slip from their grasp.

Beginning in the early fifth century BC, Punic armies engaged in a bloody two hundred years of sporadic warfare to maintain and expand Carthage's foothold in the west and south of Sicily, only to be forced to accept the domination of the rest of the island by Greeks. Despite the length and ferocity of this conflict, the opposing sides shared similarities that went back to their eastern Mediterranean homelands. Both were colonizers and inveterate seamen, the Western heirs to an ancient conglomerate of Near Eastern civilizations whose roots were older than history. But they were about to meet, in the third century BC, a newcomer from Italy that was to overtake them both—in conflicts that would make their struggle for Sicily look like child's play.

## METROPOLIS

By the third century BC Carthage was the heart of one of the greatest powers of the ancient world. Her naval supremacy in the western Mediterranean was absolute. We have already visited the city's harbor—a segmented body of sheltered water to which the world came to trade and Punic warships came to dock. Guarded in times of danger by huge chains that were stretched across its seventy-foot-wide entrance, this port/naval base was the heart of the Punic empire, the place from which the Carthaginians had set out to prove their maritime prowess. Back in the sixth or fifth century BC, a legendary explorer named Hanno the Navigator had sailed with sixty vessels beyond the Pillars of Hercules and down the west coast of Africa, establishing Punic hegemony and trading with locals.

This was the sort of exploit that put the rest of the world on notice: Carthage was not to be trifled with. The city's navy was by far the largest in the region. In addition to triremes, the Punic navy now boasted an increasing number of quinqueremes. Though its precise structure remains something of a mystery, the quinquereme, a Hellenistic invention, seems to have added more oarsmen to power a larger ship, whether by adding more decks (which seems unlikely, given the issues of balance) or by increasing the number of rowers per oar. The result, in any event, was the largest warship of its day, capable of shattering smaller triremes with its massive, bronze-covered beak. More importantly, Carthage, with its unmatched access to naval stores, was capable of turning these battleships out at a high rate.

With its navy ensuring peace on the seas and its markets bursting with exotic goods, Carthage's population had exploded between the fifth and third centuries. Behind the city's elaborate defenses, the city continued to grow—up. Literary evidence, with archaeological support, points to Carthaginian housing blocks of multiple stories, perhaps as many as six. These preceded the tenement blocks of Rome by many years and showed a capacity for bold, ingenious architecture worthy of Punic ambitions. What is more, Carthage boasted advanced cisterns and running water, as well as efficient plumbing to take away waste—a carefully planned, city-wide civil engineering system that in many ways was the envy of the ancient world.

An equally complex government had arisen to run the empire efficiently. Though originally ruled by monarchs, Carthage ended up developing a political order more in step with the interests of its mercantile aristocracy. Assemblies of the people in which

*The great city of Carthage at the height of its naval power and commercial splendor, as envisioned in the late nineteenth century.*

ordinary citizens could speak were sometimes called, but administration of the city and the direction of government rested primarily with a pair of annually elected "suffetes," who were not unlike Roman consuls. Similar to temporary kings who could veto each other, the suffetes controlled the ship of state and answered to two advisory bodies: the Council of Thirty Elders and the Council of 104, both of whose members were drawn from the wealthiest families. The system ensured stability, as did the city's wealth (in which everybody shared) and its navy (which offered plenty of gainful employment to the empire's poorest citizens).

One of the largest cities in the world, Carthage had been able to grow virtually unchecked in its western Mediterranean sphere for several centuries. It had a thriving trading empire, the greatest fleet in the known world, and no cause to fear the future. Rome, an expanding state across the sea to the north, was a land power with virtually no navy. Besides, it had already signed three treaties with Carthage, in 509, 348, and 279 BC. There seemed little reason to feel threatened from that direction.

But the Carthaginians had not counted on Sicily, the great cockpit of the central Mediterranean—where even the might of Carthage was vulnerable and an up-and-comer like Rome could try its hand at the game of empires.

## CHILDREN OF BAAL

Carthaginian religion recognized a large pantheon of gods, from those whose origins lay deep in Phoenician history to those embraced much later, including deities of Greek origin. Chief among Carthaginian gods was Baal Hammon, who seems to have represented many things to the Carthaginians: stability, morality, and the eternal nature of Punic values. Baal's female consort, Tanit, was just as sacred, while Melkart, the "god of the city," represented ancient institutions of kingship and authority that went back to Punic origins in Tyre.

Central to the worship of gods like Baal Hammon was the sacrifice of young human beings. Such practices were recorded by numerous contemporaries, informing a legend that acquired physical confirmation in modern times. In an area of ancient Carthage known to archaeologists as the Tophet, excavations have turned up the charred remains of some twenty thousand young children who were buried between about 400 and 200 BC. Clearly the cremation of children continued right up to the destruction of Carthage, its practice possibly coinciding with moments of acute crisis for the city. As to the question that invariably bedevils researchers—Were these children burned alive or dead?—there is still no answer.

## STUMBLING INTO WAR

Like Syria and Lebanon in centuries past, Sicily had become a stomping ground for armies. Its division into independent Greek city-states and Carthaginian trading colonies ensured ceaseless tension between the region's two greatest seafaring peoples—a political storm that never truly abated, offering a plethora of career-making opportunities for martial dynasts, mercenary bands, pirates, and unemployed generals.

Into this bedlam strode a group of mercenaries from Campania, in southern Italy. Having served in the employ of Agathocles, tyrant of Syracuse, during his campaigns to expand Syracusan territory, they found themselves without work after his death in 289 BC. So they marched themselves up to Massana (modern-day Messina), ruthlessly and brutally took over the town, and used it as a base of operations from which they systematically plundered the countryside. Calling themselves the Mamertines, or followers of Mars, they even took to minting coinage in a bid for legitimacy.

It was simple brigandage taken to audacious new heights. Moreover, Massana was a strategically crucial city, controlling the narrow Strait of Massana that separated Sicily from the toe of Italy. Everybody wanted it, and the Mamertines had it. By the 260s Hiero, the new tyrant of Syracuse, was regularly grappling with the Mamertines, and he finally dealt them a decisive defeat around 265 at the Longanus River. As the Syracusans prepared to march on Massana itself, the Mamertines sent appeals for help to Carthage.

To the Carthaginians, looking back on two hundred years of struggle to control Sicily, an opportunity to get their hands on a prize like Massana was almost too good to be true. They sent a small garrison to Massana—it was enough to dissuade Hiero from involving his city in a fight with the likes of Carthage.

This should have been the end of the whole affair, but history often hinges on the confusing decisions of dishonorable men—and the Mamertines were certainly that. For reasons that are lost to posterity, they grew uneasy under Carthaginian protection, threw the Punic garrison out of Massana and appealed for help once again—this time to Rome.

When the request reached the Senate, it caused a furor of impassioned debate. The Romans, having just taken over the Greek cities of southern Italy, had begun to cast a wary eye on nearby Sicily and its large Carthaginian presence. Perhaps it was time to exert some pressure in that direction before things got out of control. Better yet, they could now do it under the guise of faithful friends answering a call by fellow Italians: the Mamertines were Campanians, after all, and their homeland was part of the confederacy of Latin peoples led by Rome. Moreover, if there were any place in the Mediterranean where Rome—certainly not a naval power—could pull off an overseas expedition, it was Sicily. Massana was just a few miles of ocean away from Italy. Despite some heated opposition to the idea, Rome answered the call of the Mamertines.

Evading Punic naval squadrons by crossing the Strait of Massana in darkness, a small Roman force managed to set up camp in the vicinity of the city, only to discover that the Carthaginians and Syracusans—enemies for centuries—had entered an uneasy alliance, so severe was their concern over Roman intervention.

Three armies now camped in and around a city that was, at least notionally, still controlled by the Mamertines—bandits who were now under the official protection of the Roman state. Though the sources are sketchy about the sequence of events during this time, it is certain that the Romans scattered both the Carthaginians and the Syracusans in separate battles. Securing their position in Massana, the Romans sent a large army led by both their consuls against Syracuse in 263 BC. Hiero capitulated without a siege, his position clearly hopeless in the face of determined and overwhelming Roman aggression. In addition to coughing up a large indemnity, Syracuse was made an ally of Rome by treaty. Rome's first foray into events beyond the Italian peninsula had been a stunning success.

Carthage, despite its large navy, had failed to properly guard the strait against enemy transit and now faced a new and determined foe on the island in which it had already invested so much blood and treasure. In Syracuse the Romans now had a large and wealthy base for their Sicilian operations. Neither power foresaw a long and costly war, yet neither was prepared to yield. Sicily had become too much of a Punic preoccupation for Carthage to make peace without a greater show of force, and Romans did not typically sheath their swords until they had achieved a decisive settlement, whatever the cost. Unwittingly, they were moving toward cataclysm.

## OPENING ROUNDS

Sicily was not an easy place to wage war. Mountainous, with numerous fortified towns, it had become a kind of school of siegecraft for all those who wished to dominate it. Though more experienced in such matters than the Romans, the Carthaginians still relied as much as possible on their navy to secure and defend the empire. Ships and the expertise to maintain and sail them were the natural outlet for Punic genius. Punic armies, by contrast, were almost entirely composed of mercenaries, especially Gallic and Iberian infantry, and excellent Numidian cavalry. Though led by Carthaginian generals, the nature of such troops put a strain on the effectiveness of military operations. Language was always a problem in such a multicultural force, and because the Carthaginians, unlike the Romans, were extremely reluctant to grant citizenship to non-Carthaginians, the loyalty of such troops depended almost exclusively on pay and the respect they had for their Punic commanders.

In 262 BC, while Carthage conscripted and organized new mercenary forces, Rome got the jump on its Punic foes and struck at a place it knew could be taken without recourse to naval power. Agrigentum was a heavily fortified Punic stronghold in the south of Sicily, several miles from the sea. Without proper siege engines, the Roman army invested the place and prepared to starve it out, but Carthage managed to send a large relief army, complete with elephants. It proceeded to capture the Roman supply dump and turn the tables on Agrigentum's besiegers.

But it was not enough. Rather incredibly, the Roman legions—four of them, two Roman and two allied—overcame their hunger long enough to force the issue when the Carthaginians finally offered battle. Agrigentum fell soon afterward, in 261 BC.

It is hard to know from the sources what the two armies beneath the walls of Agrigentum were really like. Were these fresh Roman legionaries, or veterans from the fight at Massana? How weakened were they by hunger? How nationally diverse were the Carthaginians? One thing is certain: this was the first large pitched battle between the two powers on land, and Carthage was determined to make it the last. Facing Roman armies in the field was not a cost-effective strategy.

Another development that same year, however, showed how tenacious was the foe the Carthaginians were up against. For it was in 261 BC that Rome began to build a fleet.

## ENDURING THE UNENDURABLE

Perhaps Carthage, whose walls and multi-storyed housing blocks were dazzling the city's visitors when Rome was still a glorified hamlet, had become complacent. It is difficult not to perceive a trajectory in empires that inevitably pits adaptability against intransigence and complacency. For centuries Carthage had been the only show in town—who else had been in a position to send trading fleets into the Atlantic Ocean? Separated by miles of sea from the struggles of its ancient Phoenician homeland, where a veritable cascade of empires fell one upon another in bloody succession, Carthage had built a gilded consortium for itself in the calm, sunny waters of the western Mediterranean. Not until the rise of Rome had Punic civilization been forced to cope with another state capable of threatening its sphere of influence.

And now that the struggle was at hand, Carthage was not coping well enough. It was not obvious yet: Roman legions had proven too tough for Punic mercenaries, but that did not mean Sicily was lost. Redoubling the efforts of the navy could still bring victories enough to maintain a strong foothold in Sicily. In a deeper sense, though, Carthage had already failed to understand Roman culture, with its emphasis on public honor, keeping faith with allies, and defiance even in the face of hopelessness. The Romans were at once deeply conservative and keen to adapt, jealous of their ancient customs and eager to welcome others into them. Such qualities made them natural empire builders even at this early date, when their imperial policy lacked coherence or long-term direction.

For Carthage, running the state like a corporation of shareholders and maintaining a narrow base of citizens with control over foreign labor and mercenaries had brought prosperity and expansion. The navy was strong, the sea lanes secure. Changing course just to defeat a power like Rome probably seemed unnecessary or even hysterical. The simple truth, however, was that Carthage had no grasp of the storm that was about to break upon it.

In the wake of Agrigentum, Carthage kept its Sicilian garrisons behind walls and shifted to offensives at sea, launching raids with impunity along the Italian coasts. Stung by these, the Romans oversaw the rapid (in two months!) construction of a hundred quinqueremes and twenty triremes. Rome was bound and determined to break into the navy business, come what may. Aided by the expertise of Tarentum, Naples, Syracuse, and other maritime cities now tied by treaty to Rome, this amazing effort was based on the confiscation of a Carthaginian quinquereme that had run aground in southern Italy.

That they pulled off this audacious achievement in the first place speaks volumes about Roman determination, but they still had to use these new ships against experienced Punic seamen with centuries of naval tradition behind them. Once again, the Romans displayed a level of adaptability that would bedevil their Punic enemies for the next century. To compensate for their lack of maneuvering skill against the more skillful Carthaginians, they devised a means of using their vaunted legionaries at sea. It was called a *corvus*, or "raven"—a bridge, attached on a swivel to the prow of each ship, that could be lowered during battle, its far end equipped with a great spike for impaling an enemy vessel and fixing it in place, allowing Roman marines to storm aboard.

In 260 BC, off the north coast of Sicily near a place called Mylae, the two fleets faced off in a major battle for the first time. Each force probably numbered somewhere in the neighborhood of 150 vessels, overwhelmingly quinqueremes. Racing forward in their long ships like a great pack of sea wolves, the Carthaginians were confused by the towering platforms looming awkwardly from the Roman bows, and soon enough came to dread them. By the end of the fight, the Carthaginians had lost between thirty and fifty ships sunk or captured.

Time and experience only allowed the Roman crews to become more efficient, and by 256 BC Rome was confident enough to launch an attack on Carthage itself. The

Punic fleet, prepared to risk all at sea to prevent a landing of legionaries on African soil, clashed with the Roman fleet at the epic battle of Ecnomus, only to be scattered in defeat.

The Romans were able to land a considerable force near Carthage before the Carthaginians, desperate enough to forgo their ban on pitched battle, came out to meet them. The result, to the surprise of many, was a decisive Roman defeat in which a large number of elephants and the excellent Punic cavalry proved too much for the Italians in open ground. The tables had now turned completely: Rome dominated the seas while Carthage dealt its foes humiliating defeats on land.

More Roman disasters followed. In the very same year as its army's defeat in Africa—255 BC—Rome's navy suffered a dreadful defeat at the hands of the weather. Still inexperienced in naval matters despite their precocious achievements, the Romans had failed to shelter the fleet properly in Sicily and lost more than seventy-five percent of it to a furious storm. This catastrophic loss, followed six years later by a major naval defeat at the Battle of Drepana, more than offset the gradual gains they were making on Sicily itself, where a series of Punic towns had been taken.

Now as confident as it had ever been, Carthage could be forgiven for thinking that Rome's dreams of naval supremacy were over. It could not have been more wrong. In a stupendous building effort that put their previous shipbuilding triumph to shame, the Romans turned out some two hundred vessels to make good their losses. By 241 BC they were sailing to the Aegates Islands on the western tip of Sicily. And there they crushed their Punic enemies in a furious naval battle.

Carthage, absolutely defeated in the maritime environment it had once had all to itself, sued for peace.

## SALT IN THE WOUND

The First Punic War had been a disaster for Carthage but in this epic, unprecedented struggle, one fact stands out as particularly significant: in the wake of Carthage's naval victory at Drepana and the storms that utterly savaged the Roman fleet, Carthage made the remarkable decision to gradually decommission much of its own fleet. The reasoning was simple: Roman naval might was all but broken, and the Punic navy was putting undue strain on the empire's finances.

This momentous change in policy (shipbuilding had been proceeding at a furious pace for most of the war) illustrates, perhaps more than anything else, the differences between these two clashing civilizations. Offered by recent good fortune an opportunity to cut costs, Carthage did not hesitate—while, across the Mediterranean, Rome simply built a whole new fleet, even larger than the one it had lost, from scratch, spending lavishly to maintain a war effort that it never considered slackening.

For Rome, victory—not survival—was everything. Carthage, by contrast, was a state built with balance sheets. It lacked the ability to alter what it was, even now that it faced an enemy it was hard-pressed to understand.

Carthage's central weaknesses came to the fore when, in the wake of the shameful peace it was forced to sign (stipulating a huge indemnity and acceptance of complete Roman rule in Sicily), its mercenary army in Africa mutinied. Starved by defeat of the funds it depended on to pay the mercenaries, Carthage had to fight its own hired troops.

The man who was given the task of defeating these uppity freelancers was an industrious general named Hamilcar Barca. Considered by the Hellenistic writer Polybius to be the most respected tactician of the age, Hamilcar had already made a name for himself by giving the Romans a hard time in Sicily against formidable odds. He now devoted his talents to the smashing of the Carthaginian hirelings. In 238 BC he trapped the rebel army in a gorge and loosed his elephants on them, producing a ghastly slaughter and capturing the revolt's principal leaders, who were promptly tortured to death.

To the horror of Hamilcar and all his countrymen, the Romans took the opportunity of Carthage's civil disorder to seize Corsica and Sardinia—an act of blatant, dishonorable acquisitiveness that Hamilcar, for one, could never forgive.

This outrageous breach of faith by the Romans boldly announced to the world their decision to cast everything aside in the pursuit of empire. Deprived of its navy, Carthage now had the ignominious fate of acquiescing to Roman naval power when, not thirty years before, there had not been any.

In the most adaptive shift of policy in its history, Carthage responded by trying its own hand at land empire—not in Africa, but in Spain. Hamilcar Barca, now the most respected military figure in Carthage, spearheaded the expansion of Punic territory in the Iberian peninsula. This was different from the usual exploitation of harbors and coastlines—this was the absorption of villages, farmland, and especially mines (with which Carthage could pay its egregious indemnity) deep inside Spain. Undertaken by the

*Coin minted at Carthage c. 230 BC, showing the head of Hamilcar Barca.*

Barca family as much to enrich themselves as to expand the interests of Carthage, the Punic push through Spain at first took the form of naked conquest. For nine years, from 238 BC until his death in battle in 229, Hamilcar waged constant war against Celtic and Iberian peoples. Assuming control of the army, Hasdrubal—Hamilcar's son-in-law and second-in-command—employed the same tactics, along with treaties and even marriage alliances. The Barcids, in effect, had become the aristocratic medium through which Iberian resources and manpower were pledged to the Punic Empire. By the time of Hasdrubal's death in 221 BC, all of southern Spain up to the Guadalquivir River lay under some form of Punic suzerainty.

Not surprisingly, it was in Spain that conflict with Rome fired up once again.

## A PLACE CALLED SAGUNTUM

Alarmed at this Punic expansion, the Romans sent envoys to Hasdrubal in 226 BC to ask after the general's intentions. There they exacted from him a formal promise that Carthaginian armies would not cross the River Ebro—well north of the Guadalquivir, at that time the boundary of Barcid activity. Such an agreement would allow further conquest by Punic armies while putting to rest Roman fears that such activity would continue into the Pyrenees and Gaul.

After Hasdrubal's death in 221 BC, Hannibal Barca, son of the great Hamilcar, assumed command of the Carthaginian army in Spain. In his mid twenties, Hannibal was already popular with the army, in whose presence he had been campaigning since his early youth. When he was still a boy, on his father's insistence, he had sworn an oath never to be a friend of Rome. In fact, he would soon become Rome's worst nightmare.

The spark for the renewal of hostilities between Carthage and its arch-enemy was a place called Saguntum. A city-state on the Mediterranean coast of Spain, Saguntum became the focal point of the tug-of-war between the great powers, its population divided between pro-Roman and pro-Punic agitators. Invited by the pro-Roman faction to intervene, Rome promised protection for the city, in effect making Saguntum a friend of Rome—an ideal starting point for the growth of Italian interests in Iberia.

By 219 BC Hannibal was campaigning in central Spain, becoming immersed in the local politics of which Saguntum was an integral part. When one of Hannibal's client tribes got into a heated dispute with the city, Hannibal intervened and laid siege to Saguntum, which fell by the end of the year. Located south of the Ebro River, the city was fair game as far as Carthage was concerned, but Rome, having accepted the Saguntines into its circle of allies, understood the attack as a slight against Roman honor and a crystalline *casus belli*.

Hannibal had been acting largely on his own initiative, appealing to Carthage for direction when possible but following his instincts while messages passed slowly back and forth. Though the suffetes and councils of Carthage were divided on the subject of their general's conduct in Spain, they rallied as one when confronted with a typically terse Roman delegation demanding answers. Roman effrontery had become a form of Mediterranean currency, but the elders of Carthage were not buying. War was welcomed.

Twenty-three years of peace had passed, yet Carthage and Rome, between them dominating the western Mediterranean, could no longer act without provoking each other—and one's rise manifested the other's decline. Indeed, Rome's climb to empire had occurred literally over the backs of vanquished Punic combatants. From this point on, the Carthaginians would either flourish by bringing the Romans to their knees, or disappear into obscurity under hob-nailed sandals.

Against the uncompromising Roman drive to conquer, Carthage had little to offer but one man's genius. Incredibly, it very nearly proved enough.

## A MAN CALLED HANNIBAL

Given the oath he had made to his father before the gods, Hannibal may well have understood what the fall of Saguntum would lead to. He certainly had laid the groundwork for the campaign that followed—the epic, almost mind-boggling series of labors and victories that still makes his name a synonym for greatness more than twenty-two centuries later.

Hannibal's charisma seems to have stood in inverse proportion to his age: the men under his command, many of whom had fought with his father, grew to worship him. Few generals have ever blended confidence, audacity, and imagination in such ample measures. One wonders what Alexander, who had at his disposal a military machine unmatched in the ancient world, would have said of this Punic phenomenon—a man who achieved so much with an army whose weapons, formations, and training were hardly better than those of the legions sent against him.

The fact that so many today have a passing familiarity with Hannibal's crossing into Italy and subsequent victories is as suggestive of his significance as it is detrimental to the appreciation of his feats—ironically, the story of "Hannibal and the Alps" has become so commonplace that few ever stop to consider just how incredible the achievement was.

It began with hard facts. By defeating Carthage and dictating terms to her back in 241 BC, Rome had become the only great naval power in the western Mediterranean. Carthage had not only been stripped of much of its navy, but handily robbed of Sicily,

Sardinia, and Corsica as well. The waters around these islands now bristled with Italian quinqueremes on patrol. Attacking Rome meant going overland.

Hannibal's preparations were noteworthy. This was more than just a long march over difficult terrain—it was also a passage through potentially hostile peoples, all of whom may, or may not, have a stake in the clash between Carthage and Rome. Along the southernmost and quickest route to Italy lay Massilia (Marseilles), an ancient Greek city-state now friendly to Rome, not to mention a coastline convenient to Roman naval expeditions. Instead, Hannibal would need to march well inland—a journey he had prepared for as much as possible by sending friendly delegations ahead to win over angry Celts along the way.

Departing from Cartagena in the spring of 218 BC, Hannibal led a force of around ninety thousand infantry of various types and twelve thousand cavalry. To avoid having his troops desert—a common occurrence when troops are fighting in their own territory—he exchanged many of his Celt-Iberian troops for men from Africa. Hannibal also had thirty-seven war elephants. Despite its diversity, this gloriously colorful force revolved like a well-wrought wheel around the hub of Carthaginian officers who had grown to know their troops and each other through decades of hardship and victory. Hannibal stood at the center, resolute and commanding.

His army came to the Rhone River well north of Massilia, confronting a wild frontier most of the troops had never before set eyes on. There, while hostile Celts eyed them from across the vast waterway, Hannibal's men tore into the local forests to construct a fleet of rafts. Those designated for the elephants were heaped with soil and underbrush to put the animals at ease. And when the time was right, the

*Hannibal, the greatest Carthaginian general, crossed the Alps to invade Italy and take the Second Punic War to the doorstep of Rome.*

whole Punic army crossed virtually at once, its very passage so awesome as to scatter the Celts on the opposite bank without a fight.

This feat alone guaranteed Hannibal's place in the history books. Putting his determination and Punic engineering expertise on display, the crossing of the Rhone was a marvel of its time. But he had had to leave thousands of troops in the Pyrenees, where hostile tribes had threatened his advance, and he was heading into alpine territory of which he had little or no knowledge. It remained to be seen whether this outrageous role of the dice could possibly pay off.

## CANNAE

The obstacles facing Hannibal's army as it wound its way through the passes of the Alps in late 218 BC—the dead of winter—must have been awesome. Capricious weather, rockslides, and hostile mountain tribes all took their toll on the column of weary, hard-pressed soldiers and camp followers who found themselves in a world they had scarcely imagined. Attrition had been huge since the beginning of the campaign, not least because Hannibal had been forced to leave garrisons behind to secure his line of approach—and possible avenue of retreat.

As they entered the Po River valley in far northern Italy at the end of 218 BC, Hannibal's troops had more to celebrate than the orchards and balmy weather—this was *Gallia Cisalpina*, or "land of the Gauls this side of the Alps," as the Romans knew it. The region, centered on the valley, was more a part of Celtic Europe than it was of Roman Italy, settled by peoples who were perfectly capable of welcoming an anti-Roman presence and even joining it.

Hannibal came out of the Alps with some twenty thousand infantry and six thousand cavalry. Perhaps twenty of his elephants made it through. Needless to say, any Gallic warriors he could rally to his cause were very welcome indeed. After defeating Roman forces at Ticinus, he roused the local Gauls and recruited thousands of their warriors to his cause. He then exhibited his gift for fluid tactics at the battle of Trebia, where he wore down the Italian infantry before dealing it a series of blows on the flanks with his excellent cavalry. The following year, he crushed a Roman army in a perfectly planned ambush along the banks of Lake Trasimene, pouncing on the Roman legions as they marched in column and driving them against the lake in an improvised slaughter pen.

Rome was suddenly facing the very real prospect of catastrophe. By this time sixty thousand men, Romans and Italian allies, had been killed or wounded in battles against a foe who seemed impervious to everything sent against him. While Rome scrambled to produce a solution, Hannibal marched south in the hope of rousing local populations to his cause and severing Rome from its Italian confederates.

By the summer of 216 BC Rome had mustered and trained an army approaching ninety thousand strong—a clear indication of the tremendous manpower available to the state through alliances it had established in Italy. Hannibal had failed to break the ties that held this confederation together and which formed the sinews of the emerging Roman Empire. Simply put, Rome's allies refused to abandon it.

Perhaps they would with one last, spectacular Punic victory. To meet the leviathan bearing down on him, Hannibal had perhaps fifty-five thousand men in total. He had done nothing but win since descending on Italy like a plague, despite operating so far from Punic centers of power, but how long could he keep this up?

The two armies met in August near Cannae, toward the eastern coast of southern Italy. Dangerously outnumbered, Hannibal made a decision—we cannot know how deliberately or under what circumstances—that would establish him as one of history's singular military geniuses. Forming his army into a crescent with its center bulging toward the Romans, the Carthaginian general put his strongest units—the heavy infantry and veteran cavalry—on the wings, well away from the central melee that was sure to result.

The Romans came on, concentrating their attack in the center. When the Punic lines began to fall back, the Romans poured on the fury, believing they had crumpled the heart of Hannibal's army. But it was only a ruse. As the legions pressed forward, the Punic line gradually inverted from convex to concave, slowly accepting the Romans into a pocket. Hannibal's wings went forward to complete the embrace, their pincers closing with the speed of horse. Before they knew it, the Romans had advanced themselves to suicide.

To appreciate the horror of Cannae, one must understand the completeness of the Carthaginian encirclement. Hannibal had managed what every general longed for but almost never achieved: the absolute containment of an enemy army to be reduced at leisure. What followed was, even by the grisly standards of antiquity, sheer, methodical slaughter. The Punic forces now fought their way in toward the center, corralling the Italians into a killing field that soon put real physical limits on the Romans' ability to respond. Legionaries lost the space to wield their weapons properly, so closely were they pressed against their fellows. As the killing continued, ramparts of dead and wounded impeded the action, and eventually many Romans simply feigned death to escape what had become an act of mass murder. Still Hannibal's men hacked and stabbed their way in, their ranks eventually flagging more out of sheer exhaustion than anything else.

Polybius gives a figure of seventy thousand Roman dead. A more realistic estimate comes from Livy, who offers a figure of fifty thousand. Suffice it to say that the battlefield

*Following pages: Despite his elephants and larger army, Hannibal could not prevail against the Romans at the battle of Zama.*

was carpeted with Roman corpses. Rome had suffered a disaster equal to all its previous disasters combined—on one horrific afternoon.

## WHO DEFINES VICTORY?

At the hands of Hannibal, the young manhood of Rome and its confederates had suffered battlefield attrition all but unique in antiquity. The great Punic general was almost literally bleeding Rome white.

And yet, the Romans gave no sign of capitulation. This was unheard of in the ancient world. Indeed, Rome's refusal to treat with Hannibal is more important to understanding the course of the Second Punic War than the latter's amazing feats. What could it mean? How was it even possible?

To begin with, Rome, as it had shown in the First Punic War, maintained an absolute abhorrence for accommodation, but its disregard for the suffering it could incur by continuing to fight Carthage was the least of Hannibal's worries. Rome's greatest asset, in fact, was the solidarity it had created through treaties with its Italian neighbors—almost none of whom abandoned Rome in its greatest hour of need.

This was extraordinary. Far from being a brutal conqueror that simply snatched up its fellow Italian peoples and squeezed resources out of them with an iron fist, Rome had always doled out carrots and sticks with remarkable prudence. It now reaped the benefits: faced by the greatest threat to its existence since the Celtic invasion of 170 years earlier, it had little to fear in its own hinterland.

With no hope of winning the countryside to his side, Rome remained beyond Hannibal's reach. A prolonged siege of such a large city, which would have been difficult for a relatively small army such as his to begin with, was impossible in hostile territory.

Rome, rather than providing more armies for Hannibal to chew up, simply denied him the opportunity of victory while shadowing his movements. The Carthaginian general was forced to become a raider throughout Italy rather than a conqueror of Rome. Meanwhile, Roman armies invaded Spain to cut off Hannibal's supply bases. The man sent to do this, Publius Cornelius Scipio, proved the equal of Hannibal—and Scipio had a state behind him that would spare nothing in the pursuit of victory.

After securing the Spanish front for the Senate, Scipio spearheaded the campaign to flush Hannibal out of Italy by attacking Carthage itself. In October 202 BC the two generals clashed at the battle of Zama, Scipio dealing his legendary opposite a decisive defeat that left Carthage more vulnerable than it had ever been.

For a second time, Carthage had been crushed by Rome. And this time it was the end of its empire forever.

## TARGETED BY A TITAN

The treaty of 201 BC that ended the Second Punic War was harsh on Carthage, to put it mildly. Carthage was forbidden from waging war outside Africa—even warlike activity inside Africa had to be approved first by Rome, which now absorbed Carthage into its collection of subject "friends." Scipio ordered the proud vessels of the Punic navy towed out to sea and burned for all to witness. Henceforward, Carthage would be restricted to ten measly triremes. It would also be slammed with a massive indemnity of ten thousand talents of silver—a titanic fortune—to be paid over the next fifty years.

The treaty was more than just humiliating. It was the end of the Punic Empire. Spain was joined to Rome as the Mediterranean islands had been, to be administered as a pair of provinces. Carthage was left with its rich agricultural hinterland, but nothing else. The city now existed at the whim of Rome, for whom it would provide grain, markets, and annual tribute. Though the city could govern its own affairs as it always had, it was a defeated state without the power to decide its own fate.

When the last indemnity payment was made in 151 BC, unburdening Carthage of its greatest financial liability, there were already voices in Rome—especially Cato's—advocating an arrangement with Carthage that was a bit more ... *final*.

The Numidians, hostile neighbors of Carthage, offered an excuse to act. As Numidian attacks on the outskirts of Carthaginian territory increased, Punic leaders, their actions carefully circumscribed by the treaty of 201 BC, appealed to Rome for intervention. But while Rome sent delegations, they proved futile. Numidian attacks continued, and Rome eventually stopped listening to Punic appeals altogether. Carthage, frustrated and increasingly defiant in its economic renaissance, raised an army of its own and, without Roman permission, sent it out to do battle with the Numidians.

Incredibly, this perfectly pardonable act of self-defense was the only reason needed by the Roman war party to jump into action. By the spring of 149 BC a large, double-consular army had been shipped from Sicily to Utica, a Punic city just northwest of Carthage that had sided with the Romans in the interest of self-preservation.

What occurred next stands out as one of the more execrable acts in Roman history. The consuls sent word to Carthage that it was to disarm or face a siege. Now in a truly desperate state of affairs, with many of its African cities abandoning it in the face of Roman might, Carthage complied, sending caravans of weaponry and equipment—swords, spears, catapults, missiles—into Utica to be tallied and coopted by the legions there. The Romans now dropped their bomb: the Carthaginians were ordered to abandon their city and move whither they wished to establish a new community, as long as it was several miles from the sea. Carthage itself was to be destroyed.

The Romans cannot have been so naive as to think that compliance with this demand was an option for the Carthaginians, who were being ordered—rashly and in the wake of a treacherous act—to abandon their temples, tombs, and history. Having been divided over whether to resist the Roman invaders, the incredulous population of Carthage now rallied as one, mortified at the naked temerity of Rome's scam to disarm them. There would be no surrender.

## ANNIHILATION

Carthage was undoubtedly one of the best fortified cities on the planet. And though they had been largely disarmed by Roman duplicity, its citizens underwent a heroic militarization. Smiths toiled day and night, women offered their hair as ropes for the siege engines, slaves were freed and just as quickly armed, and everyone prepared to defend their city to the very last.

In the end, that is essentially what they did. It took the consular army some three years to breach the defenses of Carthage. What ensued, from the fighting around the harbors to the storming of the Byrsa, the fortified hill at the center of Carthage, was a tableau of gore and animal fury: street fighting at close quarters, resistance from rooftops and upper story windows, systematic demolition of housing blocks, the accretion of stone and flesh into ghastly heaps, an endless cycle of atrocities, and pyres of people and property coughing smoke into a blackened sky. Consul Scipio Aemilianus is said to have wept at the sight of the great city's devastation.

Soon Carthage was no more. The fires burned for ten days, and fifty thousand unfortunate survivors were sold into slavery. Rome had scratched its Punic itch for the last time.

*The Mausoleum of Bes at Sabratha from the Carthaginian period, shows the influence of Hellenistic architectural traditions.*

If a case can be made for geopolitical hard luck cases, Carthage would be at the top of the list. Like Achaemenid Persia before its evisceration by Alexander, Carthage was a well-ordered, vital empire that had the tremendous misfortune of having a tougher competitor as a neighbor. Rome's qualifications as an imperial power were unmatched: the sturdy structure of treaties that at once supported its manpower base and secured the friendship of Italian allies; the socio-political milieu of conservative pragmatism that rewarded piety as much as it fostered new ideas; the abundant resources of a large land power that bordered the sea; and the penchant for seeing conflicts through to their ultimate conclusion, rather than fighting only as long as was necessary to assume a fleeting place of dominance, as was so common in the Mediterranean world.

Rome, with its institutionalization of violence against foreigners as a principal means of political advancement, felt the urge to conquer more than any other state in antiquity. Roman magistrates, particularly consuls, were raised with a hunger for glory overseas bought at the expense of enemy lives. In fact, Roman arms, which would one day achieve an unparalleled level of deadly efficiency and organization, were no better at the time of the Punic Wars than those of Carthage. The difference was acceptance of change—Rome embraced every opportunity to grow and learn, while Carthage, confident in the longevity of its success, merely found ways to work within the systems it had: traditional Phoenician institutions that ensured stability and garnered wealth but that could not spawn an imperial machine aggressive enough to counter Rome's.

The result was all too predictable. Hannibal may have been a genius, but all he could do was delay the inevitable. Rome came to look upon Carthage as the punching bag with which it could hone its skills for the takeover of the ancient world. By 146 BC Rome was ready. And Carthage had been punched into oblivion.

CHAPTER ELEVEN

# THE SELEUCIDS

## THE LIMITS OF HELLENISM

ON a fine spring day in 301 BC, the remaining heirs of Alexander the Great met in Anatolia to decide the fate of the known world. It was not to be a polite discussion. At an ancient crossroads near the settlement of Ipsus, in Phrygia, two armies drew up in formation opposite each other on a broad plain ideal for the deployment of cavalry and elephants, which both sides possessed in abundance. Between them, these two mighty hosts represented, in person and by proxy, a who's who of the Hellenistic world—the successors, or *diadochi*, of Alexander's outsized ambition and, at least to themselves, the caretakers of his vision. And what a bunch they were.

On one side stood Antigonus I Monophthalmus, "Antigonus the One-Eyed." An obese octogenarian, his sorry physical condition belied the quick-thinking, tough tactician. He had been leading soldiers in battle for over sixty years, for most of them with only one eye—the consequence of an injury sustained while campaigning with Alexander's father, Philip. (Antigonus once executed a soldier for calling him "Cyclops.") Unlike his antagonists, Antigonus still believed in an empire that could be ruled by a single master in the tradition of Alexander. Not for the first time, he and his son Demetrius aimed to expand his realm in Anatolia and Syria at the expense of every other Hellenistic ruler in his way—two of whom faced him on the battlefield that day.

One of these, Lysimachus, was a mirror image of old One-Eye. A cavalry commander who had become one of Alexander's seven esteemed "bodyguards," he was as youthful and cautious as Antigonus was aged and bold. Governor of Thrace, Lysimachus was keen on acquiring whatever territory he could add to his modest realm. Power would ultimately make him dangerously paranoid: in old age he would murder his own son on trumped-up charges of treason.

Then there was Seleucus Nicator. Widely regarded as one of Alexander's finest generals, he had fought with the great Macedonian king, who was barely his senior, all the way to the Indus. With the vast majority of Alexander's Asian conquests under his administration, Seleucus had plenty of men and resources to draw on, and had thrown his lot in with the others to topple Antigonus and Demetrius.

Seleucus was ambitious, shrewd, and calculating. Perdiccas, regent of the unstable Macedonian Empire after Alexander's death, had named him second-in-command—a choice that would prove fateful. Not long after Perdiccas invaded Egypt in 321 BC to bring it back under Macedonian control, his troops mutinied. To restore order in the army, Seleucus and his fellow generals promptly assassinated Perdiccas. Problem solved. The

*Previous pages: Hellenic order Corinthian capital and fluted column c. 320 BC.*

governorship of Babylonia, which had been Perdiccas's, fell to Seleucus as his share of the spoils.

Conspicuous by their absence at Ipsus were the two remaining Hellenistic heavyweights. Cassander, whose holdings in Greece and Macedon were still in chaos from fighting Demetrius, had sent contingents into Anatolia to help Lysimachus and Seleucus without showing up for the fracas himself. And Ptolemy, concerned above all things with holding onto his Egyptian-based empire, contented himself with gnawing away at Antigonus's Levantine possessions while the rest of the *diadochi* slugged it out in Phrygia.

And slug it out they definitely did.

## THE CLASH OF STEEL, THE CLAMOR OF ELEPHANTS

Having broken off from fighting Cassander the previous year, Demetrius had hastened up the Ionian coast and into the Anatolian interior to meet up with his father. The combined army they were able to field was all the evidence anyone needed to see why their dream of reuniting Alexander's empire under Antigonid rule could very well come true.

It was a classic Hellenistic force based on the phalanx, whose serried ranks of forty-five thousand pike-wielding infantrymen formed the center of the line, supported by another twenty-five thousand light infantry. Before the phalanx stood a screen of seventy-five war elephants—probably so-called "forest elephants" procured from Africa, they would have been a bit smaller than the larger variety of the savannah. Antigonus put his cavalry, which numbered around fifteen thousand in total, on the wings, with Demetrius in command of the right. Significantly, these were the hard-charging heavy horsemen perfected by Philip of Macedon that had been the most feared element of Alexander's formidable Asian juggernaut.

The army on the other side of the battlefield had precious few of these heavy horsemen. Their fifteen thousand cavalrymen were of the lighter Persian type, and their speed and accuracy with the bow were no match for heavier cavalry should it come to a melee. They also had fewer infantrymen—perhaps sixty thousand or so, also formed up into a phalanx.

*Above: Seleucus I Nicator, Macedonian general and founder of the Seleucid dynasty, who established the greatest empire of the Hellenistic world.*

What Lysimachus and Seleucus *did* have were elephants—lots of them. Moreover, they were slightly heavier than those from the African forests. These were the elephants given to Seleucus by the Indian warlord Candragupta Maurya several years before as part of a peace agreement. Around four hundred strong at Ipsus, they were well trained and accustomed to battle. Little wonder Lysimachus was so glad to learn of Seleucus's march into Anatolia to join him.

Seleucus seems to have been hesitant to part with his elephants and kept the majority of them under his command toward the rear of the allied army. The rest, perhaps a hundred strong, made a screen before the allied phalanx, with the Persian cavalry on the wings. Lysimachus commanded near the center of the front line.

Demetrius commenced hostilities by launching his heavy cavalry into the enemy horse opposite him, effortlessly driving them from the field. Indeed, so hard was the chase that he disappeared from the battlefield, his lithe Persian quarry galloping hard before him while loosing a desultory response of missiles.

Seleucus then deployed the force of three hundred elephants by wheeling them about to face the rear, thereby protecting his allied phalanx against the possibility of Demetrius's return and an attack from the rear. This left Lysimachus free to engage his one hundred elephants with those of Antigonus, creating a cacophonous maelstrom at the center of the battlefield, which no doubt quickly disappeared within a storm of dust.

While the allied cavalry rained arrows down on the Antigonid phalanx, Lysimachus got the better of his old enemy in the pachydermatous duel, gradually driving Antigonus and his increasingly panicky elephants back onto his own line. Then up came the allied phalanx, slowly striding forward with their *sarissai* probing, adding immense pressure on the Antigonid ranks. And still Demetrius was nowhere in sight, having ridden off on a wild goose chase.

Antigonus, eighty-one years old and aging more quickly by the minute, recalled the promise he had made to himself earlier that day: he would not leave this field in defeat. With the shrill screams of wounded elephants crashing on his ears and the heartbreaking sight of his enemies' pikemen coming on like a moving forest, he looked to the horizon for signs of his son. But deliverance never came. Antigonus went down in the carnage, an implacable old scrapper to the last. Receiving word of the disaster, Demetrius did not return to the battle but led a group of survivors back to friendly territory.

With Antigonus dead and his son in retreat, the remaining *diadochi* breathed a sigh of relief. Ptolemy, Lysimachus, Cassander, Seleucus—these were the four survivors of a power struggle that had commenced with the death of Alexander in 323 BC and had already seen the downfall of many great men. What set these four apart from all those who were no longer in the race was a grudging willingness to compromise—an appreciation of the fact that any resurrection of Alexander's empire had died with Antigonus, and that each of them, in his own sphere, could live like a king if only he stopped thinking of defeating all the others.

This is something of an oversimplification, of course. Macedonian dynasts were not in the habit of giving up on having it all, especially those who had been schooled in imperial warfare by Alexander himself. But the pious reverence of Alexander's memory also propagated the notion that he was unique—giving a free pass, as it were, to his successors to take over his legacy without accomplishing as much. Perhaps Antigonus had been too brash? Whatever the truth, he had dared to become as powerful as the rest of them combined and, now that he was gone, his vanquishing offered a lesson that was not soon forgotten—better to rule as a king in Alexandria, or Babylon or Ephesus, than to rule as an emperor in the grave.

The *diadochi* would continue to battle, but in this new eastern Mediterranean milieu where Greek was the language of the elite and ancient imperial institutions lived alongside new modes of kingship, it was Seleucus—the man smart enough to bring elephants to a horse fight—who would build the greatest empire of the Hellenistic world.

## THE LAST OF THE OLD BREED

Seleucus's career as an empire builder had begun dubiously. Having taken part in the infamous murder of Perdiccas, the young general assumed Perdiccas's place as satrap of Babylonia. But he had barely begun to warm to the job when Antigonus kicked him out in 316 BC during the latter's initial war of attempted unification.

Taking refuge in Ptolemy's court, Seleucus satisfied himself with a naval command and raised havoc along the coastline of Antigonus's vast empire. He captured Cyprus, went inland to join up with Ptolemy and, with his help, defeated Demetrius in 312 BC, clearing the way for a triumphant return to Babylon.

It was the beginning of a slew of energetic conquests that would leave Seleucus master of the majority of Alexander's empire. Secure in Babylonia while Antigonus and his son were busy in the west, Seleucus headed east with a powerful army, snatching Media, Susiana, and Persia from governors loyal to Antigonus.

By 302 BC he had fought his way to the Jaxartes River in modern-day Kazakhstan, battled the Mauryans along the Indus, proclaimed himself *basileus*, or "king," in his own right, and founded a new capital at Seleucia on the Tigris. Essentially walking in Alexander's footsteps, Seleucus had toppled those who were disloyal to him or who had broken away from the Macedonian yoke, defining an empire of his own based on the old campaigns of Alexander.

After playing his crucial role in the defeat of Antigonus in 301 BC, Seleucus was awarded further gains in the agreement between the victors that followed. This agreement, along with further campaigns, gave him control by 300 BC of Mesopotamia, Syria, southern Cappadocia, and Armenia.

Now possessed of a gigantic empire as well as a route to the Mediterranean via Syria, Seleucus founded a new city, Antioch, on the Orontes River near the sea. Named for his father, this was to be his new capital. Seleucia became the capital of the eastern satrapies, the security of which Seleucus entrusted to his son Antiochus in 293 BC.

Anatolia now beckoned, and here he was aided by the tragic family drama of his neighbor Lysimachus. Goaded by his scheming wife, Lysimachus had ordered his eldest son by a previous marriage to be executed, ostensibly on account of the victim's disloyalty. Virtually the entire Hellenistic world recoiled in disgust. When Lysimachus's daughter-in-law, Lysandra, now a widow, showed up at the court of Seleucus, he embraced his own indignation as a *casus belli*—Lysandra's late husband would be avenged.

In 282 BC Seleucus led his army north and, at the battle of Corupedium in Lydia, defeated Lysimachus decisively. Lysimachus did not survive the clash and was allegedly killed by Seleucus himself in personal combat (which must have been a memorable and impressive sight, as both men were in their seventies by now). As he stood over the body of his onetime ally, Seleucus no doubt realized that he was the last of Alexander's generals left standing. Ptolemy had died in old age several years before, and Cassander had died in 297 BC from a debilitating sickness.

Energetically exerting control over his vanquished foe's territories, Seleucus soon found himself sovereign ruler of a territory stretching from Ionia to India. If anyone could lay claim to being the heir of Alexander, it was he.

## TOOLS OF CONTROL

In 285 BC, Seleucus dispatched a trusted general named Patrocles to the far northeast of the empire. Far from being warlike, this mission involved exploration and trade. Patrocles was charged with charting the boundaries of the Caspian Sea and finding its relation, if any, with the River Oxus. Seleucus hoped to uncover a means of transporting

*[illegible] Silver tetradrachm of Lysimachus, governor of Thrace, bearing the image of Alexander. Alexander's successors used his image to establish their legitimacy.*

goods more efficiently through central Asia—a new water route to exploit the trade with Mauryan India and the lands to its north.

Patrocles never found a connection between the Caspian and the Oxus, which empties into the Aral Sea, but his expedition and the impetus behind it show the enormous size of the new empire created by Seleucus—and the emperor's determination to understand its frontiers, master its commercial potential, and rule it effectively.

The managerial innovations of Seleucus began with his own family. By giving his son Antiochus control over the eastern satrapies, the emperor charted a middle course between co-monarchy and ensuring succession. Antiochus was less than an equal and more than an underling. Given the enormous distances in the empire, Seleucus wanted somebody on hand in the East who could make decisions not just on the emperor's behalf, but with the vested authority of the emperor himself—someone who could act at once as an appendage of the court and as an informed local. That this arrangement also gave Antiochus on-the-job training was all the better, for as everybody knew, he was going to be emperor himself one day. This policy was to be standard for most of the Seleucid emperors.

Such overt pragmatism had other manifestations. Seleucid rule came on the heels of centuries of imperial organization by other cultures, much of which was coopted by Seleucus and his successors where appropriate. Especially in the east, where distances militated against constant attention, established elites remained in place if they were able to maintain control and prove loyalty. These may have been families that went back to the days of the Achaemenids. Indeed, Alexander himself had relied on the Achaemenid system of satrapies to oversee his vast conquests, and the Seleucids followed suit, though they further subdivided the vast majority of provinces. Eventually, every province had at the very top a handpicked satrap—usually a friend of the emperor—who answered directly to the court.

Perhaps the most important means of establishing authority throughout the vast Seleucid empire was cultural. Alexander's invasion of the Persian Empire had commenced a movement of people and ideas from west to east that Seleucus continued. A Macedonian by birth and inclination, with the predilection for Greek civilization that characterized all Hellenistic leaders, he vigorously set about establishing colonies of Greek settlers in the lands he had taken charge of. In combination with those previously established by Alexander, these Hellenistic communities helped to establish a network of Western institutions throughout the empire and offered the court a conduit to interaction on the local level. Enculturation worked both ways, of course—Greeks in Bactria or Media or Syria took on local customs to varying degrees even as they changed the complexion of regional culture, but this worked to the Seleucid court's advantage, establishing an avenue of approach to subject peoples that worked in conjunction with the official satrapy bureaucracy.

Nevertheless, to rule as Greeks in an immense sea of non-Greeks would have been foolish, if not impossible, and so the Seleucids became both. With their own administration forming merely the newest of a series of ethnic layers that went back centuries, Seleucus and his successors were happy to embrace the cults, gods, and practices of the venerable states that came before them. They took on the aspect of local deities, assumed the mantle of Asian forms of kingship quite sincerely, and placated regional notions of leadership through rituals that no Greek of Classical antiquity would have tolerated. That was the spirit of Hellenisticism—the amalgamation of West and East that forged a dynamic new era. And the Seleucid enterprise was its clearest manifestation.

## POLICING A ROUGH NEIGHBORHOOD

In 275 BC, Antiochus I, son and heir to the late Seleucus, clashed with a confederation of Galatian Celts in Anatolia. Migrating from Europe via the Balkan Peninsula, these Celtic tribes had left a path of chaos in their wake as they extorted blood money from hapless dynasts and plundered the countryside of those who did not pay up. They were a fierce people with a long and proud warrior tradition, and they soon posed a real threat to the security of the Seleucid frontier in Anatolia.

Antiochus led an army out to deal with them and, in a fight known as the "battle of the elephants," loosed his fierce pachyderms on the Celts, who had never faced such beasts before and broke in a rout. To the people of the Seleucid Empire, the event was cause for celebration. Antiochus was dubbed *Soter,* or "savior."

This brief and successful campaign was one of the highlights of Antiochus's reign. Having brought the Celts to heel, he soon found them eager to serve with him as hearty mercenaries. And the emperor had plenty of work for them.

It was fortunate that Seleucus had given his son so much experience as regent, because Antiochus (r. 281–261 BC) had his hands full from the start of his reign. There were revolts in Armenia and Cappadocia, open warfare with Ptolemy II in Syria, and clashes with the breakaway province of Pergamum. All of which proved that the Seleucids had assumed power not only over a huge empire, but an empire spanning the cradle of civilization itself—the ancient, highly urbanized arena of dynastic ambitions. At no point in the history of this empire would it be free of dire threats within and without its borders.

To cope forcefully with these threats, the Seleucids could count on one of the most extraordinary military machines of the ancient world. With such a huge population under its control, the Seleucid Empire almost never had manpower issues. The core of its military forces was the Macedonian phalanx and heavy cavalry inherited from Philip and Alexander—the same units deployed by other Hellenistic states such as Ptolemaic Egypt. Seleucid commanders trained their non-Greek subjects in the skills of Macedonian warfare, using their abundant numbers to round out armies whose size would have made Alexander jealous. These units were supported not only by the elephant corps, but also by traditional Asian fighters such as the fast-riding horse archers of Persia and the light infantry that had filled out Achaemenid armies.

Such a formidable arsenal could only do so much, however, especially when the empire's enemies could draw on the same types of troops. Moreover, the Seleucids consistently had too many fires to put out all at once.

By the reign of Antiochus III (r. 223–187 BC), sixth king of the Seleucid dynasty, the empire was utterly besieged by crises. A tireless campaigner, this Antiochus battled Ptolemaic Egypt to a draw in the Levant, subdued a rebellion in Anatolia, forced the submission of Armenia, drove back an attack by Parthian nomads and forced them to sue for peace, invaded and defeated the rebellious Greco-Bactrian kingdom, reestablished friendly relations with Mauryan India (and acquired more elephants), and pushed the Ptolemies out of Judea. For winning back the rebellious satrapies of the East he would be dubbed "Great." But Antiochus's achievements are as illustrative of Seleucid woes as they are impressive. Clearly the empire was fighting for its life by the beginning of the second century BC, and only a king as tenacious, decisive, and militarily gifted as Antiochus III was capable of holding it together.

## BETWEEN A ROMAN ROCK AND A PARTHIAN HARD PLACE

Needless to say, few monarchs were as extraordinary as Antiochus the Great. But just as important in the tale of Seleucid decline, the Seleucid Empire ultimately found itself facing two formidable military powers at the very same time—and on opposite borders.

Antiochus the Great chose to build upon his successes in Anatolia by invading Greece. History has been unkind to him for even attempting this, as it required naval supremacy (which he never possessed, having an overwhelmingly land-oriented empire). There he found much more than he bargained for when, in 191 BC, he came up against legions of the Roman Republic. Defeated at the battle of Thermopylae, Antiochus retreated to Anatolia and prepared for a rematch. He did not have long to wait.

In Rome the Seleucid state had acquired a formidable opponent. Having all but destroyed the Carthaginian Empire a decade earlier, the Romans had snatched up an empire of their own. In addition, the greatest desire of their annually elected consuls

*Heliodorus is expelled from the temple in Jerusalem. He had been sent to seize the temple treasure by Seleucus IV, who was in constant need of money to buy off the Romans.*

## THE GYMNASIUM

Like any blending of cultures, Hellenization was a complex phenomenon that progressed at different rates and with widely varying results throughout the ancient world. In most cases, it involved cultures living side by side rather than being amalgamated into a single entity: Greek language, laws, and institutions remained largely unaffected by indigenous elements, forming a culture of the elite to which non-Greeks could aspire as long as they were willing to jettison their native customs.

One fundamental of Greek culture that represented a potentially contentious point of contact with Asian populations was the gymnasium. No self-respecting Greek city or colony was without one. Manifesting the Hellenistic reverence for competitive sport, the gymnasium was a large complex in which Greek men gathered to exercise, compete (strictly one on one—there were no team sports), and discuss the great issues of the day. It was where young men acquired an education and where older men passed on the wisdom of their years, all in an atmosphere of immodest physicality.

Clothes had no place in the gymnasium—Greeks experienced no shame of their bodies, and exercised in the nude. In contrast, Asian cultures found public nudity shameful and scandalous. This stark difference of opinion might have remained little more than a curiosity were it not for the fact that the gymnasium was so central to the Greek culture that it spread from the Nile Valley to the mountains of Sogdiana. One of the factors that inspired rebellion in Judea during the reign of Antiochus IV, for instance, was the outrage felt by many pious Jews at the sight of their fellows exercising naked in the gymnasium—a custom taken on by Hellenizing Jews as part of an effort to join the ruling establishment.

was to win military glory before their one-year terms was up. In this way the Roman enterprise grew at an alarming rate, sustained by a military ethos that emphasized flexible, highly trained infantry formations, methodical siege engineering, and the prosecution of wars at all cost until peace terms could be enforced to Roman advantage.

With a huge navy, the Romans easily mastered the Aegean, enabling them to cross into Anatolia. Here they found the Seleucids' Achilles' heel, for Antiochus was ruling over a diverse patchwork of ancient states and peoples that were more than willing to side with a Roman invader who not only promised to free them, but also to engage them as clients and "friends" rather than subjects. Led by the consul Lucius Cornelius Scipio and his brother, the very Scipio Africanus who had defeated Carthage, the Roman army soon swelled with soldiers from the rebellious state of Pergamum.

Around fifty thousand strong, the Roman's clashed in 190 BC with the Seleucids at Magnesia ad Sipylum in Lydia. Antiochus had his entire army with him, including twenty-six thousand phalangites, eight thousand heavy cavalry of various sorts, fifty-four elephants, and an elite cadre of Arab archers on camelback. Including the numerous light infantry units and cavalry archers, his forces outnumbered the Romans and their allies by some twenty thousand.

It was not enough. The Roman legions, bringing Antiochus to battle on ground of their choosing, proved more flexible than the ponderous Seleucid phalanxes and won the day. It was a disaster for Antiochus: not only was he forced by the ensuing treaty to consider the Taurus Range the new boundary of his empire and to pay an outrageous indemnity, but the setback also sent throughout Asia a signal of vulnerability that Seleucid subjects quickly picked up on. Revolts spread throughout the East.

From this point onward, the Seleucid Empire was on the defensive virtually everywhere. Antiochus's heir, Seleucus IV (r. 187–175 BC), spent much of his reign finding ways to pay the awful Roman indemnity and was ultimately assassinated by his own minister. He was succeeded by his brother, Antiochus IV.

Though known to history as "Epiphanes," or "God Manifest," Antiochus IV suffered one of the singular humiliations of antiquity—a loss of face that perfectly encapsulated the inexorable decline in which the Seleucid state now found itself. In 168 BC Antiochus invaded Egypt for the second time in his reign, initiating the latest in a long line of border wars between the two Hellenistic kingdoms. The Seleucid armies got the better of their opponents and drove deep into Egypt. Then, outside Alexandria, the most famous city founded by Alexander the Great, the Seleucid advance was stopped—by a single aged man.

Gaius Popilius Laenas, a Roman senator, had made the treacherous journey from Italy on behalf of the relationship that bound his republic to Ptolemaic Egypt. Rome's primary breadbasket, Egypt had been made a "Friend of Rome" by treaty. The Seleucid invasion therefore troubled the Roman Senate very deeply.

Hence the sage ambassador, who confronted Antiochus and his army as it marched through northern Egypt. The Seleucid emperor, glittering in battle array and backed by his phalanxes, stepped forward to greet the old man, only to be rebuffed by a cold stare. The senator, accompanied only by his attendants, demanded that Antiochus turn back and go home, in response to which the emperor laughed incredulously. Popilius then stepped forward and drew a circle in the sand around Antiochus with his staff. "If you do not comply with my demand before stepping out of this circle," declared the senator gravely, "consider yourself at war with Rome."

Antiochus turned around and went home.

If fear of Roman legions had undermined all Seleucid credibility in the West, things in the East were little better. Indeed, they were much worse. The Parthians, nomadic horsemen from the steppes east of the Caspian, became the bane of Seleucid dreams. Settled in Parthia, a satrapy over which the Seleucids often lost control, they were as adept at swallowing up breakaway provinces as the Seleucids of this period were at losing them. The two states became inversely related—Seleucid loss always equaled Parthian gain. By 139 BC, when Demetrius II suffered defeat and capture at Parthian hands, the entire Iranian plateau had to be written off by the Seleucids, making contact with the territories further east increasingly unrealistic.

Seleucid decline had become inexorable.

## IMPLOSION

In making peace with the Romans after the disastrous battle of Magnesia in 190 BC, Antiochus the Great lost his younger son as a hostage to Rome. The ultimate result of this, as was Rome's intention, was to divide the Seleucid dynasty into those in the empire and those with Roman backing. The two branches of the family—one now a tool of the Roman Senate—continued to battle over control of the throne.

This Roman manipulation would have been debilitating enough on its own, but the Seleucids were also facing a war of survival against the Parthians as well as Ptolemaic aggression. The combination created a drawn-out disaster. The Ptolemies had made the smart choice in siding with Rome, rising star of the Mediterranean. The Seleucids, by contrast, now found themselves besieged on all sides, and their institutions—which relied on Greek enculturation throughout a vast and profoundly heterogeneous realm—proved inadequate.

By the beginning of the first century BC the once mighty Seleucid Empire had been reduced, through internecine conflict at the court level and humiliating defeats on the frontiers, to the territory of Syria. That it lasted after this had more to do with its role as a buffer between greater states in the region than any lasting ability to defend itself. The last of the Seleucid dynasts, Philip II, was little more than the ruler of a petty state.

In many ways, the Seleucid Empire was the realization of Alexander the Great's dream of creating a state that merged West and East. Through the Greek colonies they established from Syria to the Hindu Kush, the Seleucids worked to make this dream a practical reality—to build a vast empire in which Greek colonies acted as conduits of Western ideas while taking on local Asiatic customs. But like all imperial exercises of antiquity, this vision was groundless without the force to back it up, and the Seleucids were not able to cope adequately with the titanic forces working against them from all directions. Hellenism worked marvelously as an expression of culture; it failed, but for a relatively brief time, as a modus operandi of empire.

CHAPTER TWELVE

# HAN

As it played host to the 2008 Summer Olympics, China presented the image of a vigorous titan with its eyes fixed on a bright future. The opening and closing ceremonies, thundering and grandiose, dazzled the world with performances of carefully choreographed synergy. This was a country with a message: Our nation may be immense, but it is unified and driven.

How much of that image was truth and how much propaganda? Unity is a relative and elusive concept, especially under a government that controls the dissemination of information. Nevertheless, China has been a cohesive nation-state for most of the past twenty-two centuries, offering one of the most durable examples of cultural continuity on earth.

It was not always so. In fact, while the city-states of Greece were experiencing their Classical zenith during the fifth and fourth centuries BC, the peoples of China were in a similar situation. In the heartland of what we now understand as Chinese territory sat a collection of kingdoms, each with its own court, bureaucracy, and military. They were combative and fiercely jealous of each other's territory, often engaging in warfare over borders that became increasingly fortified. And yet they were all heirs to a sophisticated and dynamic culture that grounded their religion, enriched their philosophy, defined their magnificent art, and breathed fire into the struggles that kept them divided. Overcoming such a potently contentious status quo to achieve the dream of unity would not be easy.

By the end of the third century BC, however, unity under a single dynasty had been achieved. Certainly no ordinary power could hold such a vast and unruly collection of peoples together, and the empire that resulted—China's first—was extraordinary in every way. Created by the Qin and overtaken by the Han, this empire would achieve greatness equal to that of its western contemporary, Rome.

And, like the Roman Empire, the Han Empire would collapse not because of a single disaster or invasion, but because of a confluence of factors whose combined impact was equal to the task of bringing down a complex and mighty state.

## BEGINNINGS

The concept of empire runs deep in Chinese history, though it remained more of a goal than a reality for most of antiquity. Between the third millennium and the third century BC, three great dynasties emerged in succession to assume varying degrees of suzerainty over the region known as China Proper, in the northeast of the modern-day country.

*Previous pages: Han dynasty watchtower.*

The first of these, the Xia, has appeared only vaguely in the archaeological evidence, and remains steeped in myth. Then, by around 1600 BC, the Shang rose to prominence, where they would stay for the next five hundred years. Originally believed to be as mythical as the Xia, the Shang came to light thanks to modern Chinese apothecaries, whose market for "dragon bones" gradually brought to light a vast collection of ancient bones with mysterious inscriptions. These were ultimately connected to a site called Anyang, in modern Henan province, one of many locations that would eventually produce an abundance of Shang artifacts.

Centered on the Yellow River valley, which would remain the very heart of Chinese civilization into the modern era, the Shang rose to prominence as leaders steeped in the rituals of ancestor worship. Bones inscribed with the earliest Chinese script were used by Shang leaders in divination to communicate with the dead—the very bones that, according to nineteenth-century Chinese pharmacists, possessed healing powers. Combining the moral authority of a priestly class with the administrative power of local governors, the Shang elite presided over a coalition of walled towns. Their king, however, had no eunuchs or bureaucrats to call on, nor borders as such to defend: the Shang state resembled a league of subject villages, many of which bordered lands and settlements that had yet to fall under the Shang's sway. With a modest court whose authority stretched about as far as the king's arm, expansion proceeded slowly.

The Zhou, who conquered the Shang late in the eleventh century BC, expanded on this simple formula with feudalism, granting conquered lands to loyal allies and creating an expansionist kingdom that ensured loyalty in subject populations. Of course, this went smoothly only as long as the Zhou had lands to subdue and grant—a contingency that eventually proved unreliable, not least because the parochial Zhou court had few sophisticated administrative tools for expansion on a truly grand scale. By the eighth century BC, the Zhou had become figureheads in a land of entrenched vassal states whose loyalties were localized.

These vassal kingdoms became the eponymous "Warring States" of the period that ensued. One of the most tumultuous, fertile, and fascinating periods in Asian history,

*Above: A bronze ritual vessel dating from the Shang or Zhou period.*

the era of the Warring States laid the bedrock for much of the majestic civilization that followed even as it witnessed the constant struggle of competing kingdoms locked in a cycle of a paranoia, espionage, and military adventurism. The states all pretended to pay homage to the diminished Zhou court while occasionally mustering armies to thwart nomadic barbarians on the northern and western frontiers. But their primary business involved jockeying for supremacy over each other, engaging in regular bouts of raiding and all-out war to steal each other's territory and keep opponents off balance. Gradually, as the smaller states fell to more powerful aggressors, seven contenders emerged: Han, Qin, Qi, Wei, Chu, Zhao, and Yan. Separated by defensive walls, garrisoned by huge infantry armies, they glowered at each other in perpetual animosity.

By the end of the third century BC only one would remain.

## DEFYING THE ODDS

No area of civilized endeavor experienced so much innovation during these centuries as the art of war. Armed with crossbows and iron weapons, the Warring States fought each other with increasing efficiency and destruction, creating more efficient bureaucracies and military establishments. Sun Tzu's military classic, *The Art of War*, appeared during these years, espousing an economy of engagement that stressed subterfuge and misinformation as well as tactical dexterity to overcome adversaries.

In such an atmosphere of relentless military competition, some states evolved faster than others, but none evolved as quickly as the Qin.

Based to the west of the Yellow River valley, the state of Qin was relatively small but it embraced the cutting edge developments of the era with a severity that set it apart from its six competitors. Shang Yang, influential minister to Qin rulers through the middle of the fourth century BC, became the godfather of a barracks-state the likes of which the Yellow River civilization had never seen. Under his guidance and that of his successors, Qin leaders turned their mountainous realm into a factory for the production of conquering soldiers.

Much of this warlike metamorphosis rested on a rejection of the past. Unlike the Confucian days of yore, with their emphasis on filial piety, the Qin hammered through a legalist policy based on loyalty to the state. Confucius (551–479 BC) had preached a doctrine of morality founded upon traditional ties of blood and reverence for ancestors. But to the cynical policy makers of the Warring States, only obedience to the ruler would do, compelling them to quash the growing threads of Confucianism that were winding their way through society. The result was a new order that the Spartans, half a world away but just as exclusively patriotic, would have appreciated.

Qin administration was canny in its appreciation of the links between land, peasants, and victory. Victory was possible only through the creation of infantry armies, for which vast numbers of peasants were required—and the recruiting of peasants was a great deal easier when the state promised land in return for loyal service. By dividing the kingdom into a vast grid and distributing land directly to smallholders, the Qin court undercut the authority of local lords and ensured the maximum number of males for recruitment—because the burden of military service fell on the household, a greater number of individual farmers made for a larger pool for conscription. In time all that mattered was dedication to the king and performance in battle, both of which were rewarded with more land and influence. Confucian ideals, which tended to favor the cultivation of a learned class of intellectuals, counted for little. This was a martial order, pure and simple.

Other reforms were just as effective. To maximize the realm's arable land, irrigation systems were designed and built, scoring the countryside. The court formed units of elite fighters answerable directly to the king. Power, increasingly concentrated in the ruler alone, was a palpable link between the court and the peasants in the countryside, all of whom were formally registered with local units for ease of mustering and deployment.

The effect of these programs was astonishing. By 221 BC, the Qin had conquered every other Warring State and made them subject realms in the first large, contiguous empire of China. This was a true watershed in history (indeed, our word "China" is derived from "Qin"). Qin Shi Huangdi, victorious ruler of Qin, now called himself emperor.

## CONQUEROR AND CONQUERED

Emperor Qin Shi Huangdi worked tirelessly to mold his vast realm into a streamlined state. Using the customs of Qin as a guide, he pushed through the standardization of everything from wagon axles to coinage. Road construction and weights and measures were all overhauled to adhere to new imperial guidelines in an effort to unify the various lands and their people. The emperor even had a new and simplified script created in order to lessen the confusion created by the empire's numerous dialects.

But as far-reaching and visionary as these steps were, they could not compensate for the emperor's greatest challenge: turning what had been a state built for war into a state built for government. Everything under the Qin had been carefully geared toward producing a lean, bellicose population that, in the words of Shang Yang, acted "like hungry wolves on seeing meat." So comprehensive and thorough were the Qin standards of militarization, in fact, that they denied the state the capacity to do much beyond vanquish foes and annex territory. Running a subject people was a ruthless enterprise

to the legalist Qin: keeping them on the march not only earned the state victories and fed its expansion, but also kept the peasantry from building up the sort of surplus that would invariably turn them into docile consumers or, even worse, *merchants*. Abundance was a scourge to be avoided.

It is only against this background that Qin Shi Huangdi's destructive policies on becoming China's first emperor can be understood. With no enemies at home, he turned his attention to the Xiongnu, a race of warrior nomads to the north who had amassed a vast empire of their own and who consistently made trouble on the frontier.

But this was hardly enough to absorb the attentions of an entire militarized empire, especially since these operations were intended to keep the Xiongnu at bay rather than conquer and absorb them.

Seeking to keep his subjects busy at any cost, the emperor fed his megalomania by giving them enormous building projects. They labored to build the Great Wall in the north against the Xiongnu, to construct roads and, eventually, to complete the emperor's tomb—a gargantuan pyramid concealing elaborately ornamented chambers and guarded by an army of terracotta warriors.

Such policies served to alienate the court from its people. Indeed, most Chinese, especially those in the east, considered the people of Qin simple barbarians. Now they were running the whole Chinese world. Qin Shi Huangdi's policies, for all their energy and merit, continued to treat the empire like an occupied territory, a stratified state with the Qin at the top and everyone else at the bottom. China was an armed camp, and those who might oppose the emperor in any way, particularly Confucians, were executed or buried alive, their books burned in great bonfires.

Qin Shi Huangdi amplified the scale of his empire's tragedy by seeking immortality, an obsession that prevented him from seriously preparing for a succession and also drove him to consume deadly amounts of mercury. When he died in 210 BC, his empire had just three years left before succumbing to a maelstrom of disaffected army commanders, desperate laborers, and regional aristocrats who saw their chance at throwing off the Qin yoke.

*Above: Terracotta archer, one of the army of life-like figures from the tomb of Qin Shi Huangdi, found near Xi'an in Shaanxi province.*

## NEW MANAGEMENT

Between 207 and 202 BC a civil war raged over control of the empire Qin Shi Huangdi had created. With Qin leadership in abeyance under ineffectual princes, two factions came to the fore, each led by a brilliant general of the Chu: Liu Bang and Xiang Yu.

One of the greatest, most legendary generals in all of Chinese history, Xiang Yu dominated the course of events until his wiser, more deliberate foe was able to defeat him with superior diplomacy and more thorough preparation. Liu Bang, a notorious ne'er-do-well of humble stock who had once lived the life of a brigand, managed finally to defeat Xiang Yu in 202 BC. According to legend, the great general committed suicide to escape the ignominy of defeat. Enemy soldiers, having surrounded him to watch the spectacle, fell on his corpse in a scuffle to claim it and the bounty it would bring from Liu Bang, tearing the body to bits. With his arch-enemy out of the picture, Liu Bang—now known as Emperor Han Gaozu—set about securing his vast prize. The Qin model of empire was the only one available to him; after all, a unified China was still less than two generations old. As a result, much of Han policy, particularly in the early years, was based on a continuation of Qin law and tradition.

But Han Gaozu was no Qin Shi Huangdi. A libertine who had spent most of his life acting like a thug and a whoremonger, Liu Bang achieved his position in life through his own toughness and shrewd tactical cunning. Military service in a time of national tumult had offered him a way up the imperial ladder. He was neither a traditionalist nor a merciless autocrat, and he was willing to think unconventionally to a degree that Shi Huangdi would have considered dangerous or even weak.

One of his first acts as emperor was to move his capital out of his own Chu power base to the Qin homeland. There, near the old emperor's capital of Xianyang (which had been burned and razed during the civil war), Han Gaozu built a new capital he called Chang'an. Ironically, despite the connection to Qin Shi Huangdi's notorious court, this move was a profound break with the past: unlike the Qin, the Han were severing their regional loyalties, associating themselves from this point on only with the empire. It was meant to allay fears throughout China that Gaozu would rule as a conqueror.

This association of the emperor with the whole empire instead of with just one state took other forms, as well. Gaozu, having risen to prominence in a civil war at the head of an organization of numerous allies, now found it prudent to reward his finest supporters, making them subject kings of his imperial court. This was an unavoidable expedient to assuage uneasy henchmen in a time of turmoil but it also emphasized the new emperor's willingness to reward prominent men from throughout the Chinese world, whatever their homeland.

## REVERSING THE PAST

Han Gaozu died in 195 BC, leaving behind him a secure dynasty and an empire that had changed only marginally from the one that had preceded it. His successors, however, would gradually take the Han model of rule further and further away from its Qin predecessor and, in doing so, would at once build a stronger empire and sow the seeds of their own demise.

At the heart of the Han policy was a shift away from reliance on the peasantry as the backbone of the army. With one eye on the cultivation of professional retinues and the other on the enticing fortune to be had by taxing smallholders, the Han emperors chose to break the traditional link between court and farmer that had defined the Warring States period and the success of the Qin. In its place they imposed a head tax on the peasantry that they used to recruit professional armies that could be maintained year-round.

Military reality influenced this change. The Xiongnu to the north had become immensely strong and the primary target of imperial Chinese military exertions. A nomadic people, the Xiongnu fought, as did all great peoples of the Asian steppe, on horseback, their warriors typically loosing arrows while turning in the saddle. To counter this, the Chinese state had been forced to rely on other barbarians and on those Chinese professionals who had absorbed the lessons of the frontier and were able to fight along Xiongnu lines. All of which made the seasonal conscription of unskilled peasants pointless and even counterproductive.

Though it did not happen immediately, this change in course set in motion trends that had wide-ranging effects. To begin with, taxation hit the peasants hard, driving many of them to sell off their land to raise the necessary cash. Taking advantage of this, the aristocracy bought up the surplus real estate and set themselves up as local landlords. That they were able to do this had much to do with another shift in Han society, namely the court's promotion of Confucianism. Unlike their Qin predecessors, the Han embraced the old ways, establishing an academy for the instruction of civil servants along Confucian lines. With the court now eager to accept talented young intellectuals into its orbit as bureaucrats for an expanding empire, a veritable market in talent arose: established families scrambled to send their sons into civil service in order to draw imperial salaries, which in turn could be used to expand local power at home by buying up more land, building relationships through gifts, and putting lesser households on the payroll. Angered by their tax burden and alienated from the imperial agenda by the lack of military service, the peasants began naturally to look to their local nobility for leadership. The result was a gradual but inexorable rise of landlordism throughout the empire—the emergence of an aristocracy that would one day threaten the absolute power of the emperor himself.

These developments were slow at first, as Han Gaozu's immediate successors held onto much of the legalist tradition that had been institutionalized under the Qin. But by the reign of Emperor Wu Di (r. 140–87 BC), one of the most illustrious of all Han rulers, the new reality was becoming widespread. Wu Di, still considered one of China's greatest emperors, would galvanize the reformations of the Han into a state of unprecedented expansionism.

## WU DI

The seventh Han emperor, Wu Di became the bane of China's barbarian foes. He remains emblematic of those who ruled during the first Han period.

To begin with, Wu Di bestowed on his rule divine sanction. Galvanizing a trend toward imperial glorification that had been increasing since the early days of the Han, Wu Di grounded the magnificence of his station in religious ritual, becoming his people's connection to the divine by overseeing regular sacrifices to the gods. The intent was to couch the office of emperor in a sacred light that no mortal could challenge, an elevation of government to unimpeachable grandeur.

Having safeguarded the justification for his policies in this way, he felt free to act boldly. Wu Di was the first emperor to aggressively favor Confucianism. He was also the first to push through taxation on a large scale in lieu of peasant conscription—a brutally pragmatic measure intended to help him deal, once and for all, with the dreaded Xiongnu.

Since around 200 BC, when the fearsome Xiongnu horsemen had dealt

*Emperor Wu Di leaves his palace in a horse-drawn chariot (painting on silk from a history of Chinese emperors).*

Chinese armies a devastating defeat, the Han emperors had been willing to pay regular tribute to the barbarians of the north to keep them at bay. This was the quintessence of humility. While touting themselves as the guardians of civilization, the Chinese emperors were forced through weakness to buy off a rough-hewn, leather-clad people they would just as soon have spat on if given half a chance.

By the time Wu Di was sitting on the throne, many in the court felt the time had come to throw off the Xiongnu yoke. And in the 130s BC, the emperor acted. Sweeping north with huge cavalry armies, Wu Di delivered the first serious defeats to Xiongnu forces in over seventy years, pushing them back miles from the Chinese frontier and forcing their leadership into a destabilizing crisis from which it would never truly recover. But this was just the beginning.

Wu Di turned his attentions west, into the vast stretches of sand and steppe that gave onto central Asia. Employing the veteran armies that had humbled the Xiongnu, Wu Di smashed the barbarian peoples who had dominated there for centuries, literally doubling the size of the Han Empire. No one in China had seen such military exploits since the conquest of the six Warring States by Qin Shi Huangdi.

## CHU-KO-NU

The crossbow—a deadly weapon that, using mechanical tension, could project a missile much farther and faster than could an archer relying on the strength of his arm—was in widespread use in China a thousand years before it appeared in Europe. In fact, Chinese engineers even produced a rapid-firing version: the *chu-ko-nu*.

Probably developed during the Han period, the *chu-ko-nu* featured a magazine over the bow that was capable of storing ten bolts. Operating the weapon was as easy as pulling back a lever that drew the bow, released the bolt and then—on the return motion—dropped another bolt into the groove from the magazine. All the user needed to do, in other words, was hold the weapon with one hand and loose a string of missiles with the other by pulling and pushing a lever, back and forth, back and forth. Like many great inventions, it is at once brilliant and breathtakingly simple.

Held at the waist rather than against the shoulder, the weapon sacrificed accuracy for a high rate of fire: practiced users would have been able to get off roughly a shot per second. Provided enough bolts were at hand (on the walls of a city, for instance), units of crossbowmen armed with a *chu-ko-nu* must have been devastatingly effective against massed foes.

This, besides a scandalous quest for immortality that mirrored that of the first Qin emperor, was to be Wu Di's principal legacy. He had humbled the Xiongnu and taken the culture of China to hitherto unknown frontiers. By the end of his reign he had built outposts on the Caspian Sea, invaded what is today Vietnam, and added part of the Korean Peninsula to his empire.

Though his campaigns were brilliant and unprecedented, they also took the Chinese Empire into a wider world that now required vigilance on the part of the court. And the manner in which the Han engaged the peoples beyond its expanding borders would prove fateful indeed.

## NEW BEGINNINGS, OLD PROBLEMS

By the first century AD, the Han Empire—despite a high level of stability—found itself in turmoil. A radical named Wang Mang managed to briefly secure the throne with the hope of pushing through agrarian reforms, and established a dynasty that he called Xin, or "new."

By 23 AD he had been deposed, his supporters crushed. Two years later the Han re-established their dynasty in Luoyang, commencing what has become known as the Eastern Han. The Western Han, with its capital at Chang'an, had ended with the revolution of Wang Mang.

Now ensconced in the east of the country with its rich literary and artistic heritage, the Han court began to look at itself as the nation's cultural patron rather than merely its martial leader. Confucianist academies flourished, and the emperors surrounded themselves with a panoply of functionaries, in-laws, eunuchs, and scholars. Steeped in ritual, the Eastern Han rulers came to be defined by their separateness. Gone were the ties between crown and subject, the relationship that had militarized the countryside and created the first Chinese empire. They had been left behind by untouchable autocrats whose right to rule was nothing less than a mandate of Heaven.

Under these circumstances, the great families in the provinces became more powerful than ever, filling the vacuum left by the imperial administration's retreat into courtly affairs. They purchased the loyalty of local peasants, who had few options but to attach themselves to aristocratic protectors.

Militarily, the Eastern Han at last acquired control of the northern and western frontiers. This was a process that owed as much to resettlement as it did to victories in the field. During the first century AD the Xiongnu diverged into two distinct groups, with those in the north maintaining a traditional way of life hostile to China, and those in the south resettling within the borders of the Han and becoming subjects of the

empire. The court, in essence, now had a client population of expert cavalry, and wasted no time employing it against the empire's enemies. In 87 AD the southern Xiongnu were instrumental in dealing their northern kin a decisive defeat that at last pacified the northern frontier for the Han.

This momentous success was emblematic of the complex relationship that had grown between the Han and its barbarian neighbors. Swift and deadly, the Xiongnu horsemen became a mainstay of Han armies, especially when offensive operations were called for. Letting them settle within the borders of the empire in exchange for their military service became official policy. A similar strategy was employed in the west, where large populations of outsiders regularly petitioned imperial authority to settle inside Han borders. In response, the Chinese established frontier provinces under military governors who were charged with defending the borders as well as pacifying foreign settlers like the Qiang, who typically offered themselves as fighters or laborers once they had been accepted into the empire.

In this way, a broad arc of militarized territory stretched from the north to the west—a vast, permeable frontier administered and patrolled by armies, where Han Chinese lived uneasily alongside foreigners with different customs. Remote from the centers of power in distant Luoyang, the Han in these territories showed a willingness to forge local bonds and seek local solutions.

To be sure, the Han had found something approaching security on their borders, but at a price that would soon prove too high to pay.

## MOUNTING CRISES

By the second century Han China was an empire that old Qin Shi Huangdi, had he been able to emerge from his great tomb, would not have recognized. In his day, private ownership of land had been regulated to prevent any one family from acquiring too

*Above: Figure of a horseman of the early Han Dynasty, from northern China.*

much. Now, throughout China, landlords controlled the fates of helpless tenant farmers, monopolized imperial offices, and amassed private armies.

When he had been emperor, Qin Shi Huangdi had appointed generals who served for one campaign only. Now, in the capital and on the frontiers, great armies whose ranks were swelled by felons, mercenaries, and barbarians swore fealty to their commanders—now appointed for life—rather than to the emperor.

In the north and west, where Qin Shi Huangdi had been happy to let loose his dogs of war, there now stretched great swaths of territory that seemed neither barbarian nor Chinese—a no-man's land from which Han villagers, horrified by their resettled foreign neighbors, removed themselves en masse to points south, denuding the countryside and leaving a buffer zone where oppressed barbarian subjects and tyrannical military commanders vied for control.

And the imperial court, which had been a nerve center for vigorous government under Qin Shi Huangdi, was now so removed from its people as to be all but unaware of the crises that besieged its realm.

None of these things on its own could have brought down the Han dynasty. Indeed, the empire was thriving in many ways: the arts flourished, peace was the rule rather than the exception throughout the vast expanse of China, trade and commerce brought goods from throughout the known world, and the empire's scientific and engineering achievements were as advanced as any on the planet.

Together, however, these developments spelled disaster. The Han emperors' policies of distancing themselves from the peasantry, leading the army by proxy through lifetime appointments of professionals and barbarian mercenaries as leaders, attaching their fortunes throughout the provinces to an unchecked aristocracy, and at court allowing the gathering of self-interested advisors who presented a further buffer against outside reality, all came together in the second century to weaken the dynasty's facade of control. All that was needed was a good kick to bring it tumbling down.

It came soon enough—and the people wearing the boots came to be known, rather infamously, as the Yellow Turbans.

## THE COLOR OF DISASTER

As the peasants of the late Han saw it, prosperity for the empire was coming at their expense. Taxes used to build fortifications, equip armies, pay bureaucrats, and build outposts along the eastern tributaries of the so-called "Silk Road" had been taking their toll on the countryside. By the middle of the second century, the peasants were simply waiting for someone to ignite their smoldering resentment into a conflagration.

In northern China, a group of radicals decided to do just that. They were Taoists, espousing an ancient doctrine of peace through egalitarian principles that included the universal ownership of land, and they wrapped their heads in scarves of dark yellow to show their attachment to the soil. Their leader, Zhang Jue, hoped to set in motion a veritable revolution against the aristocratic status quo and its apathetic imperial protectors, to orchestrate an empire-wide rebellion.

In 184 the Yellow Turbans struck, sending waves of violence throughout the empire. Numbering perhaps in the hundreds of thousands, they fell upon imperial offices and outposts, slaughtering countless victims and filling the countryside with great columns of black smoke. The imperial court, guilty of allowing such disaffection to ignite into widespread revolt, soon found itself having to rely on a military from which it had become dangerously estranged.

By the spring of 185, the Yellow Turbans were subdued, their peasant hordes slaughtered or scattered by professional, ruthlessly efficient imperial armies. But the war had shown every one of the Han court's weaknesses in bold relief. Though

## THE SILK ROAD

To the Chinese, silk was more than just the finest of textiles. Its production and trade was central to the imperial economy.

The proper extraction of silk filaments—produced by worms with a fondness for the leaves of the mulberry tree—was an art in itself, requiring such close and constant examination of the worms that silk producers usually lived with them. And once woven into cloth, silk became one of the most valued of all luxuries, a currency in itself. The Han court often paid its troops with silk, and large amounts of the cloth were usually enough to buy off barbarian armies on the frontier.

The demand for silk ensured that it would find its way to markets as far away as Rome. Nevertheless, the famous "Silk Road" of ancient Eurasia was hardly a single road funneling bolts of silk and other Asian luxuries west to Mediterranean ports. Though Romans knew that the precious textile came from the East, they had no notion of the immense distance it had traveled, nor any knowledge of imperial China. Sold by the Chinese on their frontier, bolts of silk were then traded to central Asians, who in turn might sell it in India to buyers who would sell it in Arabia, then it would be taken to Alexandria, and so on, with each merchant doing business locally and, by small steps, moving merchandise across continents. It is probable that no single caravan ever made the journey from China to the Roman world along the so-called Silk Road.

responding to orders from the capital at Luoyang, commanders—their troops bound to them through long years of posting on the frontier—acted with autonomy in the field, knowing that the emperor, Ling Di, was utterly dependent on their efforts. As they and the aristocratic factions that supported them maneuvered and fought throughout the empire, the court could only look on as a deeply interested, and somewhat powerless, party. The sinews of empire had shifted from the person of the emperor to the factions, warlords, and aristocrats who had been allowed to assume primacy over the generations. Immersed in a fugue of intriguers and backstabbing opportunists, the emperor was all but impotent in the crisis that threatened his very inheritance—and from which he was saved by a collection of wealthy nobles and warrior adventurers who were plotting their own treacheries even as they subdued the greatest threat to imperial peace since the days of Wang Mang.

In the years following the Yellow Turban rebellion, Emperor Ling Di carried on as usual, seemingly unaware that a new caste of generalissimos was now calling the shots. He died in 189. Dong Zhuo, a warlord from the northern frontier whose army had become little more than a massive bodyguard, marched on the capital that same year, burning it to the ground and seizing the imperial heir as a hostage. At this point, the Han Empire essentially collapsed, though the idea of it lived on in the young, Xia Di, who grew to manhood as a prisoner. Manifesting the imperial order that had slipped away, he was literally passed as a pawn and prize between warlords who wanted to restore the unity he represented but that none of them was powerful enough to achieve. By the time he died in 220, under the control of an infamous general and self-appointed king named Cao Cao, China had reverted to a collection of independent realms.

Though its policies failed in the end, the Han Empire set the pattern for all Chinese imperial systems to come, from the acceptance of Confucianism to the elaborate glorification of the emperor. And to this day, most Chinese refer to themselves as Han—a fitting tribute to a golden age.

CHAPTER THIRTEEN

# PARTHIA

## FEUDAL EMPIRE IN A WORLD OF ADMINISTRATIVE STATES

THE Roman leader Licinius Crassus had grown impatient. Having come to Mesopotamia all the way from Rome to achieve military glory, he had found only a desolate countryside, pounding heat, and enemies that faded before his advance like a mirage. Now, at the banks of the Balikh River near a town called Carrhae, his legions begged for a breather and a meal.

Crassus demurred. The men would be allowed to eat, but there would be no respite from the chase. As soon as the legionaries had scoffed down enough food and water to thwart exhaustion, the column decamped, heading south after the broad trail of hoof prints in the dust. Crassus was too close to slacken the pace now.

It was May of 53 BC. His evasive foes were Parthians, a powerful eastern people who had been sparring with Rome over Armenia, an ancient and independent kingdom that both empires sought to control as a client. Though tensions had been at a fever pitch, the situation had failed to explode into all-out war.

Crassus was here to change that. Seven years earlier, he and two other of Rome's leading citizens, Gaius Julius Caesar and Gnaeus Pompeius Magnus (Pompey), had altered the course of the republic's history by forming an alliance, or triumvirate. Until then Crassus and Pompey had been rivals—wealthy, influential men, each of whom threatened to control events in Rome for himself through manipulation of clients, resources, and street violence. The Senate, wary of succumbing to a potential tyranny, had played them off against each other to guarantee Roman freedom. But then, in 60 BC, they cunningly turned the tables by agreeing to act in concert along with Caesar, a friend and protégé of Crassus, to get what they wanted. The Senate was powerless to stop them.

Caesar soon headed to Gaul, where he quickly became one of the most famous conquerors in history. Pompey, already Rome's preeminent military hero for his earlier triumphs in the east, was given control of distant Spain, which he was happy to govern through legates while he stayed in Rome.

Crassus, by contrast, had no such martial achievements to boast of. His earlier experiences in command of troops were forgettable next to the achievements of his two esteemed colleagues, and his fortune, though the largest in the empire, could not buy what military reputation earned in Roman society.

Besides, at sixty years of age, he was running out of chances. So in 55 BC, having secured the proconsulship of Syria, Crassus—accompanied by his son Publius—marched off to raise an army and clobber the Parthians, crossing the Euphrates River in spring of 53 BC.

*Previous pages: Capital from the Great Temple at Hatra.*

# CARRHAE

The sun cooked the Roman soldiers in their gear as they trudged away from the river into the dry Mesopotamian countryside. Seven legions strong, they numbered around forty thousand, the vast majority of whom were infantry. Scouting parties had been sent out and they now came galloping up in a hurry. Their intelligence was straightforward enough: the Parthians were coming.

Crassus, knowing how fatigued his legionaries were, opted to form them up into great squares to fend off Parthian cavalry charges. Dangerously short of cavalry himself, the proconsul intended to use what he had wisely and sparingly lest he lose the only mobile element he had in this flat, open terrain. For now he ordered light infantry skirmishers out front to screen the main body.

Presently the Parthian horsemen came into sight, their shimmering figures moving fast over the hot plain to the unnerving rhythm of kettledrums. Dust rolled along with them in huge clouds, enveloping the trotting mass in a translucent veil of khaki. Crassus, hard pressed for information in the sudden onslaught while his legions hastened to complete their defensive maneuver, saw the light infantry screen falling back in panic and realized the battle was well and truly upon him.

The Parthians came fully into view now as they drove the Roman skirmishers back onto the still-forming squares. When the dust cleared, it exposed an unforgettable sight: a broad wave of galloping, ironclad horsemen, a thousand strong and in tight formation. These were the legendary cataphracts—warriors equipped with a great helmet and scale mail, riding a steed draped in leather or scale armor, and holding a great lance with which to skewer as many as two opponents in one charge. With the sun glinting off their iron scales and their faces hidden behind the masks of their helmets, they made an alien sight to the Romans, for whom such hard-charging, heavily equipped fighters were a new and terrifying experience.

Their charge against Crassus's skirmishers having succeeded, the cataphracts wheeled and departed like metallic beasts into the dusty swirl. The Romans strove to complete their squares while anticipating the next attack, which came soon enough. Announcing their arrival with the thunder of galloping hooves, a great mass of horse archers swept about Crassus's army, nearly encircling it while keeping their distance. Then the arrows came in a deluge. Roman officers barked orders to form the *testudo*, a formation in which legions made a makeshift carapace with their great shields to deflect enemy missiles. Almost immediately the sky whistled with death, bringing forth a cacophony of deflected arrows and screams from the unfortunate. Then another wave came, bringing more of the same. And another.

Crassus needed time to complete the squares and sent for his son, Publius. Giving him command of the cavalry, Crassus sent him out to scatter the horse archers while the legions sorted themselves out. The squadron, perhaps 1,300 strong and supported by a large contingent of archers and infantry, rode out into the maelstrom.

By the time Crassus had seen to the deployment of his legions, urgent requests for help were coming in from Publius. Too far away now to be seen, the proconsul's son had gotten himself into trouble. He would not get out of it. While Crassus made preparations for a second sortie to save him, Parthian riders came up and lobbed a grim token into the Roman ranks: the head of Publius.

His son dead, his cavalry all but annihilated, Crassus slowly sank into a slough of despond while his dwindling legionaries endured the attrition wrought by Parthian arrows beneath the cruel Mesopotamian sun. The *testudo* worked to a point, but it could

## THE PARTHIAN SHOT

Were it possible to go back in time and witness cataphracts in action, the modern time-traveler would doubtless be struck by their similarity to a common Western archetype: the mounted knight. A thousand years before armored horsemen with lance and sword came to define the rules of warfare in Europe—and ultimately the rules of proper aristocratic conduct—they were ranging across the mountains of Iran, even employing a tactic, the mounted charge, that would become the hallmark of the knight.

This was no coincidence. Of course, the cataphract was not a knight: he was not necessarily a member of the nobility, he rode into battle without stirrups (a later invention that would revolutionize warfare), and his lance, though held under the arm, was actually fastened to the horse's neck by a rope or chain intended to maximize its kinetic force on impact. But the Parthian cataphract so impressed Westerners that this type of warrior eventually found its way into Roman and Byzantine armies, where it would be preserved until it emerged in Europe in a form only slightly transformed by centuries of prominence. That quintessentially European warrior icon had its roots on the high Iranian plateau.

Another element of Parthian culture has made it all the way into our own time. Generally defined as any hostile remark made in the process of leaving, the so-called "Parthian shot" has become the preferred tactic for anyone in the process of losing an argument and wishing to make an exit. And its origins go all the way back to the Parthian horse archers, who typically feigned retreat while turning in their saddles to loose arrows at pursuing enemies. Today it may be irritating or a little passive-aggressive, but back in antiquity it was downright deadly.

do only so much without relief from any other quarter. When Crassus and his men saw the long train of camels laden with arrows that the Parthians brought up for support, they despaired. The Romans had become, in effect, the targets in a great shooting gallery, to be savaged at Parthian leisure.

Darkness brought relief. Abandoning their wounded on the battlefield, the Romans withdrew to Carrhae itself, and the following day hastened to the hills nearer Syria. Unfortunately, succor proved elusive. While advance elements of his army would make it back to Roman territory, Crassus and his main force found themselves surrounded by the horsemen who had humiliated them outside Carrhae.

The Parthian general, known to history as Surenas, presented Crassus with an offer to parley, during which a scuffle led to the proconsul's death. The campaign had been a colossal defeat: twenty thousand Roman soldiers had been killed and ten thousand taken prisoner.

## HIGH PLAINS DRIFTERS

The battle of Carrhae stands out as one of the greatest military disasters in Roman history. Moreover, the Parthians had been outnumbered four to one. Surenas was not even leading the main Parthian army, which had marched to Armenia with the king in anticipation of a Roman advance there. With just one thousand cataphracts and nine thousand horse archers, Surenas had smashed a large Roman army and slaughtered its proconsul, one of the most powerful men in the world. (His accomplishment was so great, in fact, that his king—jealous of a potential rival—had him murdered.) Clearly the Parthians were not to be trifled with—a lesson the great Crassus had learned the hard way.

By the time Crassus and his seven legions were crossing the Euphrates, the Parthian Empire was almost a century old. The story of its emergence is yet another thread in the densely woven tapestry of Near Eastern history. In the middle of the third century BC, the Seleucid Empire ruled over most of the Asian territories conquered by Alexander the Great before his death. It was during this time that Andragoras, satrap of Parthia, rebelled against imperial authority in the hope of carving out a kingdom of his own.

Though he had defied the Seleucids, Andragoras soon encountered bigger problems that were entirely local. The Dahae, a confederacy of Scythian steppe nomads from the eastern side of the Caspian Sea, had moved into the regions of Parthia and Bactria, becoming a sort of transient and independent population within the borders of the empire. One of these tribes, the Parni, found a dynamic leader in Arsaces, who took advantage of Seleucid wars in the west and Andragoras's vulnerability as a rebel to seize control of Parthia itself. The Parni were now masters of a whole satrapy.

Parthia in effect became the kingdom of the Parni, who continued to exploit Seleucid troubles in the west by annexing more territory in the east. Though Seleucid retaliation materialized on several occasions in the following years, matters in the west proved too formidable to allow anything like a concentrated reconquest of Parthia. By the final decades of the third century BC, the Seleucids and Parthians seem to have worked out an uneasy arrangement whereby the Parni governed locally on behalf of the empire, almost like vassals.

This simmering status quo boiled over during the convulsive reign of the Seleucid emperor Antiochus III. The greatest conqueror of his dynasty, Antiochus marched east to deal with the rebellious satrapies there and reassert Seleucid control over his vast realm. In the process he stripped Parthia of much of its new territory before heading back to the Mediterranean. Though humbled and reduced, Parthia had survived as an autonomous state—a condition that served it well when Antiochus's defeat by the Romans at the battle of Magnesia in 190 BC sent ripples of disorder across the empire. When the emperor died three years later, the Iranian satrapies broke away one by one, setting themselves up as petty states. The Seleucids were collapsing—and the Parthians were stepping into the breach.

## GREATNESS

Until now the Arsacid dynasty had been rulers of a relatively small corner of northern Iran that had managed to become a regional power. But in 171 BC Mithradates assumed the throne, and his plans for Parthia were far more ambitious.

In 163 BC the king embarked on a series of campaigns that abruptly cut short the independence of many of Asia's breakaway satrapies. Bactria was the first to fall, securing Parthia's eastern flank so that Mithradates could lead his army west—into the ancient heartland of some of the world's most fabled empires. Media fell next, depriving an already staggering Seleucid Empire of one of its most crucial provinces. By 141 BC virtually nothing stood between Mithradates's swift-riding armies and Mesopotamia itself, opulent birthplace of cities. The Seleucids, floundering under the leadership of an adolescent ruler named Demetrius II, could do little but watch as Parthian warriors occupied the city of Seleucia.

By autumn Mithradates had annexed all of the rich alluvial plains of the Tigris and Euphrates, and Babylonia itself had become a Parthian prize. Elam fell soon after. The Seleucid response, though delayed, was furious and well timed. While Mithradates was back east fighting Bactrians, Demetrius II led a force out to reclaim Mesopotamia, where he was aided by a large revolt against Parthian occupation. After trouncing his enemies in the east, however, Mithradates offered stunning evidence of Parthian mobility by sweeping west to confront the Seleucids personally. His defeat of the Hellenistic armies was complete—he even captured Demetrius for good measure.

Interestingly, Mithradates treated his young prisoner quite well. Though Demetrius was sent into permanent exile in the northeastern region of Hyrcania, the Parthian king gave him his own daughter in marriage. Mithradates was certainly an extraordinary figure: in addition to conquering an enormous realm for his people, he undertook a codification of Iranian law and minted Parthia's first coins.

Conquering an empire was one thing. Keeping it, especially in the contentious world of Hellenized Asia, was another matter entirely. The Seleucids were not yet willing to write off their Iranian possessions and, in the east, rampaging nomads of the steppe known as the Sakae were storming out of what is today Russia.

Widely regarded as the last Seleucid emperor of any ability, Antiochus VII Sidetes (r. 138–129 BC) raised an army of enormous size, intent on putting an end once and for all to the seesaw conflict with Parthia. Antiochus harkened back to the first of his dynasty—Seleucus Nicator, a man who had campaigned with Alexander himself and who had known more than a thing or two about instilling fear in enemies. His march eastward seemed unstoppable as Antiochus reclaimed Babylonia and Media for his empire, his success sowing unrest in other areas of the Parthian realm. In late 130 BC he sent his troops into winter quarters around Ecbatana in Media, where the residents soon revolted openly against the billeting. The following year King Phraates II of Parthia sensed the time was right and struck, decisively defeating the Seleucid army and sending its emperor back home in a casket. Antiochus's family fared almost as poorly: his son was imprisoned and his niece was delivered into Phraates's harem.

Things did not go quite as well for the Parthians in the east. The Sakae, fellow horsemen with an appreciation for hard-hitting mobility, proved more than a match for the Arsacids. In fact, the Parthians used their Seleucid prisoners in 128 BC as captive mercenaries against the Sakae, only to find that the two had managed to make common cause, creating a military disaster on Parthia's eastern border that claimed the life of King Phraates himself. The empire was clearly on the verge of becoming little more than a flash in the pan.

## AN EMPIRE REBORN

In 124 BC Mithradates II assumed control of Parthia. A gifted administrator and soldier, this Mithradates galvanized his people's imperial ambition. He took Babylonia back from the Seleucids, attacked Armenia and captured the son of its ruler, and subdued all Mesopotamia by 113 BC. He achieved equally impressive gains in the east, where he retook the province of Aria and pushed Parthian influence well into central Asia.

By the time of his death in 88 or 87 BC, Mithradates II had secured the Euphrates River as his empire's western border, concluding an uneasy peace treaty with Rome. He had placed his own puppet on the throne of Armenia, established relations with the Han Chinese court, and secured control over the Silk Road by which goods were exchanged between the Roman West and China. Parthia was now a world power of the first order—a fact that Mithradates was happy to advertise with his coins, which portrayed him, in the fashion of the old Achaemenids, as "king of kings."

Parthia, however, was no Persian Empire. The Achaemenids had cultivated a bureaucracy that reached to the ends of their huge realm, helping them create a homogenous state structure even as they permitted regional variation, but the Parthians ruled as overlords of a patchwork of vassals. The Asia over which they had risen to dominance was a complicated place, with numerous different ethnicities inheriting the religions and customs of a dizzying parade of fallen empires. Language offers a good example of this. To connect themselves to the glory of the Achaemenids, Parthians at court spoke Persian, employing a Pahlavi script based on Aramaic characters. Greek, however, was spoken virtually everywhere as a result of the Hellenization that followed Alexander's conquests. Greek colonies throughout the empire were treated with respect by the Parthian conquerors, not least because of their commercial connections. Indeed, the Parthian emperors put *philhellenos*, or "friend of the Greeks," on their coins—and it was written in Greek letters, even in the final days of the empire when few could still read Greek.

Constrained by the diversity of their possessions, the Parthians forged what amounted to a loose conglomeration of subject states under the direction, such as it was, of the Arsacid king. Eighteen vassal rulers ultimately paid homage to Parthia, in some cases having received their states as fiefdoms in exchange for loyalty, service, and tribute. Some of these, like Armenia, were ancient kingdoms while others were mere cities. The Parthian heartland, a modest empire unto itself, relied on the Silk Road to fill its coffers with tolls and tariffs, while outlying areas were allowed to maintain whatever economic ties they had maintained in Seleucid days. Parthian administration was absent from subject territories—only the refusal of tribute or

*Silver tetradrachm showing Mithridates II of Parthia, who ruled the East from Babylonia to the Oxus (Amu Darya) River.*

military service, if called upon, would bring direct attention, which would take the form of a punitive expedition charged with reasserting Parthian dominance. But religiously, culturally, the vassal lands of the Parthian Empire were afforded a striking degree of independence.

Like the Achaemenids, Parthian emperors traveled from city to city, eventually relying on Ctesiphon, founded by Mithradates II, as their primary capital. Other major urban centers, among them Babylon, Seleucia, and Ecbatana, were treated as virtual capitals by the roving court. Such peregrinations were suggestive of the Parthians themselves—a nomadic people who had secured a vast empire of ancient settlements and who retained their distinctive identity while ruling over many other peoples.

## NEMESIS OF ROME

The Parthian Empire had no standing army. Like a feudal kingdom of the European Middle Ages, it relied on the personal retinues and private armies of the emperor's numerous vassals, each of whom was responsible for mustering a force equal to the wealth and abilities of his particular state. In times of crisis, the Parthian court called on its subject rulers to raise whatever warriors they could and meet at an appointed time and place for the purposes of campaigning. Surenas, the noble who killed Crassus and savaged his army, had personally raised the ten thousand horsemen he led to victory at Carrhae. They were his retainers and dependants.

Cavalry dominated Parthian armies almost completely, and not merely because of the origins of the Parni on the Eurasian steppe. With such a vast empire to defend and a steady stream of threats from both east and west, the speed of horse was crucial for getting armies from Bactria to Babylonia and back again. The Parthians employed two types of horsemen: the heavy cataphracts, for charging and melee, and horse archers. The latter, manifesting centuries of Indo-Iranian excellence in mobile warfare, loosed their missiles from the saddle with a composite bow, whose fusion of wood and horn in a recurved design produced a force more than equal to regular bows that were much larger. As Crassus discovered to his doom at Carrhae, the archers typically traveled with a train of arrows in tow for maintaining a barrage that was as continuous as it was devastating.

Few men were to test the efficacy of the Parthian way of war more thoroughly than Mark Antony. In the wake of the disaster at Carrhae, Rome continued to spar with its eastern neighbor in Syria and northern Mesopotamia. In one of these conflicts, a Roman general named Publius Ventidius succeeded in defeating several Parthian armies and even managed to capture some of their leaders. Ventidius was given a triumph back in Rome—a fact that Antony, his superior, noted most enviously.

Having split the Roman Empire with his rival Octavian, Mark Antony had all of the eastern provinces at his disposal for an invasion of the Parthian heartland. In 36 BC, at the head of a hundred thousand fighting men, he marched into upper Mesopotamia, virtually in the footsteps of the unfortunate Crassus, with the intention of winning himself some immortality by smashing the Parthians.

Things did not go quite according to plan. Advancing into Media, Antony divided his huge army, leading the major part of it ahead while the baggage train lagged behind with the siege equipment under the protection of two legions. Such a dispersal of forces played nicely into the hands of the Parthians, whose rapid horsemen were capable of preying on the slow-moving, divided columns in a manner of their own choosing. While Antony laid siege to the city of Praaspa without proper siege engines, his train was set upon by Parthian cavalry and slaughtered in droves, costing him ten thousand soldiers and all his heavy equipment and supplies. The Romans gave up on the siege with the approach of winter and headed for Armenia, harried by Parthian bowmen the whole way. From Armenia, in the midst of winter, Antony led his forces back to the safety of Syria. By the time they arrived, more of them had died of starvation and exposure than Crassus had lost at Carrhae.

Mark Antony was no Crassus. The most trusted lieutenant of the recently assassinated Julius Caesar, he was a seasoned campaigner and favorite of the soldiers. Some of the most experienced legions in the Roman army revered him unquestioningly. Yet even he found Iran too tough a nut to crack. Indeed, the Parthians had defeated him soundly.

Antony's abortive invasion encapsulated what soon became the status quo between Parthia and Rome. In the open vistas of Mesopotamia, Roman legions with their slow-moving infantry and siege equipment were at the mercy of Parthian cavalry. But just as importantly, Parthian horsemen were vulnerable in the hilly regions of Roman Asia Minor and the Levant, where they were at a disadvantage against experienced footmen. Moreover, the Parthians had no knowledge of siege engineering, making their lunges into Roman territory little better than raids that were incapable of taking fortified cities. For these reasons, the struggle between these two radically different empires would continue for more than two hundred years.

## A COURT IN CHAOS

This was unfortunate for Parthia, not only because Rome was a military superpower, but also because it had plenty of problems of its own.

Like so many imperial courts in antiquity, the Parthians suffered from succession issues that could, depending on the personalities involved, assume disastrous proportions.

The year before Mark Antony invaded Media, King Orodes of Parthia stepped down, choosing the eldest of his thirty sons, Phraates IV, to take his place. Determined to ensure his seat on the throne, Phraates promptly murdered his father and all his brothers. Nor did he stop there. Seized by rampant paranoia, he started knocking off members of the nobility as well, driving many of them into exile. Antony got the inspiration for his Parthian enterprise from a disaffected Iranian noble who was happy to guide the Romans on their march through Parthian territory.

In fact, the reign of Phraates IV could have stood as a morality tale about the wages of sin. Widespread revulsion at his tactics eventually manifested itself in the person of a usurper named Tiridates, with whom Phraates would fight a bitter struggle for control of Parthia. Forced to flee north, Phraates relied on Scythian mercenaries to retake his realm in a fight that raged back and forth and in which Tiridates relied on Roman backing. At one point in 26 BC a counterattack by Tiridates came so rapidly that Phraates murdered the women of his harem rather than see them fall into the usurper's hands. By capturing one of the king's sons and spiriting him off to Rome as a hostage, Tiridates brought Octavian, now the Emperor Augustus, into the heart of the conflict. The Romans offered to return him in exchange for all the "eagles," or standards, that Parthian units had captured during the wars with Crassus and Mark Antony. Phraates complied in 20 BC, by which time Tiridates had been decisively vanquished.

With relations between Parthia and Rome at an all-time high, Augustus offered an Italian slave girl named Musa to Phraates as a gift for his harem—a token of thanks for the return of the eagles. In addition to giving Phraates a son, soon to be known as Phraataces, Musa proved the equal of any court intriguer. She eventually convinced the king to send his oldest sons to Rome as noble emissaries, freeing up the succession for Phraataces. Around 2 BC she sealed the deal by poisoning Phraates. Phraataces promptly assumed the throne. Within a few years the two conspirators, Musa and her royal son, actually married each other, further horrifying western observers, who regarded such a thing as the purest scandal. Clearly many Parthians were sickened by the spectacle as well, because Phraataces was assassinated by AD 4. Musa disappeared from history. Just three years later Orodes III, Phraataces's successor, was also assassinated. For the next hundred years, this innate turbulence at the highest level of the Parthian Empire was exacerbated by two foreign elements: Armenia and the selection of its king, and the offspring of Phraates IV who had been sent to Rome by the machinations of Musa.

At the heart of the Parthian people and realm was a handful of esteemed clans whose various relationships to the Arsacid ruling family dominated aristocratic affairs. Additionally, any healthy, unmarked male of the Arsacid line—even an ancillary branch—could become heir, depending on the reigning ruler's wishes. These two factors provided the real prospect of crisis at every imperial succession, as various claimants and their noble backers jockeyed for the crown.

This was a dangerous enough situation on its own, but when the Romans, eager to manipulate the Parthian court, started sending the sons and grandsons of Phraates IV into the east as claimants, the stage was set for generations of bedlam. A Latinized branch of the Arsacids, these men—friendly to Rome and familiar with its ways—were viewed as potential puppets by Roman emperors. On at least one occasion, a Parthian monarch faced an opposition candidate within the Iranian world and one sent from Rome at the very same time.

Against this contentious and unpredictable backdrop, the ongoing chess match for control of Armenia heated up. By AD 63, in the wake of a Roman attack sent to punish the Parthians for once again putting a puppet on the Armenian throne, Vologases I and Nero reached an agreement: an Armenian candidate could stand as long as he had approval from Rome, whose emperor would actually place the crown upon the king's head in Rome itself.

Behind the peaceful compromise, however, were ominous cracks in Parthian strength. Though Vologases had eventually been able to check the Roman legions that had advanced into Armenia, it had come after three years of Roman victories during which the Parthian emperor was too busy coping with the secession of Hyrcania in the north, revolts throughout the empire, and—not surprisingly—the campaigns of a potential usurper named Vardanes. Only after patching his crumbling realm back together was he able to counterattack in Armenia to force Nero to the table. Parthia, in other words, was getting battered from within and without. And it was only going to get worse.

## SHIFTING REALITIES

In AD 113 the Emperor Trajan made war on the Parthians. One of the greatest soldiers ever to rule the Roman Empire, Trajan was seeking military glory but was nevertheless happy to have a pretext in Armenia, where the Parthians had rashly set up another king without his approval. The campaign was a stunning success. Marching into Armenia, he deposed the king (and probably had him quietly murdered) and annexed the kingdom as a Roman province—a neat solution to the problem that had been pitting Romans and Parthians against each other for decades. He then marched south and did the same to Mesopotamia, sweeping aside those local dynasts who did not flee. In 116 he crossed the Euphrates, conquered enough territory to comprise the new Roman province of Assyria, sailed his army down the Tigris, successfully besieged Ctesiphon, and then kept moving down through Babylonia and Mesene, both of which were annexed

But his gains were not to last. When he died the following year, Trajan was succeeded by Hadrian, as gifted in defense and consolidation as his predecessor had been in conquest and annexation. Hadrian returned Trajan's conquests to their original rulers, and even Armenia was left in the hands of a king chosen by the Parthians. To Hadrian, concerned with creating borders he knew he could defend, such far-flung possessions were a luxury he could not afford.

Nevertheless, Trajan's whirlwind *tour de force* marked a watershed in Near Eastern history. To begin with, it put Parthia's vulnerability in bold relief. For most of the fighting, King Osroes had been unable to do much more than incite revolts against the Roman conquerors, so busy was he with internal struggles to secure his crown. Indeed, the period leading up to Trajan's invasion witnessed a profusion of feuding claimants to the Parthian leadership, making it as vulnerable as it had ever been. After generations of strife, the monarchy was losing its authority to an increasingly acquisitive aristocracy. Centralization, as was the case with so many ancient empires, was difficult to maintain over time, especially in a feudal state that depended so much on the loyalty of nobles who were eager to bargain for greater power in tumultuous times. Even more rigidly organized states encountered this; Parthia, with its limited bureaucracy and lack of formal administration, fell prey all the more rapidly.

Just as importantly, Trajan's enterprise showed how far the Romans had come from the grim days of Carrhae. After years and years of conflict with Parthia, which many Romans considered the most formidable of all Rome's foes, the legions and their generals had learned to campaign successfully in the oppressive, arid regions that had once been their doom. While always masters of siege warfare, they had learned to complement their infantry in the east with more cavalry, and to train their troops to a sharp fighting edge before commencing operations. The Roman military had become ever more organized, structured, and professional.

In contrast to this, the Parthians were still a warrior elite ruling over a cosmopolitan empire through contracts of vassaldom and coercion, with a military infrastructure that reflected this reality. As they had done so many times before, the Romans adapted. The Parthians continued to rely on the same institutions, and though their horsemen were still to be feared, they had their limits.

*Detail of a bronze statue of a Parthian warrior found in a sanctuary at Shami, south of Kerman in southwestern Iran.*

All of these factors pointed to Parthia as an empire that was gradually losing the strength to thwart the forces arrayed against it—as a state whose rudimentary system of overlordship could do nothing about its own interior power struggles and very little about the evolving foreign nemesis that seemed to grow only stronger through the years of jousting. As the Arsacids continued to leak prestige and the leverage that came with it, these corrosive elements became irreversible. Parthia, despite the occasional triumphs of its warrior elite, was facing a decline it was not designed to stop.

## THE GRIP IS LOST

The decline and fall of Parthia came in slow motion, probably because of the ability of its armies to steal victory from the jaws of defeat. Throughout most of the Parthian Empire, especially Mesopotamia, the combination of heavy cataphracts and mobile archers made a daunting combination well into the common era.

In 162 Parthian Emperor Vologases IV, acting on years of Roman inactivity, invaded Armenia with the hopes of placing an Arsacid on its throne. It was a gamble, based on an assumption that Roman attention had drifted away from the east. After defeating local Roman forces, the Parthian armies turned south and ravaged Roman Syria.

Events as alarming as this always brought a dedicated Roman response, and this was no exception. In 163 a huge Roman army flooded Mesopotamia with legionaries, resulting in the conquest of Babylonia and the plundering of Seleucia, before plague broke the operation utterly, forcing a Roman retreat and weakening both sides. The Parthians soon counterattacked, retook the lost territory, and then lost it again to the attacks of Emperor Lucius Verus in 169. Much of the region between the Tigris and Euphrates became an armed Roman camp.

For Parthia, these seesaw conflicts amounted to death throes. Heedless of his empire's woes, or perhaps hoping to draw attention away from them, Vologases V availed himself of internal Roman troubles in 192 to pick a fight. For one of the last times in history, Parthia's horsemen descended on Mesopotamia, only to summon the wrath of Roman Emperor Septimius Severus, who sacked Ctesiphon in 198 and then stalled at the investment of Hatra, where the lengthy siege operations tested his armies to their limits.

If Rome had reached its military limits, Parthia was utterly on the ropes. As historian Malcolm A.R. Colledge put it, "Political stability and central authority had been sadly undermined by generations of dynastic struggles. The destruction wrought by three Roman invasions of Mesopotamia and Babylonia within eighty-five years was incalculable."

The Parthians, however, had one final military triumph left in them. In 217, reacting to a Roman invasion of Media, Artabanus V sent an army into Mesopotamia and there bested a Roman army, forcing the Emperor Macrinus to sue for peace. It mattered little, however, for the bane of the Parthian state was emerging within its own borders.

The Parthian throne had been so debased by Roman invasion, internal strife, and the suspect loyalty of vassal states that its nobility could exact privileges with near impunity. Indeed, all but devoid of respect, the Parthian kings now had little with which to back their demands, so reliant had they become on the feudal hosts of lords who now could do as they pleased. To the kingdom of Persis, ancient homeland of the Persians, this state of affairs was too tempting to pass up. King Ardashir, relying on the widespread reverence for the Achaemenid heritage that Persis represented, made common cause with fellow rebels in Media, Adiabene, and Kirkuk. Artabanus V, king of Parthia, was all but helpless to stop them. Ardashir soon took Parthia and, after killing Artabanus in battle in 226, had himself crowned emperor in Ctesiphon. The Sasanid dynasty was born.

With so little in the way of centralized administration, Parthia was perhaps doomed once it found itself locked in a perpetual struggle with a state as well ordered and adaptable as Rome. A feudal enterprise that harkened back to the earliest empires of the Tigris–Euphrates basin, Parthia survived only as long as its warrior nobility could enforce and defend the loose status quo over clients. Against this background, the Parthians' collapse seems inevitable. It is no coincidence that the Sasanids who toppled them brought a centralized, bureaucratic government with them, reinstating the golden age of Achaemenid Persia.

*The so-called "Hellenistic" temple at Hatra, a large fortified Parthian town near the border with Roman Mesopotamia.*

CHAPTER FOURTEEN

# ROME

## *CUI BONO?*

IN September of AD 9, Publius Quinctilius Varus, a Roman noble sent north to establish the new province of Germania, led his army of three legions and their supporting elements toward winter quarters on the Rhine. En route, word came to him that a revolt among local Germanic tribes had broken out. Guided by Arminius, a native German who had received a military education in Rome as a hostage, Varus headed off toward the rebellion through the Teutoberg Forest, in what is now northwest Germany.

It was a ruse. Arminius had feigned loyalty to Varus while secretly building a loose confederation of local tribes, which now gathered to strike a blow against Roman imperialism.

Having taken the bait, Varus's legions marched heedless into a great slaughter pen framed by carefully prepared fieldworks. When the signal went up, the Romans, drawn out in column, could do little but fall back before the bellowing barbarians pouncing on them from concealed positions. The sounds of butchery soon filled the woods. Those legionaries fortunate enough to escape the initial carnage fell prey to pursuers over the ensuing days, their fighting retreat becoming a grisly denouement in the verdant gloom of Lower Saxony. Of the twenty thousand plus soldiers who had marched north with Varus, virtually none survived. Roman forces returning five years later to the miles-long field of debris were struck by the white bones and cloven skulls, the remains of legionaries nailed to the oaks as ghoulish totems.

It is said that Caesar Augustus (r. 27 BC–AD 14), first emperor of Rome, took to wandering the halls of his house at night, howling, "Quinctilius Varus, give me back my legions!" The designations of Varus's three destroyed legions—the XVII, XVIII, and XIX—were permanently retired, never again to appear in the history of the Roman Empire. It was almost as if they had never existed.

Partially because of the Teutoberg Forest horror show, the Roman Empire eventually made a fateful decision: thenceforth, all of the Rhine and most of the Danube would remain barriers to Roman settlement. Central Europe's Germanic populations would remain neighbors, rather than subjects, of the empire.

Two obvious factors informed this decision. First, the large Rhine and Danube rivers themselves made excellent barriers, at once preventing easy crossing while facilitating transportation of defensive forces along their lengths. Second, the Germanic peoples proved resistant to conquest. Heirs to a fierce warrior tradition, they cherished local freedom above all else. Indeed, this inability to organize themselves into anything larger

*Previous pages: Roman order Corinthian capital from the Pantheon in Rome.*

than small villages prevented the creation of concentrated strongholds against which Roman leaders could act decisively. Without great fortified towns such as those of the Gauls that had fallen to Julius Caesar, the Germans remained as difficult to quell as a swarm of flies. A campaign into Germania promised to last indefinitely, costing far more than it was worth. Such calculations proved decisive, especially when backed by the hard lesson of the Teutoberg Forest.

Unfortunately, the Romans were laying the groundwork for a tumultuous future with this policy. As Tacitus later wrote of the Germans:

*In truth neither from the Samnites, nor from the Carthaginians, nor from both Spains, nor from all the nations of Gaul, have we received more frequent checks and alarms; nor even from the Parthians: for, more vigorous and invincible is the freedom of the Germans than the despotism of the Persians.*

This was written in the first century AD—by the fourth century, the "German problem" had grown much worse and far more complicated.

The fall of the Roman Empire in the West has been the subject of heated debate for centuries. Doubtless it represented the convergence of many factors, including political, economic, and military considerations, and even individual human failings; complex phenomena usually require complex explanations. But if there was one factor without which the process probably would not have occurred when and where it did, it was the long, permeable frontier that bifurcated Europe along the divide between civilized and barbarian cultures. The Rhine–Danube border and the nature of the peoples along either side of it was the *sine qua non* of Roman decline—the geopolitical idiosyncrasy that focused Western Roman weaknesses into a general collapse.

## THE WAY OF THE ANCESTORS

According to legend, the brothers Romulus and Remus founded Rome in 753 BC. Romulus, who murdered his brother soon afterward in a power struggle, was traditionally remembered as the settlement's first king. Monarchy, however, wore out its welcome in

*According to Roman myth, the founder of the city, Romulus, and his twin brother, Remus, were abandoned as infants and suckled by a she-wolf.*

the city on the Tiber, and the last king of Rome, Tarquinius Superbus, was overthrown around 510 BC.

What gradually emerged to take its place was one of the most complex systems of democracy ever devised—a structure of checks and balances that, while favoring oligarchy, bent over backwards to thwart the reappearance of an autocracy and its inherent risk of abuse.

Two orders of Roman families sparred for influence over the ensuing generations, shaping a sporadic conflict that managed to give birth to stable democratic government. The patricians, from Rome's oldest and wealthiest bloodlines, dominated affairs until the plebeians effectively rebelled by removing themselves from society to create a parallel state. This "struggle of the orders" during the fifth century BC ultimately settled into a political structure that merged the two classes and their respective governments while safeguarding the interests of both.

This was the birth of the Roman Republic—a state that, as it evolved, eventually reflected as much a preservation of tradition as a deep-seated suspicion of power. Between the fifth and second centuries BC, it coalesced into a collection of leadership posts and popular assemblies, the salient details of which offer some idea of the scheme's overall sophistication.

A handful of magistracies, or elected offices, evolved to operate the machine of government—quaestors, on the bottom rung of the ladder, with minor financial responsibilities; aediles, charged with overseeing public events and the smooth operation of marketplaces; praetors, who functioned something like low-ranking military officers; and consuls (only two), most powerful of the magistracies, incorporating the highest levels of political and military power. Collectively known as the *cursus honorum*, or the "run of offices," these positions—for the most part open to both patricians and plebs who had attained a certain level of wealth—added more responsibility with each office, drawing the most gifted men of the state toward supreme power by giving them increasingly more influential posts to run for.

Another office, open only to plebeians, wielded considerable influence. Called "tribunes of the plebs," each of these ten men had veto power over any law passed by the state—a strangely powerful function that arose out of the plebeian concern for checking patrician dominance.

All officers were elected for a one-year term by democratic assemblies, three of which were particularly important. The Centuriate Assembly, organized into voting blocks that openly favored the wealthy, elected praetors and consuls and could pass laws. The Tribal Assembly of the Plebs, open only to plebeians, voted by tribe (based primarily on where one lived) to elect tribunes and issued plebiscites—laws that were binding on all citizens, whether patrician or plebeian. And the Tribal Assembly of the People, composed of both plebs and patricians, elected aediles and quaestors and passed into law proposals made by those officers. (The difference between plebeians and patricians in fact decreased over time into virtual insignificance. The noble families that dominated Roman life through their wealth and influence eventually included families from both orders.)

Finally, there was the Senate. Originally a form of council for the early Roman kings, the Senate evolved to become the premier clique of Rome—an elite congress composed almost exclusively of former magistrates. Though the Senate could not pass legislation, its recommendations—which carried immense weight—were typically championed by an officer for passage in the assemblies. A proclamation from the Senate was not unlike a firm suggestion from the community's elders.

Because of the Roman reverence for *mos maiorum*, or "the way of the ancestors," older concepts, which were held sacrosanct, were not altered, and new institutions were added to the already crowded government platform. Hence the blur of counterbalancing offices and assemblies, the compromises reached between points of authority by trial and error. The Senate could not declare war (which required a vote of the Centuriate Assembly) but controlled foreign policy. Tribunes held no *imperium*, or military authority, but were the only ones who could call a meeting of the Assembly of the Plebs and the only ones who could propose legislation to that important body. Consuls held tremendous executive power, but only for a year—and only in a collegial arrangement in which each of the two office-holders could counter the other's reckless policies. And so on.

But *mos maiorum* played another role in the Roman state: it offered a guiding hand to the process of government. Far from having a written constitution, the republic had a collection of laws held together by custom. Nothing but public censure and individual conscience prevented anyone from charting a new and untried course through the maze of checks and balances. And once men started doing just that, the republic itself was found wanting.

## ITALIAN ENEMIES AND FRIENDS

In 280 BC King Pyrrhus of Epirus landed in Italy with a large army and a mission to crush Rome. A great warrior monarch of the Hellenistic Age, he had been invited by the citizens of Tarentum to save their ancient Greek city from its belligerent neighbor to the north, whose legions were expected any day. Pyrrhus was a military opportunist of the old school, and he welcomed the excuse to try his lean, mean phalangites in an Italian adventure—and perhaps snatch up some territory along the way.

That year he fought the Romans at Heraclea and, the following year, at Ausculum. On both occasions his Macedonian-style phalanxes—supported by thousands of archers and cavalry and twenty war elephants—won the day, but at a terrific cost in lives: thus the term "Pyrrhic victory." After a diversion into Sicily to humiliate the Carthaginians, he returned to Italy and clashed with the Romans once more at the battle of Beneventum in 275 BC. Though largely inconclusive, the battle convinced Pyrrhus, arguably the finest general of his day, that fighting Romans was simply too costly. He returned to Epirus across the Ionian Sea, leaving Italy to the legions.

Pyrrhus's futile romp put Roman military assets in bold relief. By the time he showed up, the city on the Tiber had already quelled most of its neighbors in Italy, including the Latins, the Etruscans, and the Samnites. And Rome's treatment of these humbled enemies spoke volumes about the type of enterprise the city had embarked on.

Until then, ancient empires had always attempted to subjugate defeated populations to varying degrees, whether by wiping them from the face of the earth, letting them carry on under new management answerable to the imperial center, or something in between. By contrast, Rome chose a unique course. Exhibiting a legalistic approach

*Imperial courtiers are shown in procession on the north side of the* Ara Pacis Augustae, *a monumental altar erected in 13 BC in honor of Augustus.*

that reflected the Republic's domestic government, Rome bound its vanquished Italian enemies to itself through bilateral treaties.

These documents, secured with individual communities and varying dramatically, doled out bits and pieces of Roman citizenship—or the promise of such in the future—in a way that ensured loyalty. The process also divided Roman allies because the various forms of treaty kept them sundered into different communities. The result was a patchwork of states whose only common feature was a link to Rome.

All treaties, however, shared one important feature: the contribution of recruits to Rome in times of war. By securing quiescence with treaties and exploiting manpower through military contributions, Rome created a state capable of martial exploits out of all proportion to its relatively small size. On paper, it was a city-state with neighboring client states; in reality, it was the hub of a well-oiled machine of expansion drawing on Italy's considerable population in new and effective ways.

Two other things helped in driving Pyrrhus back across the sea. The first involved the legions themselves, which employed a maneuverability on the battlefield that lumbering Hellenistic phalanxes could not match. Though they took a hammering from Pyrrhus's tough professionals, the legions gave nearly as good as they got in quantity of wounds. The other deciding factor is considerably more difficult to define, even if evidence for its existence was everywhere in antiquity: Pyrrhus encountered in the Romans a people who refused to play by the rules of other civilized states. Having twice trounced them in 280 and 279 BC, the king of Epirus should have been able to bring his Roman enemies to terms. But they simply rebuffed his entreaties, deciding instead to raise new armies and fight on and on until they were able to deal on *their* terms—or, as in the case of Pyrrhus, drive their enemies from the scene of action. If the Romans were not invulnerable, they were certainly defiant, stubborn, and imperious.

## BUILDING AN EMPIRE ON PUNIC CORPSES

Pyrrhus of Epirus was Rome's first overseas foe. With his exit, all Italy fell to the legions, including the rich Greek cities of Magna Graecia in the south.

The Roman Republic now found itself master of an Italian realm. It might have remained little more than this were it not for the complex situation in Sicily, in which the Carthaginian Empire fought for supremacy with Greek cities that had thrived there for centuries. With Sicily just a few miles by sea from Rome's southern Italian "allies," Rome became involved in the Sicilian power struggle, taking on both Greeks and Carthaginians from 264 BC. It was the beginning of an overseas struggle that would change Rome forever.

War raged across Sicily for years, its Greek communities forever losing their independence to Punic and Roman armies locked in a winner-take-all fight for the Mediterranean's most strategic island. And it was not long before the fighting spread to the sea itself.

Carthage had every reason to feel confident in such a war. After all, its navy was the mightiest in the known world, sustained by safe harbors throughout the western sea in Spain, Sardinia, Corsica, and North Africa. With access to unlimited naval stores through its trade routes, a large manpower pool skilled in seamanship, and centuries of shipbuilding expertise, Carthage had little to fear on the waves.

But the Carthaginians had not counted on Roman tenacity. During the First Punic War (264–241 BC), Rome displayed adaptability that, centuries later, still seems incredible. Though the Romans were not entirely ignorant of maritime warfare, they should have been no match for a contender like Carthage, for while Roman expansion within Italy and Sicily brought under its control ancient Hellenistic cities with formidable naval traditions, these communities could contribute little toward a navy capable of taking on the mighty Punic fleet. None of this mattered to the Romans, who set themselves the task of turning their budding little empire into a naval power virtually overnight.

Audacity and sheer drive were not the only Roman qualities that came to the fore in this daunting endeavor. Imagination also figured prominently. Someone devised a brilliant invention to allow Roman legionaries, the city's greatest military asset, to fight at sea. Called a *corvus*, it was a swiveling boarding bridge sporting a great spike at its end and mounted on the prow of Roman vessels. Once alongside an enemy ship, a Roman crew would release the corvus from its upright position, sending its spike crashing through the enemy's deck and joining the two vessels with a ready-made bridge for boarding. Legionaries could then rush the enemy crew, effectively turning a battle at sea into a land melee.

With the help of the *corvus*, Rome's miracle fleet—built with astonishing quickness—more than held its own against the Carthaginians, dealing them several crippling defeats. Just as impressively, Rome merely rebuilt its fleet after storms smashed it to bits off the coast of Sicily, once again displaying an uncanny resilience and willingness to commit against an enemy in the face of staggering adversity. When Carthage finally surrendered in 241 BC, the great city lost not only Sicily but nearly all its fleet, forever ending its reign as the supreme naval power of the Mediterranean.

The next great war with Carthage began in Spain, where Punic expansion—intended to compensate for the empire lost during the first war—clashed with Roman interests in the peninsula. What followed in the Second Punic War (218–202 BC) was an epic clash with Hannibal Barca, Punic general and military genius, which further proved

Roman implacability. In a slew of abject defeats in Italy itself, Roman legions suffered abominable losses, their hapless consuls groping for a way to trap and somehow check Hannibal. At the battle of Cannae alone, an estimated fifty thousand Roman and allied combatants lost their lives. But rather than treat with the Punic menace, Rome relied heavily on its subjects in the Italian Confederation to feed men into the ranks, dug in its heels, and turned to unconventional tactics—such as drawing Hannibal out of Italy by attacking Carthage itself in Africa.

No ancient power had ever suffered so many complete battlefield disasters and refused to seriously consider negotiation. Rome's doggedness would seem reckless, even unbalanced, if it were not for the fact that it worked. The price of Carthage's second submission was even harsher than the first, stripping it of all its overseas possessions and turning it into a virtual dependant of Rome.

By the dawn of the second century BC, the city on the Tiber ruled Sicily, Sardinia, Corsica, and Spain—an impressive empire stolen from the power it now supplanted as supreme in the western and central Mediterranean.

## THE BURDENS OF CONQUEST

Rome was not finished with Carthage. Convinced that their defeated enemy was making a gradual comeback, the Romans sent an army over to Africa to stamp out Carthaginian civilization forever. After a three-year siege, the magnificent Punic city was razed to the ground and its citizens sold wholesale into slavery.

The year was 146 BC—the very year that Rome did the same thing to another glorious and ancient city at the other end of the Mediterranean: Corinth. The Achaean League, an organization of Greek cities under the influence of Rome, had rebelled against their Italian overlords. In response, the Romans, after crushing the revolt, made an example of Corinth by annihilating it.

Rome was now up to its neck in the cares of empire, the result of military achievements that spanned the Mediterranean world. Incredibly, while it had been fighting the Carthaginians in the final decades of the third century BC, Rome had also sent an army east to Macedon, which had rather foolishly allied itself with Carthage. Between 215 and 204 BC, Roman legions fought Macedonian phalanxes for control of Macedon and northern Greece even while Hannibal Barca raised hell in the Italian countryside.

This sort of cool-headed campaigning on multiple fronts (and in the wake of disastrous defeats inflicted by Hannibal) exhibited the ease with which the thriving republic warmed to the task of projecting its prowess abroad. Such confidence and bold-faced disdain for foreign arms lay at the heart of Rome's imperial impulse. It can be argued that Rome's initial empire was accidental in nature; that is, it found itself confronting unwanted crises through military intervention and acquiring territory in the process. But, from their earliest struggles against the Etruscans and Latins, the Romans had cultivated a policy of domination over others, whether overtly or by implied threat, and Roman consuls were expected to make a name for themselves not by penning epics or consecrating bathhouses, but by defeating foreigners in battle.

Force was provided by a military machine that relied on the "maniple"—the fundamental unit of the Roman army, composed of 120 men, or two "centuries" of sixty men each. Unlike the phalanxes preferred by Hellenistic armies, Roman legions were much more flexible, their maniples capable of breaking off and exercising more sophisticated maneuvers than the forward assault typical of huge, lumbering phalangite formations. Though Roman armies suffered defeats, their maniple system proved the more efficient in the long run.

What did *not* prove efficient in the long run was the connection between property and military service. Like so many states in antiquity, the Roman Republic relied on small landowners to fill its armies. Such men were able to afford the equipment and, it was believed, serve more effectively because they had so much at stake. Though city-dwellers without property were recruited for auxiliary units, Rome relied on its farmers to make up the legions.

But as Rome's imperial ambitions extended as far afield as Spain, Africa, and Greece, legions were required to fight for longer and longer periods. Given the distances involved and the nature of ancient warfare, recruits might be away for years at a stretch. Consequently, many—increasingly too many—of these recruits came home to farms that had become dilapidated or been abandoned altogether. The simplest solution for such veterans was to sell their farms and join the faceless urban mass—where they fell below the property qualification for military service. Rome eventually found itself disenfranchising its bedrock yeomanry, running out of recruits, and creating an urban crowd of ex-legionaries whose misfortune could easily spark disaffection or worse.

Other fundamentals of the republican system were also under strain as well. Consuls, Rome's field marshals, found their ability to conduct lengthy operations abroad compromised by the one-year terms to which they were limited. Eventually the Senate was compelled to extend consuls' terms, not only offering a window of opportunity for abuse but also fostering, through longer periods of service, the relationship between commanders and the men who served under them—creating bonds of loyalty in the field that might someday trump loyalty to the state.

It was against this background that some of Rome's most ambitious and opportunistic men tested the limits of the *mos maiorum*, and in the process shook up the establishment.

The result was a generations-long saga of violence and political upheaval that, in the end, laid the republic itself to rest forever.

## THE RADICAL

In 133 BC Tiberius Sempronius Gracchus served as a tribune of the plebs. Brash and politically astute, Gracchus saw the plight of the smallholder as Rome's central issue and hoped to ride it into immortality.

His plan was simple, if drastic: rebuild Rome's military manpower by creating more farms. To do this, he proposed a law limiting the amount of land any one citizen could own. Those owning too much would have the excess seized by the state for distribution to others, especially former soldiers who had fallen on hard times.

Fair enough. Surprisingly, Gracchus's proposal even had some support in the Senate, where powerful landlords abounded. Nevertheless, his plan for getting the bill passed was historic. Rather than taking the idea to the Senate first, where it could be vetted by the state's most respected patriarchs, he took it directly to the people by calling a meeting of the Tribal Assembly of the Plebs, which was his right as a tribune.

This was unprecedented. Until then, custom—the *mos maiorum*—had dictated that the Senate be consulted first so that its august members could debate the bill's worth. But Gracchus, eschewing custom and adhering strictly to the letter of Roman law, chose to exercise his powers as tribune to the maximum. Nothing prevented him from bypassing the Senate, so he did, knowing that his proposal would be popular with the masses swollen by runaway imperial expansion.

The Senate responded by opposing Gracchus in the assembly with their own toadying tribune, whom Gracchus cannily then had deposed by plebiscite—another first, as no magistrate had ever used his influence with voters to have an opposing magistrate sacked. To pious senatorial eyes Gracchus was looking very much like a revolutionary.

Maybe he was. Or maybe he was just an ambitious Roman willing to test the limits of his society in the pursuit of greatness and popularity. Whatever he was, the Senate had their own opinions about Gracchus, and they were not flattering. Once his land bill had passed, irate senators undermined its implementation by pulling tight the purse strings against its funding, as was perfectly within their power.

Again Gracchus struck. Coincidentally, the new province of Asia was in the process of being formed, the ruler of Pergamum having willed his kingdom to Rome upon his death. Gracchus proposed a law diverting the windfall profits to fund his land commission, pushing the envelope of custom once again in one stroke by trespassing on the Senate's traditional control over finances and foreign policy.

*The forum, the centre of Roman life under the empire, was surrounded by temples and civic buildings, including the Senate House.*

Already treading on thin ice, the radical tribune went another step further by declaring his intention to run for an unprecedented second term. The Senate snapped. With visions of tribunate tyranny dancing in their heads, senators and their retainers crashed one of Gracchus's rallies in the forum, breaking up the benches to make clubs and openly assaulting everyone within reach. Gracchus and three hundred of his supporters soon lay dead in the streets.

## "FIRST CITIZEN"

The drama of 133 BC set dangerous precedents for the future of Rome. To begin with, the Senate had lost some of its cherished preeminence. Because it was composed of former magistrates and foreign policy had been its customary sphere of influence, the Senate had grown powerful over the years of war and conquest. Now Gracchus had shown how a man with the right connections and popular appeal could use the Tribal Assembly of the Plebs to circumvent the Senate altogether.

An even worse precedent involved the Senate's desperate response. From 133 BC onward, violence gradually became a standard feature of Roman politics. (In 121 BC, Gaius Gracchus met the same fate as his brother Tiberius, along with three thousand supporters.) Street gangs started hiring themselves out to the highest bidder, and no magistrate left his home or appeared in the forum without his personal toughs in tow.

Taken together, these unfortunate consequences of the Gracchus affair exposed the worst weaknesses of the republican system. Moreover, they paved the way for enterprising men who could both manipulate the system *and* command the ultimate trump card in a world shaped by force—soldiers.

Toward the end of the second century BC, a man of humble origins named Gaius Marius rose to prominence in Roman society through sheer military ability. Elected to a run of six nearly contiguous consulships, he smashed Rome's enemies in Africa and in southern France, becoming a war hero in the process. To prosecute his campaigns, Marius, a naturally gifted soldier and administrator, reorganized the Roman army. Centuries and cohorts replaced maniples as the basic elements of the legion, permanent professional legions were created to foster unit traditions and competitiveness, and training was standardized. But more important than all of these reforms was the decision by Marius to recruit men from the urban masses and equip them at state expense.

The reward for such volunteers was a land grant upon demobilization. In effect, Marius reversed the relationship between real estate and military service: property was now the enticement rather than the requirement. As a result, soldiers now looked to their general not just as a commander but also as a patron who held out the promise of a future as long as they were loyal. At a stroke, the legions had been politicized.

Lucius Cornelius Sulla was the first consul to realize the ultimate potential of all these ominous developments. A successful military leader, he returned from war in Asia in 83 BC to a Rome controlled by his political enemies, one of whom was Marius. What followed was a war in the streets between two implacable factions, each led by a general who commanded an almost proprietary mastery of his troops. When Sulla emerged victorious, he ushered in a period of unprecedented terror. Proscriptions flowed in long lists from his headquarters, condemning to death all who were suspected of siding with Marius and his allies. For two years, murder ran wild through Rome and its environs while Sulla himself rewrote the laws of the state to rejuvenate senatorial power.

The reign of Sulla ended anticlimactically. Satisfied that he had done enough to put the Roman state back on course, he quietly retired from public "service" in 79 BC and died the following year. In the coming decades, most of his revolutionary decrees were undone. Nevertheless, he had drastically lowered the bar on standards of behavior in the pursuit of order. Not since the long-gone days of the kings had Romans lived under an absolute autocrat with complete and capricious control over life, death, and the limits of his own power, but in the coming years they would get used to it.

The decline of the Republic came with the rise of those who marched in Sulla's footsteps: Gnaeus Pompeius Magnus (Pompey), a military hero and egomaniac in the Marian mold; Marcus Licinius Crassus, insatiable landlord and one of the richest men in the history of the Roman Republic; Gaius Julius Caesar, brilliant protégé of Crassus and conqueror of Gaul who would try to become nothing less than a Roman king; Marcus Antonius (Mark Antony), Caesar's most trusted and valuable lieutenant and heir to his affair with Cleopatra, queen of Ptolemaic Egypt; and, the most gifted of the bunch, Gaius Julius Caesar Octavianus (Octavian), legally adopted son of Caesar upon the latter's death.

In their long, bloody death match, these men killed what was left of republican government. Crassus, having launched Julius Caesar upon the world stage, marched east to claim military glory against the Parthians and met his end in the

*Bust of Julius Caesar, who dealt the final blow to the Republic and paved the way for Augustus to found the Roman Empire.*

Mesopotamian desert. Meanwhile, after forming a power-sharing triumvirate with Crassus and Pompey, Caesar added the huge territory of Gaul to the empire, crushed his only real opposition—Pompey—and leveraged his immense popularity with the masses into a reckless dictatorship, only to be stabbed to death like a sacrificial pig by patriotic senators. Mark Antony used his association with the late Caesar to become ruler of half the empire, only to see himself trumped by the man who ruled the other half—Octavian, whose formal adoption by Caesar gave him the sort of cachet in military circles that only the Julian name could bring. The duel between Octavian and Antony marked the final chapter in the Republic: at the epic sea battle of Actium in 31 BC, where the joint forces of Antony and his lover Cleopatra met with defeat, the real loser was Roman democracy.

Octavian, soon to be known as Caesar Augustus, emerged as the unlikely winner of the decades-long brawl over Rome. Sickly in his youth, he was still somewhat frail in young adulthood, a trait that did not endear him to the Roman masses with their hero worship of the strong. However, he soon proved to be one of the greatest, most influential rulers of all time.

The republic was dead. In its place came an ingenious young tyrant who chose to call himself *princeps*—"first citizen."

## AN EMPIRE IN CHAOS

Caesar Augustus had begun life as a rather ordinary young man. Julius Caesar, however, saw other things in the boy and formally adopted him, making him heir to the Julian name and fortune. But what Augustus built with those assets was all his own—a vision of centralized rule that relied on devotion to home and state.

What the years of chaos during the so-called "Roman Revolution" proved to Romans was that the system had broken down. Centrifugal forces within the republic, personified in powerful, predatory men who claimed to have everyone's interest at heart, were compromising the peace. Sadly, the most fundamental lesson to be learnt from this long, gory process was that force equaled stability. And for all his cunning artifice, the first emperor of Rome never made a deal, settled an agreement or backed an agenda without the implied threat of legions in the folds of his toga.

The army had become the underpinning of stability. Augustus did much to divert attention from this, casting himself in the role of father figure. Rather than simply grab power at the top and rule openly like a monarch, he exercised his *auctoritas*—authority, influence, stature—to steer events through the existing system of magistracies and assemblies. Like a good conservative Roman, he manipulated the existing government instead of replacing it, taking on consular and tribunate powers and leaning on others to effect his policies.

It was something of a sham, but it worked—partly because of Augustus's genius, but also because everyone knew whom the legions answered to. Succession, however, forever posed a problem. Genius would come and go in the coming centuries; the legions, by contrast, were a constant.

Under the Republic, elaborate checks and balances had guarded the state against strife and greased the wheels of government. Now the army did both. In AD 41, soldiers of the Praetorian Guard arranged the assassination of Emperor Gaius Caligula, replacing him via military fiat with his uncle, Claudius. Caligula was almost certainly a sociopath, but the larger issue was the nature of his demise: armed warriors close to the center of power had not only decided to bring his reign to an end but also managed to secure the smooth transfer of power to his successor. From now on, emperors of the "principate" could impress the army, woo the army, suborn the army, or overawe the army. But they certainly could not ignore the army or run from it. Augustus had crafted an arrangement with the Roman people that suited his taste for inconspicuous power. His death in AD 14 left a state that, bereft of his charisma and guile, required hard and loyal men in armor to hold it together—for better or worse.

In 68 the Emperor Nero was deposed by the military, his servant helping him commit suicide to avoid a worse fate. Civil war ensued, out of which Vespasian ultimately

*Emperor Caligula's assassination by the Praetorian Guard, as portrayed in a painting by Lawrence Alma-Tadema.*

emerged to found the so-called Flavian Dynasty. A tough soldier of humble origins, Vespasian brought renewed stability to an empire quaking with court intrigue.

Not all emperors were so successful. Maintaining the army's loyalty became paramount to all other considerations. Provincial administration remained stable largely because of bureaucratic reforms pushed through by Augustus, but at court it was anyone's guess at

# ON THE ROAD

Rome conquered its immense empire with an army based overwhelmingly on heavy infantry legions—units that were not known for their swiftness relative to the cavalry or horse archers of other peoples. How could the Romans possibly have maintained the ability to transfer armies quickly from one end of the empire to the other?

The answer, in a word, is "roads." Like aqueducts, Roman *viae* bore testament to the imperial penchant for efficiency and engineering innovation. Though they became the avenues of commerce throughout the provinces, carrying everything from merchant carts to dispatch riders, the roads were originally built for—and by—the legions themselves. Every legionary was also a laborer, and engineers skilled in all manner of field works typically accompanied an army on the march. At the empire's height, more than fifty thousand miles of roads connected its far-flung subjects.

The roads themselves, many of which survive to this day, were marvels of engineering. Construction began with the excavation of a trench, or *fossa*, that would serve as the roadbed. After tamping down the surface of the bed, builders put down a layer of sand to create a level base, called a *pavimentum*. The *statument*, composed of medium-sized stones fixed in a layer of cement, came next, and over that was poured another layer of concrete called the *rudus*, in which pottery shards had been mixed. Then came the *nucleus*, a concrete-gravel mixture, shaped to slope away from the center to ensure the camber of the road. Finally, a layer of flat stones was set into the *nucleus*, their contiguous pattern forming the *summum dorsum* over which years of traffic would pass until maintenance necessitated replacement.

This procedure would have been followed for major thoroughfares in Italy and those in high-traffic areas. Roads on the distant frontiers, though durable, varied in construction. Width also varied throughout the empire. One feature common to all *viae*, however, was linearity. The Romans built their roads as rigidly straight as possible, facilitating their ability to deliver traffic between cities rapidly. The Fosse Way, whose original course forms the basis of several of Britain's highways, offers a good example, never varying more than six miles from a linear course between Ilchester and Lincoln—a distance of more than 180 miles.

the beginning of an emperor's reign how things might turn out. He might be a vigorous campaigner like Trajan, a vapid gadabout like Commodus, or a tyrannical warrior like Severus. Severus's advice to his sons on his deathbed speaks volumes: "Love each other, pay the soldiers well, and despise the rest."

This reliance on appeasing the legions combined with the chaotic nature of the succession to ensure that Rome was never far from the threat of a coup or all-out civil war. By the third century the situation had become fragile enough to collapse completely as no fewer than forty-eight contenders for the throne, many of them shameless usurpers, vied for control between 235 and 285. With soldiers in the field attaching themselves to generals they had come to know and who controlled their fate, any would-be emperor could find an army to back his claim. The result was a bloodbath and political fragmentation on an unprecedented scale. By 270 three states existed where once there had been only one: the Roman center based in Italy, the Empire of the Gallic Provinces, and, in the east, a breakaway dynasty based in Palmyra that controlled territory from Egypt to Asia Minor. The Roman Empire had flown apart.

But the so-called "crisis of the third century" was more than just domestic. In fact, it had much to do with Rome's foreign enemies—especially Germanic peoples from central Europe who had gradually become inextricably intertwined with the tumultuous empire on their border.

## A PERMEABLE FRONTIER

By the third century, Roman rule extended from Britain to the Nile Valley and from the Pillars of Hercules to the Anatolian Plateau. It was an empire of immense size, sophistication, and diversity. But only in Europe did the empire maintain a long border with barbarian peoples who were populous and always at least potentially hostile. In Africa, the encroaching desert was sparsely populated, its peoples often bribed by Roman authorities to check hostile movements. In the east were the Parthians, and then the Sasanids. The Persians, however, were fellow imperialists with urban centers, bureaucratic administration, roads, and a professional army. Though war raged more often than not in that direction, it was fought more for the expansion of borders in Armenia and Mesopotamia than anything else. There was never any real chance that Persian populations would flood the border to displace Roman communities, for the two cultures were too distinct and cohesive to allow this.

Mutual civilized strength prohibited anything more than a back-and-forth clash over territory. And in Britain, the border with Scotland along Hadrian's Wall was narrow, its neighboring barbarian peoples far too few to pose a danger to the empire at large.

The Rhine–Danube border stretching from the English Channel to the Black Sea, however, posed unique problems. This boundary, though closely watched and fortified at strategic points, was a permeable one—a frontier that allowed controlled commercial interaction and that worked as much to gradually absorb Germanic manpower as to keep it at bay.

Since the days of the Republic, Roman armies had eagerly recruited auxiliary units of foreign peoples to augment the legions. They might be slingers, horse archers, or light infantry, all of which could bring to the battlefield abilities and tactics that the Romans themselves were not keen on developing. Though most of these troops were recruited from populations within the empire, some came from beyond the borders.

The Germans were no exception, being welcomed by Roman recruiters at first into auxiliary units and eventually into the legions. The benefit to Rome was twofold: in addition to exploiting Germanic warrior proclivities to forge tough soldiers, the Romans eased local tensions along the border by injecting local economies with steady military pay and offering opportunity to those who might otherwise be hostile.

Yet what seemed like an easy situation to control during the first century BC had changed by the dawn of the third century AD. At the beginning of the empire, the Germanic peoples were obsessively independent, their culture of local autonomy creating a patchwork of villages scattered across central Europe without any discernible organization—an ideal scenario for Rome, which only rarely had to deal with large raids from across the rivers.

But proximity to the Roman Empire brought trade and ideas across the Rhine and Danube to alter the nature of Germanic culture. Notions of centralized power and kingship, along with the military discipline willingly offered by Roman recruiters, conspired to drive the Germans into ever larger groups. Chieftains and eventually petty kings emerged, building ties of loyalty to lesser headmen and holding court in mead halls where those bonds were reinforced against the background of a warrior ethos. Without knowing it, Rome—by its very nature and presence—was turning the barbarian peoples along its longest border into a formidable threat.

Loyalties, moreover, were always an issue. As Arminius proved as early as AD 9 when he wiped out Varus and his legions, talented Germans with a Roman education might just prefer elevating their own peoples at Rome's expense. By the third century officers of Germanic origin who had fought their way up the ranks were common in the Roman army—and many of them, along the permeable frontier, became kings among their own tribes, cultivating a kind of dual existence.

Rome had created its own catch-22. It could not conquer Germania, nor could it simply welcome the Germanic peoples within its borders for fear of losing control of them. It could not prevent the export of its culture, it could not command the vast Rhine–Danube frontier for want of manpower, and it certainly could not count on Germanic quiescence. Throughout its history Rome launched punitive raids into the Germanic lands, whether to capture slaves, punish brigands, or broadcast a message of strength—but these seemed only to exacerbate the situation, reminding those in Germania who wanted to enjoy the fruits of Roman civilization that they would probably have to be taken by force.

## THE DOMINATE

One element remained to turn Rome's thorny problem into an all-out catastrophe. In the third century, while the empire was tearing itself apart over the succession, a nomadic people of the Asian steppe known to history as the Huns began migrating toward Europe. Deadly accurate archers armed with the recurved bow and mounted on durable ponies inured to the hardships of the plain, they drove all before them, starting a domino effect that sent waves of migrants streaming across Europe and, ultimately, to Rome's borders.

By this time the vast majority of Germanic peoples had all but completed their gradual transformation into large confederations, two of which now crashed across Rome's porous frontier to wreak havoc. In the west the Franks invaded over the Rhine, commencing a devastating five-year raid into Gaul and Spain. The Goths moved south in enormous numbers, hitting Asia Minor and Greece, and even plundering Athens.

Invaded by barbarians, sundered into three autonomous sub-states, the empire seemed doomed but, as was the case with so many empires in antiquity, the threat of disaster produced extraordinary men of action. In the last quarter of the third century, a run of hardened emperors—chief among them Aurelian (r. 270–275) and Probus (r. 276–282), both of whom were assassinated by their own soldiers—reunited the empire through breathless campaigning and helped to deal with the bands of Germanic warriors raiding through the countryside.

By the reign of Diocletian (284–305), those nearest the court understood how close the empire had come to extinction, and were ready for drastic change in imperial administration. Diocletian gave them just that, and plenty of it.

Often referred to as the "dominate," to distinguish it from the principate established by Augustus, the new imperial order pushed through by Diocletian created a leaner, meaner empire, geared for a world that had become constantly and pervasively hostile. Taxes were increased rather drastically, mostly to fund the creation of a new, mobile army based mostly on cavalry. Administration was ruthlessly centralized, and the person of the emperor himself was virtually deified, wreathed in the divine approval of Jupiter, head of the pagan pantheon. This was an absolute monarchy in truth *and* theory.

Diocletian also founded a tetrarchy, or rule of four, intended to solve the succession issue. Each half of the empire, East and West, would be ruled by an emperor, each of whom was aided by a subordinate co-emperor who would take over upon his superior's retirement or death. Though it worked briefly, the system mostly had the effect of amplifying the succession problem by drawing in more participants who insisted they had a right to rule. The result was yet another civil war whose ultimate victor, a usurper, was the great Constantine. From 324 until his death in 337, he ruled the entire empire on his own, furthering the centralizing reforms of Diocletian and ultimately decriminalizing Christianity, a faith he himself embraced.

Constantine also founded a new city in the East, based on the old Greek settlement of Byzantium. Called Constantinople, "Constantine's City," it became its founder's most cherished preoccupation. Using every influence at his disposal, the emperor drew the rich and talented to settle there, turning his city very quickly into a center of the empire. In time it would become his capital and the capital of all who would rule in Rome's name in the East—the seat of a great empire that would escape the fate bearing down on the Western Empire.

## ALARIC AND STILICHO

Despite the reforms pushed through by Diocletian and Constantine, the second half of the fourth century saw the empire's problems grow. At the heart of the issue was Sasaniad Persia, which under King Shapur II embarked on an aggressive series of campaigns against the Eastern Empire. This could not have come at a worse time, as it forced the empire to draw soldiers away from the Rhine and Danube frontiers in order to form effective armies in Syria and Mesopotamia.

Perhaps worst of all, Hun activity instigated another wave of refugees. Chief among these were the Goths, whose sufferings at the hands of Hun armies drove them to desperation: they appealed for settlement within the Roman Empire itself. Saddled with more important military requirements in Asia, the empire agreed, allowing the Gothic migrants to take up residence en masse in the old province of Moesia as a distinct ethnic group.

What followed was a narrative of Rome's mounting problems in microcosm. As supplies grew scarce after the arrival of so many refugees, Gothic settlers fell prey to abuse. Unscrupulous imperial officials sold them dog meat, forced them to sell their children into slavery for food, and undertook other despicable acts, gradually driving the Goths to the point of hysteria. In 377 the Goths revolted, rising as one to take by force what they could not acquire otherwise.

Emperor Valens temporarily abandoned his campaigning against the Sasanians to quell the uprising. Near the Balkan town of Adrianople on August 9, 378, Valens clashed with the Germanic army and fell into a trap, the enemy cavalry appearing suddenly in his rear as he and his imperial force (full of Germanic recruits, incidentally) engaged the Gothic defensive ring of wagons. Valens fell amid the complete rout of his army.

Rome's response to such a horrific setback was a shocking sign of the times. Incapable of defeating the Goths, the empire negotiated a settlement, resettled them within the borders of the empire, and cleaned up the bureaucratic abuses that had sparked their disaffection in the first place. Moreover, the Goths became a nation within the state—a semi-autonomous people who now produced for the empire regiments of their own, all of whom fought under Gothic standards and answered to Gothic leaders. A very dangerous precedent had been set: if you have a gripe with the Roman authorities, violent rebellion will not only settle it but probably win you even greater rewards.

In 395 the issue of succession once again reared its ugly head when Emperor Theodosius I made the division of the empire into eastern and western halves official, leaving them to his sons. Arcadius, seventeen years old, assumed control in the East, while eleven-year-old Honorius inherited the West. Of all those who took advantage of these naive youths placed in control of the Roman world, the man known as Stilicho was undoubtedly the most notorious.

A Vandal by birth, Stilicho joined the Roman army and rose through the ranks by virtue of sheer ability and cunning, personifying the "barbarization" of the Roman military and all that it represented. Appointed *magister militum* (supreme military commander) under Theodosius, he ended up assuming broad powers under Arcadius and Honorius, commanding all armies from East and West. Stilicho was ambitious, to say the least, establishing in both capitals troops and agents who reported only to him.

*Above: Stilicho may have been born a Vandal but he became supreme commander of the Roman armies in both East and West.*

With this network and armed presence, he intended to leverage his influence into a high position at court, perhaps through a marriage arrangement.

Another man who was emblematic of the times was Alaric, a former officer in the Roman military who also happened to be king of the Visigoths—a mostly Gothic nation whose distinctive identity, forged through migration and trial, encompassed all manner of peoples who had fallen foul of the chaos that now shaped events on the frontier. Turned down for command of the Eastern armies, Alaric decided to get what he wanted by force, leading his people on a rampage through Macedonia and Greece in 395. Stilicho, summoned east by the court at Constantinople to do something, showed his true colors by negotiating with Alaric. Though he probably had the force to destroy the Visigoths, he understood the role they could play in his personal power play. Instead of fighting them, he settled them as federated client peoples in Epirus on the Ionian Sea. They would not remain there for long.

The Roman world now suffered from the ambitions of two men on the make: Alaric, who hoped to use the predations of his Germanic subjects to get him a command in the Roman army, and Stilicho, who could use his ability to do something about the Visigoths in order to blackmail the emperors.

Goaded by the court of Arcadius in Constantinople, who hoped to expose Stilicho as a cur and humble the Western court, Alaric—now fully convinced that almost anything could be extorted from the Roman Empire—headed for Italy. Stilicho, still convinced that he could somehow use the Visigoth king's peregrinations as a bargaining chip, continued to negotiate while strengthening his own forces—by drawing units from the Rhine frontier. This was a tremendous mistake. On New Year's Eve 406, the Rhine River froze completely. With the Roman garrisons hopelessly weakened by Stilicho's unforgivable calculations, the Germanic confederations that had been pressing on the frontier for years in the hope of fleeing migratory pressures and joining the Roman world came streaming over the ice in the tens of thousands.

The Western Roman Empire would never be the same again. The old question asked by Roman magistrates in court, *Cui bono?* (Who benefits?), now drew a whole range of foreigners from without the empire. And for them, streaming into a world that promised a richer life and cheap plunder, the answer was most definitely "We do."

## A BARBAROUS WORLD

Stilicho came to a bad end in 408 when Honorius had him summoned and executed. As for Alaric, he filled the Italian countryside with fear and rapine, descending on Rome in 410. Though incapable of mounting a siege, his large horde of itinerant malcontents blockaded the great city and ultimately forced it to open the gates. A rather bizarre form of sacking ensued, mostly devoid of burning and violence, in which much of Rome's moveable wealth was systematically mugged from its citizens. Alaric died later that year in southern Italy.

With his death, the Western court—having fled to Ravenna—felt they could deal with the Visigoths honorably. And deal they did, essentially outsourcing Roman security: Emperor Honorius hired the Visigoths as a mercenary people to take on all the *other* barbarian nations that had flooded the empire.

With Franks and Burgundians in Gaul, and Vandals and Suevi having made it all the way to Spain, the Visigoths had their hands full. But Rome had run out of options. Intermittent civil war and its attendant ills—depopulation, decreasing industry, epidemics—had hobbled the Western Empire. When added to the crippling taxation required to revamp the military and confront Persia, the situation became dire.

But just as significant was how much stronger, organized, and more motivated the Germanic confederations had become. Moreover, as the barbarian armies carpeted the countryside, they cut off whole areas of the empire from the imperial center, further limiting its ability to react decisively. The court at Ravenna had little choice but to buy off some Germanic peoples to fight off the others.

By 418 the Visigoths, having restored some sense of order to much of the Western Empire, were rewarded with a grant for settlement in southern Gaul. There they were granted a large share of local taxes, the privilege of governing their own affairs, and the responsibility of arming their own warriors. They had become federates—client peoples who ruled locally on Rome's behalf because Rome no longer had the power to do so.

In fact, Rome in the West no longer had the power to do anything but pit one barbarian people against another. The final and perhaps most egregious example of this involved the Huns. Though their nomadic movements had been affecting European populations for generations, they did not themselves appear in Europe until the fourth century.

The Romans quickly took to using them as mercenary allies against dangerous Germanic tribes, aiding the Huns in establishing a large domain of subject peoples from whom they extracted agricultural produce, labor, and raw materials.

By the middle of the fifth century, however, the Huns had taken to extracting their money out of Roman coffers by a more direct approach. Under their King Attila, an especially dynamic leader, the Huns raided the Eastern Empire, only to be stopped at the formidable walls of Constantinople. Attila then headed west in 451, essentially turning the Roman frontier and its federated Germanic peoples into a giant cash box to be looted at his leisure.

Having had their most important mercenary client turn freelance, the Romans were helpless before the "Scourge of God," as Attila became known. Only by turning to the Visigoths in Gaul once more could Roman authorities turn back the Hunnic tide. At the bloody battle of Chalons in 451, Attila was checked for the first time with Gothic help. He descended on Rome itself the following year, only to be talked out of a general siege by Pope Leo I (who was probably helped by an outbreak of disease among Attila's armies). Attila died the same year under mysterious circumstances after celebrating his marriage to a new wife.

Rome would be sacked again—and from the opposite direction. Proving how decayed the imperial apparatus had become, Vandal forces, having conquered all of Roman North Africa, *sailed* an army to Italy and took the heart of the old empire in 455.

*After 476 the mighty city of Rome fell into ruins, a perfect allegory for the fall of the Roman Empire, as depicted in this eighteenth century painting*

Europe had become a Germanized world. Whether attacking Romans or defending them, the Germanic barbarian peoples had assumed a preeminence that Rome had long since lost the ability to reverse. Ultimately all of the Western Empire would be settled and defended by federated tribes that received the same treaty the Visigoths had signed: Franks, Alemanni, Ostrogoths, and Burgundians settled within the empire, effectively replacing Roman armies and, in some cases, Roman administration. In 476 Odoacer, a Gothic king, compelled the last "emperor" of Rome in the West to stand down. His name was Romulus Augustulus, hauntingly recalling the legendary founder of Rome as well as its first emperor. Odoacer became king of Italy.

The fall of Rome could not have been the sole result of Germanic barbarians and the stresses they put upon the European frontier. Nevertheless, in asking how the western half of the empire came to its fate, one is constantly drawn to the fact that the eastern half, based at Constantinople, endured for hundreds of years after 476. The Eastern, or Byzantine, Empire had several unique assets. To begin with, it included ancient cities such as Alexandria, Antioch, and Ephesus, and its population and taxable income dwarfed those of the much less urbanized West—especially after the civil wars and gradual depopulation of western cities from the third century onward. And Constantinople itself was much more difficult than Rome to assail, possessing awesome landward fortifications and a navy to command the Bosporus.

But of all the differences between East and West, none was as conspicuous as the weakness of the Rhine–Danube frontier. Byzantine emperors had to confront challenges from the barbarian steppe, but along a much narrower border and from peoples who were more interested in looting the empire than settling within it and changing its character. In the West, the presence of that thin line separating so many generations of curious, aggressive peoples from a civilization that was for them incredible, menacing, useful, and wanton by turns produced a string of crises that the imperial administration, with all its peculiar faults, was eventually incapable of handling.

Yet one of the reasons scholars still debate this topic so heatedly is Rome's significance in the creation of our modern world. The empire's influence is all around us, from the Arc de Triomphe in Paris to much of the vocabulary of the English language. The organization of the Catholic Church is a direct descendant of Roman imperial administration, and as late as the twentieth century two European empires called their rulers "Caesar": Russia's *tsar* and Germany's *Kaiser* both had a form of absolute power going back to Roman late antiquity even while contemporary nations were democracies with various systems of checks and balances that owed much to the Roman Republic. Little wonder that many question whether Rome fell at all.

CHAPTER FIFTEEN

# SASANID PERSIA

## EXHAUSTED BY WAR

ON the ancient road connecting the Iranian provinces of Persis and Elam lie the ruins of Bishapur, founded by the Persian King Shapur I. Those who visit this crumbling place on the Iranian Plateau are sure to seek out the nearby river gorge, on whose walls Shapur had carved the achievements of his reign some eighteen centuries ago.

One of these reliefs stands out for its graphic depiction of Romans—three Romans, in fact, all of whom are bona fide emperors. Shapur, sitting majestically upon his warhorse in their midst, is conspicuous for his Persian raiment. One of the Romans, Gordian III, lies dead beneath Shapur's horse, his corpse literally frozen in the act of being trampled. Another, Philip the Arab, rests on one knee before the mounted Persian, begging for mercy (or peace). And the third stands beside Shapur, who rests one possessive hand on the emperor's bound hands. This last is a depiction of Valerian, captured in AD 260 and brought back to Persia as a prize.

As the relief attests, Shapur was a Roman nightmare made manifest. The truth behind the fates of these three emperors is open to debate: Gordian III certainly died while campaigning against the Persians, although he may have been assassinated rather than killed in battle, while nothing was ever heard of Valerian after he became a captive in the East. But Shapur's boast in stone is essentially valid, connecting him with the death and/or humiliation of three Roman emperors.

Hundreds of miles north of Bishapur, on the western coast of the Caspian Sea, is an ancient site of a very different nature. Overlooking the Russian coastal city of Derbent, the stout fortifications of Narin Kala look nearly as formidable today as they must have looked in the sixth century, when they were built. The citadel formed part of a massive wall that stretched westward from the sea, guarding regions to the south—Azerbaijan, Armenia, Iran—from invasion by nomadic barbarians. Initiated by Khosrow I, emperor of Sasaniad Persia, the walls were paid for in part by funds from the Byzantine Empire, which had learned to hate invaders from the north as much as the Persians. Interestingly, funds for the

*Previous pages: Column capital from Bishapur.*
*Above: Following the triumphant theme of the relief at Bishapur, a carving at Naqsh-i-Rustam shows the Roman Emperor Valerian kneeling in front of Shapur I after his capture at Edessa.*

fortification effort eventually stopped coming from the Byzantines, helping to spur yet another war between Persia and its powerful western neighbor.

These two monuments bracket Sasanid Persia's military history like bookends. Created three hundred years apart, they show a state skilled in war and connected with Rome, which is a good précis of the Sasanian Empire. This second Persian Empire, recalling the first under the Achaemenids, thrived for some four hundred years, witnessing a glorious flowering of Iranian culture and laying the groundwork for Islamic empires to come. These were golden years in the history of Iran—a period in which Hellenization was halted and reversed, Persian literature and art flourished, and the mightiest rulers of Europe feared the advance of Persian armies and corresponded with their leaders as equals.

But the Sasanids, for all their cultural achievements, seemed immersed in the narrative of war. Though revered to this day for the sophistication of their civilization, it was conquest that occupied much of the Sasanids' energy—and ultimately paved the way for their collapse.

## RESURRECTING THE GLORIOUS PAST

When Ardashir I overthrew the crumbling Parthian Empire in AD 226, he transformed his native Persian realm from a vassal of the Arsacid dynasty into an imperial power in its own right. To him and his fellow Persians, it marked the resurgence of Iran's proper overlords—a revival of the golden age of the Achaemenids. Named for Sasan, an ancestor of Ardashir, the dynasty came to be known as the Sasanids.

Crowned at Ctesiphon as "King of Kings," Ardashir embarked on an expansion of his Iranian kingdom, conquering the western provinces of the Kushan Empire, centered in the Hindu Kush, and absorbing by force parts of Armenia and northwest Arabia. When he laid siege to Hatra in Roman territory he literally served notice to his Roman neighbors and began a combative relationship with them that would endure, with few respites, for four centuries. By publicly laying claim to the vast areas in Syria, the Levant, and Asia Minor that had once answered to the Achaemenids, Ardashir believed he was merely restoring the old Persian Empire. The Romans, however, would not go quietly.

Shapur I, Ardashir's son and heir, assumed the throne in 241, just after the capture of Hatra. It was he who would first endure the full fury of a Roman response to the border skirmishes that now blew up into all-out war—and he proved more than a match for his Latin foes.

In 242 Emperor Gordian III marched east and his general Timesitheus scored a victory against the Sasanians at the battle of Rhesaina. But by 244 Gordian was dead,

his army routed by Shapur at Misik, and his successor, Philip the Arab, had little choice but to conclude a humiliating peace that included a massive indemnity. More Persian successes followed: the conquest of Armenia, and victorious advances into Roman Mesopotamia and Syria. In 260, at Edessa, Shapur trapped and captured a Roman army, along with its commander, the Emperor Valerian. According to legend, Valerian was taken east to be kept at court like a trophy, the Persian emperor using him as a footstool when mounting his horse. It was perhaps the single most humiliating reverse in Rome's long history.

Shapur's subsequent advance into Cilicia and Cappadocia reaped thousands of Roman captives, all of whom were resettled in the growing Sasanian Empire, their skills put to good use by the Persians (Roman soldiers built Shapur's new city of Bishapur). Having added so much territory to his exploding realm, Shapur created a new and decidedly vainglorious title for himself: King of Kings of Iran and non-Iran. It became the standard designation for his successors.

Interestingly, Shapur's worst military reverses came at the hands of an enemy of Rome. Odaenathus, ruler of Palmyra and bane of the Roman east, defeated Sasanian armies in the field several times and twice marched to the outskirts of Ctesiphon before

*Above: The royal palace of Shapur I at Ctesiphon included a magnificent vaulted audience chamber (shown on right).*

his assassination in 267. But these were little more than inconveniences in an otherwise stunning wave of conquests.

Shapur was more than just a soldier. He founded numerous cities, many of them with captives from the west, and ordered the construction of dams and fortresses throughout the empire. Moreover, he was committed to the cultivation of ideas: in addition to having numerous works from the West translated into Persian, he enforced an official policy of religious tolerance. Zoroastrianism eventually became the state religion, but Christians, Jews, Hindus, Buddhists, and others could all worship freely.

Having conquered a vast stretch of real estate from Bactria to Mesopotamia, the first two Sasanid emperors had gone a long way toward reinstituting the imperium of the Achaemenids. In little more than a generation, Persia had been reborn under Persian sovereignty. Though conflict with Rome continued for most of the rest of the third century, neither empire was able to secure an advantage that could bring decisive results. Armenia, ever a bone of contention between East and West, changed hands several times, and raids into enemy territory were a standard modus operandi for both sides. By the dawn of the fourth century, the conflict had sapped enough out of both Rome and Persia to force an uneasy cessation of hostilities.

## SHAPUR II

Though administered by a much more centralized bureaucracy than its Parthian predecessor, the Sasanian Empire was still a state dominated by noble families. In fact, many of the prominent Parthian households had merely acquiesced to Sasanid rule, becoming part of the aristocracy that provided educated young men for positions in the imperial hierarchy.

But as in so many kingdoms in history, the relationship between a king and the aristocracy upon which he relies for peace and security can be a difficult one. The case of the Sasanids was no exception. Great families had been a part of reality in Iran for centuries, and no monarch could hope to pacify the countryside without enlisting their support and resources. Should the ruling dynasty exhibit weakness, however, it could easily come under attack from the nobility. Iranian princes needed a monarch who was pious and strong in war, who could justify his seat on the throne through stability at home and conquest on the frontiers.

At the beginning of the fourth century, the Sassanid Persian Empire risked having neither stability nor conquest. In 298, King Narseh was ambushed by Roman forces and compelled to sign a treaty that deeply weakened Persia's position in the west. His successor, Hormizd II, was besieged by revolts in the east, and his death while hunting in 309 could well have been an assassination. What followed upon Hormizd's demise was a perfect illustration of aristocratic interference in the ruling dynasty's affairs. Determined to rid themselves of the current leadership (Arab raiders were striking into Persis itself, further impugning the ability of the court), disgruntled nobles killed one of the late king's sons and blinded another. A third escaped into exile. They then "elected" Hormizd's unborn son king, appointing the boy's mother to act as regent with the help of the court until he was old enough to rule.

This ninth king of Sasanid Persia, Shapur II—one of the few monarchs ever to be crowned *in utero* (according to legend, the magnates actually placed the crown upon his mother's pregnant belly)—ruled until 379, presiding over a golden age in Iran. His primary concern, true to the wishes of those who had brutally paved the way for his succession, was war. First on his list were the Arab tribes, which soon came to regret their decision to mug Persis. The Persian king swept down into the desert, crushing a combined Arab army so savagely that he came to be known there as "Piercer of Shoulders." By the time he returned home, he had left a fortified defensive line along the border of southern Mesopotamia to thwart future Arab raids.

In the West, a treaty had ensured peace with the Romans for forty years. Shapur would have none of it, and in 338 promptly recaptured Armenia. After that, however, things went poorly. Though capable of defeating Roman armies with his heavy cavalry in the open spaces of Mesopotamia, Shapur found the Roman fortresses of the area, particularly Nisibis, too tough to crack. Such places, guarding the approaches to Rome's far eastern possessions, had been made all but impregnable.

Making matters worse were the continued interruptions from the other side of the Persian Empire, where nomadic peoples were tearing up the countryside. Though Shapur was able to stop these incursions and force a peace upon their instigators, it did nothing to help his flagging operations against Rome.

These took a dramatic turn when the Roman Emperor Julian, guided by the same Persian prince who had escaped assassination by the men who had crowned Shapur, marched down the Tigris River in 363 with an army more than eighty thousand strong and trailing an impressive siege train. Arguably the equal of Shapur in terms of generalship, Julian had taken matters into his own hands after the Persians finally managed to take several of the formidable citadels in Mesopotamia that had once given them so much trouble. But after defeating a Sasanian army at the battle of Ctesiphon, he was unable to carry the city and died during the retreat. Shapur then forced a humiliating peace on Jovian, Julian's successor, in which all the Mesopotamian lands lost to the Romans in 298 were returned, Nisibis and other strongholds were surrendered, and the Romans promised to give Persia a free hand in Armenia.

Armenia soon fell to Sasanid invaders, and in 377 a peace was arranged that divided the kingdom between Persia and Rome. Shapur also campaigned in what are today Pakistan and Afghanistan, further expanding the borders of the empire. By the end of his reign, he had ushered his state into a period of newfound strength and prosperity.

But not for everyone.

## A STATE OF RIGID HIERARCHIES

Sasanid society seems to have been divided into three classes, or castes: priests, warriors, and commoners. (A fourth class, "secretaries," is sometimes referred to as well, being above commoners but below the warriors and priests.) This system was fairly strict and clearly delineated. And if the nature of Shapur II's rise to the throne is suggestive of the power of the warrior nobility, the religious intolerance of his reign offers some idea of the influence of the Sasanian priesthood.

Like the Achaemenids before them, the Sasanians were Zoroastrians, worshiping a god—Ahura Mazda—who represented universal goodness and wisdom. Ahura Mazda was a god of light, and his temples blazed with fire. One of the greatest accomplishments of Shapur II's reign was the completion of the written *Avesta*, bringing together the texts, and oral traditions about Ahura Mazda going back centuries to the deity's greatest prophet, Zoroaster (or Zarathustra).

The Mazdean priesthood that had overseen this tremendous accomplishment had grown immensely powerful over the years and was now capable of exerting as much influence at court as the landed nobility. Associated with the investiture of power in the king, they were involved in politics as well as religion—two concepts that were one and the same to the Sasanids (hardly unique in an ancient empire). When, during Shapur II's reign, the Roman Emperor Constantine made himself the protector of Christians everywhere, it was interpreted in Iran as a direct threat to Persian stability.

This was because the Sasanid Empire ruled over many Christians. While previous Sasanid kings had tolerated different faiths, Shapur II, with the urgent support of the priesthood, clamped down on Christians as a veritable fifth column. Throughout the empire, Christians were rooted out and persecuted, raising alarm bells in Rome and further exacerbating tensions between the two empires. The persecutions ended with Shapur II's death in 379, but only temporarily—Sasanid religious tolerance would change with nearly every emperor in the coming centuries.

A strong ruler in the conqueror's mold, Shapur had built cities, commanded pious obedience, expanded and fortified the borders of his realm, and struck terror in the hearts of Roman opponents.

## THUS SPAKE ZARATHUSTRA

According to legend, Zoroaster laughed rather than cried upon being pulled from his mother's womb. It is a magnificent story that compels us all the more because so little is known about this prophet of a religion that bears his name.

Even the age in which Zoroaster (or Zarathustra) lived is fiercely debated, with suggestions ranging from 1500 BC to 600 BC. Not until the height of the Sasanid Empire were his numerous preachings and fables written down in the *Avesta*, transforming a disunited faith, typically referred to as Mazdaism, into what we know today as Zoroastrianism—the cohesive religion based on the words of Zoroaster as immortalized in the texts of the *Avesta*.

Though Zoroastrianism today emphasizes a kind of monotheism, it was overtly dualistic in antiquity. Ahriman, representing evil and darkness, struggled for supremacy against Ahura Mazda, the epitome of justice, truth, and goodness. The latter was worshipped formally at fire altars whose light manifested the god's wisdom.

One of the earliest—if not the earliest—forms of worship involving a clear division between heaven and hell, moral and immoral living, Zoroastrianism has left an immense impact on other religious traditions throughout the world. One of the unlikeliest involved the cult of Mithra, a minor deity in early Mazdaism, which found new life in the Roman world. Known as Mithras in the West, the deity joined the expansive Roman pantheon as a sun god whose roots in Zoroastrian ethics appealed to Roman soldiers looking for a righteous being to guide and sanctify their dangerous profession. Mithraism became a major subculture in the empire, its temples acting as points of contact for networking soldiers and former soldiers.

He also established a strong, centralized administration that survived him and saved his lesser successors from disaster. Largely devoid of wars with Rome (which had formally bifurcated into the Latin West and the Byzantine East), the fifth century produced a plethora of fascinating characters on the Sasanid throne, from Bahram V (421–438)—known for hunting onagers, chasing women, and throwing lavish parties—to Kavadh I (488–531), whose support of a prominent heretic sect landed him in prison, from which he escaped and reclaimed the throne at the head of an army of Huns. This period saw only two brief and inconclusive wars with the Byzantines, but in the east and north the Persians continued to fight the increasingly concerted incursions by nomadic peoples, especially those of the so-called "White Huns," or Hephthalites.

The relative durability of the empire, however, could barely conceal tensions that threatened to rip it apart. Most of Shapur II's successors resisted oppression of religious minorities, a practice that earned them devotion in some quarters but that put them at

odds with the powerful Zoroastrian priesthood—who in turn defeated any attempts by the crown at further centralization. Aiding the clergy in their fight against imperial control were the nobles, whose close ties to military matters made them suspicious of emperors who did not take up the sword against the perennial foe in the West. Given this background and the continuing manipulation of the succession by powerful figures, only strong emperors were capable of countering the centrifugal forces pulling at Persia and its vast territories.

The answer to these problems was war—the sport of kings that galvanized clerics, appeased the warrior aristocracy, diverted domestic aggressions abroad, and acquired booty and territory to win popularity with everyone who mattered. Sasanid Persia was hardly unique in this way but its peculiar mix of knightly heritage, religious tension, and geographical proximity to a cultural and military equal—Rome/Byzantium—that offered regular, almost ritualized warfare, all conspired to make Sasanid Persia's embrace of war that much closer.

Not surprisingly, the sixth century proved much more violent than the fifth.

## ALL-OUT WAR AND THE REFORMS OF KHOSROW I

In the century begun by Kavadh I's reign, Sasanid Persia would fight three long, costly wars with the Byzantine Empire in 502–532, 540–562, and 572–590. Though their causes varied, these wars reflected a situation where two great states were incapable of understanding each other without resorting to aggression. As historian Michael Axworthy recently put it, "The wars and the disputed provinces had taken on a totemic value—they had become part of the apparatus by which Persian shahs and Roman emperors alike justified their rule." By the end of the century, this process had at once changed the Sasanian state and committed it to a course that would lead to its own destruction.

At the heart of this process was the most celebrated Sasanid emperor of them all, Khosrow I, known in Persian as *Anushirvan*, "the immortal soul" (r. 531–579). Remembered as a true philosopher king, Khosrow vigorously oversaw the translation of works from Indian and Greek, and commissioned an astronomical almanac. His

*Above: Head of a Sasanid king with his elaborate winged crown, sixth century* AD.

reverence for intellectuals was legendary: when the Byzantine Emperor Justinian closed down the academy of philosophy in Athens, its Neoplatonist scholars were welcomed in Khosrow's court. Inquisitive, assertive, just, Khosrow came to epitomize good kingship in the East for centuries afterward.

Just as important, Khosrow completed the government reforms begun by his father, Kavadh I. During Kavadh's reign, a heretical movement called Mazdakism had swept the empire. Born of the miseries suffered by an exploited peasantry, it espoused the communal sharing of all property, undermining the authority of Persia's wealthiest families. Class war swept the land, fought between desperate nobles and the Mazdakites who would topple their fortunes.

Toward the end of his reign, Emperor Kavadh used the chaos as leverage to institute tax reforms that lessened the power of the aristocracy. Abolishing exemptions that had previously favored the landed nobility, he created a new tax code that assessed real estate more equitably, channeling monies that had previously gone to local lords into the emperor's coffers. To ensure the efficiency of collection, Kavadh sowed the villages with minor nobility, enfiefing them with land in exchange for their services. These *dehqans*, or rural gentry, became the chivalric backbone of Persia's armies—the mailed, mounted knights who charged in battle, now paid and equipped by the enlarged imperial treasury that their empowerment made possible rather than by local lords who might coopt their loyalty.

By Khosrow I's ascension to the throne, he could rely on a well-drilled military establishment built around the dehqans. The empire had been divided into four great zones, each commanded by a *spahbod*, or military commander, and a building program eventually secured the frontiers with formidable fortifications like those that survive today at Derbent on the Caspian. With the nobility cowed, the priesthood appeased, and a large, efficient bureaucracy, the Sasanian Empire had become arguably the mightiest power on earth.

If there were any doubts on this point, Khosrow soon set about putting them to rest. Breaking a negotiated peace with the old nemesis Byzantium, the king marched on Syria in 540 and captured the great city of Antioch. He battled pro-Byzantine forces in Lazica, in modern-day Georgia, and sent an army by sea south to Yemen, freeing it of Ethiopian occupation and installing a Persian governor. In the east, he united with the Turks to destroy the Hephthalites, a Hunnish people who had been a thorn in Persia's side for centuries.

As impressive as these achievements were, it would fall to another Khosrow to show the world what the Sasanian military machine was really capable of—and, in the process, expose the Sasanid throat to the knife of new enemies.

## THE VICTORIOUS

Khosrow II's chaotic rise proved that while his grandfather and namesake had centralized and strengthened the Persian state, he had not banished the machinations of noble families altogether. Khosrow I's successor, Hormizd IV (r. 579–590), relied a bit too heavily on brutality to quash dissent in priestly and aristocratic circles, paving the way for Bahram Chubin, a noble general of old Parthian stock, to play the role of kingmaker. Around 590 or 591, Bahram conspired with other disaffected aristocrats to have Hormizd murdered, and put the late emperor's son, Khosrow II, on the throne.

What followed was the sort of drawn-out court intrigue that has plagued myriad thrones throughout history and given the likes of Shakespeare an embarrassment of riches to work with. Bahram, enticed by a whiff of destiny, retracted his support of Khosrow and nominated himself king, sinking the empire into a civil war. Khosrow turned to an unlikely source for support: the Byzantine Emperor Maurice. Not one to squander an opportunity to put on the Persian throne a man who was beholden to him, Maurice sent Khosrow back east with an army. Bahram fled to the company of the Turks, where he fell to an assassin's blade. Khosrow's enemies put other pretenders in his way, all of whom were disposed of. Little wonder he came to be known as *Parvez*, or "Victorious." His future accomplishments, however, would make these forgettable by comparison.

Securely in power by around 600, Khosrow II would become the greatest conqueror in Iranian history since Cyrus the Great. It began with the death of his Byzantine backer, Maurice, in 602 at the hands of a usurper named Phocas. Employing his outrage as a *casus belli*, the Sasanid emperor marshaled his forces for war against a Byzantine Empire that had descended into chaos.

By 605 Khosrow had captured all of Mesopotamia, with its fortified settlements and immense wealth. Between 611 and 613 he took Syrian Antioch, Tarsus, and Damascus. Jerusalem soon followed, its defiant population subjected to sack and slaughter and its holiest relic, the True Cross, spirited to Ctesiphon as a war prize. And in 619, completing a whirlwind campaign, the armies of Khosrow conquered Egypt itself, depriving the Byzantine world of its primary grain supply.

Despite its incredible conquests, the Sasanian Empire now teetered on the knife's edge. Khosrow II, shaped by the succession battles that had rocked the beginning of his reign, ruled with an iron fist. He oppressed the nobility to squelch the threats they posed to his authority, and he squeezed the commoners for all they were worth in the pursuit of money for his wars. With prudence and luck, he may have been able to secure his vast conquests (which recalled those of the Achaemenids, always a Sasanid goal)

and his position at home. But at this crucial moment in Persian history, the Byzantines produced a ringer of their own.

Heraclius (r. 610–641) reorganized the Byzantine state and military, rejuvenating an empire that had suffered dreadfully from Persian predation. By 622 his situation was secure enough to embark on foreign expeditions, and he proceeded to batter the Persian menace on all fronts. Taking the field himself, he freed Asia Minor from Sasanian

*Above: Khosrow II conquered swaths of Byzantine territory but then lost it all to the victorious Byzantine Emperor Heraclius (illustration from a fifteenth century manuscript by Vincent of Beauvais).*

control, then dealt the Persians a decisive defeat at the battle of Nineveh, while his forces in Constantinople repulsed a combined attack by Sasanians and Avars, a nomadic people who had hitched their wagon to the Persian horse. The peace that resulted, negotiated by Heraclius with Khosrow II's successor, Kavadh II, returned nearly all the territories conquered by Persia during Khosrow's spectacular run to the Byzantines. It was a stunning reverse.

Kavadh compounded the sufferings of his country by murdering all his brothers to secure his own position. Clearly Sasanid Persia had fallen off the knife's edge.

## CONQUERORS FROM THE DESERT

The costly, far-ranging campaigns of Khosrow II had all but bankrupted the empire and brought its ruling dynasty to the brink. A strong ruler at this point might have thwarted disaster, but that is not what the empire got. Now immersed in plots by the various noble houses to control the empire's future, Sasanid Persia—its costly wars having weakened the dehqans and their usefulness in opposing aristocratic ambitions—suffered from a series of weak, short-lived monarchs. In 632 the final Sasanid king, Yazdegerd III, assumed the throne as a child. He faced a threat from Arabia that would have tested the mettle of a king with twice his years and experience.

This threat was Islam. United as never before by the proselytizing message of Mohammed, the tribes of Arabia—already a formidable military force—came together to create a destabilizing front in the Near East. Byzantium would suffer greatly from the advance of Muslim forces but Sasanid Persia, having weakened itself through generations of warfare, was much closer to the Islamic threat than the Byzantines. And it felt the full onslaught of Islamic armies.

The year 636 commenced a cycle of woe for the embattled Sasanian state. At al-Qadisiyah and Nehavand, once-great armies were routed, exposing the empire to Islamic raiders. Resistance to the desert invaders was at certain places quite intense, but it could not prevent the general collapse of Sasanid power. Yazdegerd III was assassinated in 651 by his own subjects, bringing a bloody end to Iran's greatest imperial dynasty. Galvanized by their religious mission, the Muslim armies fought with a tenacity that set them apart from the civilizations that fell before them. For Sasanid Persia, they could not have come at a worse time. Having drained so much of their people and countryside in the tremendous seesaw battles with the Eastern Romans and the nomads of the steppe, the Sasanians were in no position to withstand the waves of Arab horsemen that now came upon them with a spiritual purpose. Historical contingency had conspired with the Persian need to reclaim its Achaemenid past through war in the creation of a disaster.

CHAPTER SIXTEEN

# THE MAYA

## THE DEATH OF DIVINE KINGSHIP

IN 1839 American President Martin Van Buren tapped a New Jersey-born lawyer and traveler named John Lloyd Stephens for the post of Special Ambassador to Central America. The job offered no small number of thorny challenges; in fact, the short-lived "Federal Republic of Central America" was erupting in civil war amid an annexation attempt by Mexico. But Stephens would become famous not for brokering a momentous peace, nor for negotiating a lucrative trade agreement. Instead, he would make history by following rumors of a lost civilization into the jungles of Honduras and Belize and finding, to his amazement, breathtaking glories in the vine-choked gloom.

"Of the moral effect of the monuments themselves," he later wrote, "standing as they do in the depths of a tropical forest, silent and solemn, strange in design, excellent in sculpture, rich in ornament, different from the works of any other people, their uses and purposes and whole history so entirely unknown with hieroglyphics explaining all, but being perfectly unintelligible, I shall not pretend to convey any idea." Stephens, one of a select few Westerners to have beheld these magnificent stone buildings since their heyday, was profoundly moved: "Often the imagination was pained in gazing at them."

Accompanied by British architect Frederick Catherwood, Stephens visited and documented numerous sites, ultimately acquiring an inkling of just how large this ancient civilization really was. Its age, however, could only be a matter of conjecture, though he would not have been surprised to learn that the ruins of Copan—which he bought for fifty dollars in the vain hope of shipping them to American museums—had not been occupied since the ninth century. Other great complexes of pre-Columbian America were known to the public, from Teotihuacan in Mexico to the mountain fastnesses of the Inca in Peru. But for Stephens, the majestic structures of Honduras were all the more fascinating for the gnarled wilderness that surrendered them with an almost sentient reluctance. "In Egypt," he wrote, "the colossal skeletons of gigantic temples stand in the unwatered sands in all the nakedness of desolation; here an immense forest shrouded the ruins, hiding them from sight, heightening the impression and moral effect, and giving an intensity and almost wildness to the interest." How could the world know so little about a people who had once kept the rainforest at bay and dwelt in such splendor?

How indeed? Swallowed by the lush countryside, most of the Maya ruins would have to wait until a more technical age could muster the dedication and resources to truly expose them. Much has happened since Stephens's adventure in Central America—the last few decades alone have witnessed a veritable explosion in Maya studies. Even

*Previous pages: Standing Atlante from the Palace of Masks at Kabah Puuc near Uxmal.*

the Maya hieroglyphic language has been deciphered, opening a window on their history and culture as never before. And what scholars have been able to piece together is truly remarkable.

By the time the Spanish arrived in the sixteenth century to brutally usher in a new age for Mesoamerica, the Maya could look back on some two and a half thousand years of urban civilization. Throughout that period, numerous dynasties and kingdoms had risen and fallen, defining a long and tumultuous history of clashing polities. The conquistadors may have crushed, once and for all, the Maya's centuries-long autonomy beneath the boot of New Spain, but it was hardly the first time that this ancient Mesoamerican people had fallen.

## FARMERS, BUILDERS, MERCHANTS, AND LORDS

Encompassing parts of modern-day Mexico, Belize, Guatemala, and Honduras, the ancient Maya homeland covered an area of 125,000 square miles. Roughly the size of the state of New Mexico, it is a region of extraordinary environmental diversity, from the rugged mountains and highlands in the south to the vast lowland expanse of the Yucatan Peninsula. River valleys, jungles, deserts, and forests all compete for space, rainfall varies tremendously, and air temperatures range from chilly to stifling.

*Above: Temple I rises from the jungle in the midst of the Maya ruins in Tikal National Park, Guatemala.*

Rich volcanic and alluvial soils can be found throughout the region, where the Maya learned to grow maize, beans, squash, and chile. They dwelt in thatched houses (still called *xanil nah* today), each of which featured a three-stone hearth that represented the triangular "Cosmic Hearth" on which the gods had centered the world. In time their community buildings, built in a central courtyard of the village, evolved from large thatched structures to raised earthen mounds or pyramids topped with shrines and temples.

By 500 BC, influenced by older cultures to the north, such as the Olmec, the Maya began turning their modest settlements into cities, complete with paved courtyards, causeways, and stone temples. Trade routes, some of them extending beyond the Maya homeland, allowed the exchange of goods such as cacao, obsidian, chert, bird feathers, and sea salt. Images in plaster soon adorned Maya buildings, capturing and codifying the rituals of public life. And sometime around 400 BC, the Maya made perhaps their most enduring and significant discovery: kingship.

## POWER PERSONIFIED

Archaeologists divide Mesoamerican history into a handful of more-or-less distinct periods. The first two, Early Pre-classic (2000–1000 BC) and Middle Pre-classic (1000–400 BC), witnessed the emergence of Maya civilization, while the third—Late Pre-classic—began with the appearance in some Maya cities of kings.

A response to the growing disparity in wealth that came with greater commercial activity, kings emerged as a legitimization of class. They were called *k'uhul ajaw*, or "Divine Lord," putting a holy stamp on the stratification of society, and they eventually became the most important person of every Classic Maya city-state.

In exchange for absolute obedience to his authority, the king provided crucial services that represented his perfect synthesis of the sacred and the profane, the god-like and the worldly. The *k'uhul ajaw* was a virtual demigod—he not only ruled and protected the people of his polity, but he also connected them to the universe of the gods. Like a Mesoamerican pharaoh, he was priest, general, and prince all in one. Standing at the pinnacle of society, the *k'uhul ajaw* was power manifested, ensuring stability and prosperity by his very presence.

It was no easy job. The office was totemic in nature, inextricably tying the ruler to his realm and forcing him to embark upon labors that would trumpet success to the world, intimidate rival polities, and assuage the worries of his people. Ritual played a major role in this process. Like the lead player in an ongoing theatrical production, he would don elaborate costumes and dance to assume the image of a god. The *k'uhul ajaw* dedicated new temples, presiding at the burning of incense or letting of blood—deemed the finest offering to the deities. He commemorated the conclusion of calendar cycles, and formally announced the selection of an heir to ensure the survival of his dynasty.

The ruler was not the only member of the elite in the Maya hierarchy—nobles abounded, filling roles as courtiers, scribes, priests, artists, merchants, and military leaders, all of whom enjoyed a privileged existence—but the *k'uhul ajaw* did not share power: his authority was absolute. To emphasize his elevated nature, he bore signs of office such as an elaborate headband and scepter, affected an aloof, ethereal demeanor, and took a name appropriate to his station: Sun-Faced Lord, Jeweled Skull, Stormy Sky, or Smoke-Monkey, for instance.

Life was a spectacle for the *k'uhul ajaw*, his solemn acts lying at the center of a drama for all to witness. Forming the perfect environment for this cult of performance, Maya architecture emphasized the grand and the public, and it remains the most visible link to the brilliance that thrived in the ancient Maya homeland.

## AN EPIC IN STONE

By the beginning of the Early Classic (AD 200–600), great Maya settlements such as Tikal and Copan were producing exceptional buildings, perfecting the architectural grandiosity that had arisen in leading Pre-classic polities such as El Mirador and the magnificent foreign city to the north, Teotihuacan. The Maya calendar abounded with public rituals, dances, and festivals, all of which emphasized the outdoors; the common buildings that shaped a king's capital were designed either as platforms or stages to frame the cycle of events. Only a select few persons, however, were allowed to ascend the pyramids themselves, whose pinnacles offered homes to the gods—dark inner sanctums of hushed reverence.

Administrative buildings and palaces featured large inner spaces with galleries, corbeled vaults, and curtain walls. But, like the pyramids, they served to enhance the open spaces around which they clustered, presenting artistic expressions intended to convey the purpose of the place to all who approached. Parapets and roofcombs (ornamental capitals that increased the height of the building) evolved to add even greater luster to important buildings, and artists in the Classic Period became extremely skilled at executing ornate murals and reliefs that were carefully painted in a glorious range of colors.

Materials and techniques changed from place to place, depending on the environment—highland or lowland, wet or dry—in which the city was located. Buildings with a rubble core became common in lowland areas, for instance, because platforms made of earth were vulnerable to heavy rainfall. But all Maya architecture espoused a similar aesthetic, presenting a physical manifestation of the same hierarchical worldview that elevated the *k'uhul ajaw* and bound him to his people. It was meant to impress, and that it did—and does.

Tikal offers an excellent example. Located in the lowland base of the Yucatan Peninsula, about eighteen miles from the modern city of Flores in Guatemala, Tikal dominated much of the Classic period and remains one of the largest archaeological sites of Maya origin. Here a breathtaking assemblage of gray stonework lies in mute defiance of the rainforest, including six enormous stepped pyramids, most of which were built during the Late Classic (600–800) and Terminal Classic (800–900). The largest of these, known as Temple IV, stands an impressive 230 feet high and dates to around 741, commemorating the reign of a *k'uhul ajaw* known as Yik'in Chan Kawil. At the site's center, flanked by pyramids, is the Great Plaza, whose monumental causeways radiate outward to join it with other public spaces. More architectural treasures abound at Tikal, including the enormous North Acropolis. Measuring some 330 x 260 feet, it supports a cluster of funerary temples, the dazzling work of three hundred years of engineering excellence. There are ball courts, where the Maya played a game that celebrated the beginning of the world and brought the players and their spectators closer to the gods. And south of the Great Plaza lies an awe-inspiring collection of royal palaces arranged around a series of courtyards. Incredibly, these and the numerous other structures that have been excavated at Tikal constitute a tiny fraction of the entire site, which seems to cover an area of nearly fifty square miles.

To stand in the midst of such wonders is to appreciate the power of Tikal's kings. The buildings' height, stability, technical artistry, and geometric alignment all speak to a state that had achieved an extraordinary degree of order and industry under a ruler who organized his people, protected their borders, and inspired them to greatness. Without draft animals or the wheel, Maya builders relied on human labor and ingenuity—along with a lot of local stone and lime mortar—to guarantee their immortality.

But Tikal was just one of hundreds of polities in the Maya world, and all of them believed in their greatness. In such an environment, competition—warfare—was assured.

## THE GREAT GAME OF WARRIOR KINGS

The cities of the succeeding period show just what this world of sparring kings was to lead to. To visit sites like Tulum, on the Caribbean coast of Yucatan, or Mayapan, further inland on the peninsula, is to see almost a caricature of Maya greatness. At these settlements, which flourished during the Post-classic period (900–1500), monumental architecture on the Classic model had become a distant memory. The residents of these places knew a different Maya world from that which had blossomed at Tikal, and their buildings place the gulf between the two periods in bold relief.

What had happened? In a word, collapse. The eighth and ninth centuries witnessed an epic disruption of the Maya heartland, complete with massive depopulation and the abandonment of Mesoamerica's most glorious cities.

Scholars have been searching for a definitive reason for this collapse for decades. John Lloyd Stephens could only indulge his imagination in the effort to understand what had brought down the builders of the wonders he saw. However, the efforts of epigraphers and archaeologists in the late twentieth and early twenty-first centuries have gone a long way toward dispersing much—though certainly not all—of the mystery that surrounds this subject. And one of the pieces of the puzzle is that most ancient of pastimes—war.

No self-respecting *k'uhul ajaw* could expect to sustain his reign without prestige, that elusive yet all-important fulcrum of successful rulers. A Maya king could commission steles to record his deeds, have a new temple complex built, and even draw blood from his own penis with the barb of a stingray to appease the gods, all of which were part and parcel of the business of authority. But he and his polity also needed displays of might and the humbling of foes to complete the image of health and ensure the support of his people. There was never a shortage of foes.

Empire, as it was understood in the Old World and, much later, in the Aztec and Inca kingdoms, did not exist among the Maya. In the Pre-classic period, the polity centered at El Mirador came close to achieving a level of dominance that might in time have made it into a kind of imperial capital but, for reasons that are not fully understood, El Mirador fell, passing dominance to a few cities, principally Tikal, that vied for control of trade routes, farmland, and sources of labor. Throughout the Classic Period there would always be a handful of dominant city-states but the aura of kingship prevented any of them from annexing their neighbors; rather, a conquering polity would subsume a defeated enemy into its collection of tribute states, ensuring the defeated dynasty's continuation and therefore its ability to offer the tribute—in everything from cotton to human labor—that formed such an essential part of the economy. This process guaranteed a vast patchwork of scheming, clashing polities locked in a pseudo-feudal cycle of war, retribution, and dynastic intrigue. At no time in their history did the Maya, for all their genius, produce a Rome or a Tenochtitlan. True authority was a local affair.

In such a climate of jostling petty kingdoms, the cult of war-won reputation turned the Maya homeland into a cockpit. Centered on, but not exclusive to, the southern lowlands that border the mountains, the Classic period's heartland included such royal capitals as Copan, Tikal, Calakmul, Caracol, and Palenque, whose cultural and political

preeminence stood amid a flurry of lesser kingdoms, many of which played the role of vassal states. By the fifth century, the complex web of alliances had produced two loosely organized, rival factions led by Tikal and Calakmul, whose dynasties clashed over the tribute that made them centers of greatness.

Violence had once taken the form of raids, but increasingly in the Classic period greater expeditions were launched by opposing polities to seize control of borderlands, capture prisoners for sacrifice and repatriation, and—the greatest of all goals—capture enemy lords and kings. For a captive *k'uhul ajaw*, a special form of execution was required: decapitation. The rarest of war trophies, enemy kings were ritually slaughtered in a public display meant to maximize their humiliation and their usefulness as sacrifices. If possible, however, their dynasty would live on under the dominance of the conqueror, who would either leave the vanquished alone in their ruination and humiliation or begin exacting tribute. Either way, the winner came out on top.

Armies, some of which were led personally by kings, relied heavily on the experience of nobles, who headed ranks of commoners—farmers, craftsmen, laborers—called up in times of war like militia. Fighting with obsidian-spiked clubs, bows, javelins thrown by *atlatls* (spear-throwers), and stone axes, advancing hosts usually targeted outlying

*Above: A fresco painting depicting elaborately caparisoned Maya warriors in action, from a Maya tomb at Bonampak, Mexico.*

residential districts. Population centers, with their temples and palaces, tended to be defended by earth and stone ramparts, requiring a much greater deployment to overcome. But whether or not land was conquered, captives were always taken, for the blood sacrifice that was needed to please hungry gods, as well as to fulfill the nobility's need for servants. With such trophies, victorious armies returned to cheering crowds, showering glory upon their *k'uhul ajaw*. The ruler's authority was again regenerated, ensuring his people's favor and willingness to follow him wherever fate might take him. And the cycle then began all over again.

## A SPIRAL OF DOOMS

War certainly contributed to the tangle of mishaps that brought down the Classic Maya. In their quest for stability via violence, the Maya kings ironically sowed the seeds of instability and perpetual chaos.

But such developments alone cannot explain the cataclysm of the eighth and ninth centuries. War, after all, had been an integral part of Maya society since the Pre-classic. The development of divine kingship had exacerbated and institutionalized warfare as never before, but the record suggests a combination of war with other crises, rather than an apocalyptic conflagration that can be pinned on a penchant for war alone.

Of the theories that archaeologists are increasingly drawn to, the one that has become prominent attributes the downfall to the proliferation of the Maya people themselves. Particularly in the southern lowlands, the successful cultivation of land and relative security offered by strong kingships had sown the seeds of a population explosion. By 700, the population of the Maya heartland alone, regardless of the flourishing outlying areas, had reached the tens of millions. This speaks volumes about the ability of the Maya to exploit the land, profit from trade, and establish secure homelands.

But it also threatened future prosperity. Though they could not know it, the Maya farmers were taxing the land as never before, forced by swelling populations and ever-greedier rulers into getting more out of less. To feed growing populations, they moved beyond the age-old proven arable lands into less fertile territory, producing smaller yields. Faced with growing hunger, the *k'uhul ajaw* forced farmers into even worse lands, perpetuating the cycle.

The realities of Mesoamerica played a role, as well. Without horses, oxen, or any of the other domesticated creatures whose labor formed the basis of Old World empires, the Maya kingdoms—never united—were incapable of harvesting the enormous yields that would have been guarantees against future famine. It has been argued that the greatest structure of ancient Egypt was not the pyramid, but the granary. Maya states, founded on maize—a crop that, with Mesoamerican methods, could never produce the caloric output of Eurasian wheat—were barely able to store enough to get them through calamities like Caribbean hurricanes or droughts. When these occurred frequently or were long lasting, the results could be devastating. Rulers faced with such challenges naturally turned to war to compensate for the loss of prestige and food, thereby guaranteeing a self-perpetuating descent into strife and further disorder.

Under such circumstances, the singularity of the divine king suffered dramatically. After all, he was responsible for everything—so how could the masses not blame him? The *k'uhul ajaw*, confronted with adversity on all fronts, appeased angry nobles by giving them power, dispersing the once-unassailable sovereignty of the king among his aristocracy. And the process of dynastic feuding continued apace.

## THE AMAZING MAYA CALENDAR

Masters of mathematical calculations and astronomical observation, the Maya produced a calendar as exact as any in the history of the world. Indeed, it is more precise than the Gregorian calendar used today.

Comprising eighteen months of twenty days each, the *haab* charted a year of 365 days, including five days that were considered very unlucky. But the Maya also had a 260-day almanac that charted the procession of sacred days and ceremonies. Taken together, these two cycles produced a round of fifty-two years—the amount of time that passed before the two cycles described the same day once again.

A third calendar, called the Long Count, began on a fixed date in the distant past and operated independently of the *haab* and the sacred almanac. Reckoned in great cycles, each of which comprised thirteen *bak'tuns* (about 5,128 years), the Long Count anchored Maya cosmology to the beginning of their civilization—a date, corresponding to 3114 BC, that ushered in the current great cycle that is calculated to end on December 21, 2012. There was also the *k'atun*, a period of 7,200 days. Thirteen *k'atuns*—some 256 years —formed a cycle whose ending was viewed as a sign of momentous change.

In fact, some scholars have suggested that the cyclic nature of this elaborate system of reckoning time may have played a role in the downfall of the lowland cities during the Terminal Classic. Each *k'atun* in the 256-year cycle had a distinct name and prophecy, and the Maya viewed its recurrence as very significant. When *k'atun 11 ajaw* began in AD 790, the Maya may have attached great significance to it: *11 ajaw* had last occurred in 534, just before the decline of Tikal. Could they have fatalistically accepted the changes, however destructive, that began shaking their world to its foundations?

Is this enough to explain the rapid decline of the Terminal Classic (800–900)? Probably not. Evidence of drought, however, has led many experts to add it to the reasons for Classic Maya decline. In fact, scientific evidence for such a drought during the Terminal Classic is compelling enough for many experts. What seems more than plausible is that drought, combined with the inherent weaknesses of the culture, produced a crisis brought on by a critical density of population—and perpetuated by war.

## GREATNESS REDEFINED

Maya civilization was too strong to disappear with the crisis of the ninth century. In fact, while many of the population centers in the southern lowlands disappeared altogether, many others, farther north in the Yucatan Peninsula, either continued to thrive or began anew from scratch.

These polities were, in many ways, a mirror image of the Classic culture that preceded them. More concerned with long-distance trade than anything else, the Post-classic polities relied on maritime commerce rather than river trade, dispersed central power more equally among a settlement's elite, and concentrated more on pragmatic matters and earthly wealth than on monumental architecture to ensure stability. Their architecture attempted to model that of the Classic Maya, but rarely succeeded.

This was the culture that greeted the Spanish in the sixteenth century. Hernan Cortes had recently conquered the Aztec capital of Tenochtitlan, acquiring suzerainty over a mighty empire rich in gold and silver. The Maya, however, presented neither tremendous caches of gold nor centralized capitals that could ease the process of their own subjugation. For these reasons, the Spanish conquest of the Maya was far lengthier and less dramatic than the fall of pre-Columbian America's other great civilizations.

Using cavalry, armor, and infamous Toledo steel, Pedro de Alvarado conquered the southern Maya in the 1520s, while the Montejo family subjugated the Yucatan in a long campaign that did not end until the 1540s. But if these campaigns highlighted the vulnerabilities of the Post-classic Maya, the defiance of the Itza, last of the independent Maya peoples, offered a very different story. Based in the southern lowlands that once cradled the mighty Classic polities, the Itza resisted Spanish encroachment until the very late seventeenth century. In 1697 they were vanquished, ending forever the independent Maya civilization that had begun twenty-five centuries before.

Last of the Maya resisters, the Itza manifested a resilience shared by all of their ancient people. The fate of the Maya may still challenge experts who wrestle data from uncooperative jungles, valleys, and highlands, but the Maya's prowess and passion, still manifested in the Maya of today, shout across the expanse of time to enthrall us still.

## ACKNOWLEDGMENTS

A huge thank-you must go out to Murdoch Books for producing such a terrific book out of what must have seemed at times an unwieldy project. I am especially grateful to Diana Hill and Emma Hutchinson for their extraordinary patience and encouragement.

## PICTURE CREDITS

AKG images: 4, 52, 84, 94, 131, 140–1, 202, 216, 228, 241, 259, 265, 268, 272, 279, 291
Corbis: 51, 114, 213, 282, 292
Getty images: 165, 194
Photolibrary: pages 12, 15, 19, 22, 24–5, 32, 35, 44, 59, 60, 68–9, 81, 101, 111, 118–9, 124, 146, 150, 157, 160–1, 168, 174, 177, 184, 187, 190–1, 199, 206, 219, 245, 254-5, 257, 274, 287
Picture Desk / The Art Archive: 38, 76, 90–1, 96, 105, 142, 154, 222, 234, 239, 248

## BIBLIOGRAPHY

Axworthy, Michael. *A History of Iran: Empire of the Mind*. New York: Basic Books, 2008.
Bonnet, Charles & Valbelle, Dominique. *The Nubian Pharaohs: Black Kings on the Nile*. New York: The American University in Cairo Press, 2006.
Bryce, Trevor. *The Kingdom of the Hittites*. New Edition. Oxford: Oxford University Press, 2005.
Castleden, Rodney. *Minoans: Life in Bronze Age Crete*. London: Routledge, 1994.
Colledge, Malcolm A.R. *The Parthians*. New York: Frederick A. Praeger Publishers, 1967.
Connolly, Peter. *Greece and Rome at War*. London: Greenhill Books, 1998.
Cook, J.M. *The Persian Empire*. London: Orion Publishing Group, 1983.
Curtis, John E. & Tallis, Nigel, eds. *Forgotten Empire: The World of Ancient Persia*. Berkeley: University of California Press, 2005.
Davis, Paul K. *100 Decisive Battles from Ancient Times to the Present: The World's Major Battles and How They Shaped History*. New York: Oxford University Press, 2001.
Dawson, Doyne. *The First Armies*. London: Cassell & Co., 2001.
Dignas, Beate & Winter, Engelbert. *Rome and Persia in Late Antiquity: Neighbours and Rivals*. Cambridge, England: Cambridge University Press, 2007.

Fagan, Brian M., ed. *The Oxford Companion to Archaeology*. New York: Oxford University Press, 1996.

Fitton, J. Lesley. *The Minoans*. London: The Folio Society, 2004.

Freeman, Charles. *Egypt, Greece and Rome: Civilizations of the Ancient Mediterranean*. New York: Oxford University Press, 1996.

Gardiner, Alan. *Egypt of the Pharaohs: An Introduction*. Oxford: Oxford University Press, 1961.

Goldsworthy, Adrian. *The Fall of Carthage: The Punic Wars 265--146 BC*. London: Cassell, 2000.

Goldsworthy, Adrian. *The Complete Roman Army*. London: Thames and Hudson, 2003.

Grimal, Nicolas. *A History of Ancient Egypt*. Malden, Massachusetts: Blackwell Publishing, 1992.

Gurney, O.R. *The Hittites*. London: The Folio Society, 1999.

Hanson, Victor Davis. *The Wars of the Ancient Greeks*. London: Cassell and Co., 1999.

Hanson, Victor Davis. *A War Like No Other: How the Athenians and Spartans Fought the Peloponnesian War*. New York: Random House, 2005.

Heather, Peter. *The Fall of the Roman Empire: A New History of Rome and the Barbarians*. New York: Oxford University Press, 2006.

Holland, Tom. *Persian Fire: The First World Empire and the Battle for the West*. New York: Doubleday, 2005.

Kern, Paul Bentley. *Ancient Siege Warfare*. Bloomington, Indiana: Indiana University Press, 1999.

Lancel, Serge. (Translated by Antonia Nevill). *Carthage: A History*. Oxford: Blackwell Publishers, 1997.

Lehner, Mark. *The Complete Pyramids: Solving the Ancient Mysteries*. London: Thames & Hudson, 1997.

Lewis, Mark Edward. *The Early Chinese Empires: Qin and Han*. Cambridge, Massachusetts: Harvard University Press, 2007.

Macqueen, J.G. *The Hittites and Their Contemporaries in Asia Minor*. Revised and Enlarged Edition. London: Thames and Hudson, 1986.

Markoe, Glenn E. *Phoenicians*. Berkeley, California. University of California Press, 2000.

Martin, Thomas R. *Ancient Greece: From Prehistoric to Hellenistic Times*. New Haven, Connecticut: Yale University Press, 1996.

Meiggs, Russell. *The Athenian Empire*. Oxford: Oxford University Press, 1972.

Mysliwiec, Karol. *The Twilight of Ancient Egypt: First Millennium BCE*. Ithaca, New York: Cornell University Press, 2000.

Oates, Joan. *Babylon*. Revised Edition. London: Thames and Hudson, 1986.

Roux, Georges. *Ancient Iraq*. 3rd Edition. New York: Penguin USA, 1993.

Saggs, H.W.F. *The Might That Was Assyria*. London: Sidgwick and Jackson, 1985.

Saggs, H.W.F. *The Greatness That Was Babylon*. London: Sidgwick and Jackson, 1988.

Salway, Peter. *The Oxford Illustrated History of Roman Britain*. New York: Oxford University Press, 1993.

Schele, Linda and Freidel, David. *A Forest of Kings: The Untold Story of the Ancient Maya*. New York: William Morrow and Co., 1990.

Sharer, Robert J. with Traxler, Loa P. *The Ancient Maya*. Sixth Edition. Stanford, California: Stanford University Press, 2006.

Shaughnessy, Edward L., ed. *China: Empire and Civilization*. New York: Oxford University Press, 2005.

Shaw, Ian, ed. *The Oxford History of Ancient Egypt*. New York: Oxford University Press, 2000.

Sherwin-White, Susan M. and Kuhrt, Amélie. *From Samarkhand to Sardis: A New Approach to the Seleucid Empire*. Berkeley, California: University of California Press, 1993.

Strassler, Robert B., ed. *The Landmark Thucydides: A Comprehensive Guide to The Peloponnesian War*. New York: Free Press, 1996.

Taylour, Lord William and Chadwick, John. *The Mycenaeans: And the Decipherment of Linear B*. London: The Folio Society, 2004.

Thapar, Romila. *Asoka and the Decline of the Mauryas*. Oxford: Oxford University Press, 1963.

Treadgold, Warren. *A History of the Byzantine State and Society*. Stanford, California: Stanford University Press, 1997.

Warren, Peter. *The Aegean Civilizations*. Oxford: Equinox, 1989.

Webster, David L. *The Fall of the Ancient Maya: Solving the Mystery of the Maya Collapse*. London: Thames & Hudson, 2002.

Welsby, Derek A. *The Kingdom of Kush: The Napatan and Meroitic Empires*. Princeton, New Jersey: Markus Wiener Publishers, 1998.

# INDEX